Unequal Development and Labour in Brazil

This book is about unequal development and labour in Brazil, with particular reference to the economic and social development of the Northeast region, which has suffered persistent disadvantage. It combines a historical approach, which shows how economic, social and political institutions have been restructured over time, with an analysis of changes in the pattern of production, employment, unemployment and inequality up to the present day. It draws on detailed case studies to examine the connections between local and national production systems and critical labour market outcomes such as informality in employment, precarious work and disparities between genders, races and regions. The case of the Brazilian Northeast illustrates processes, relationships and policy debates that are important not only in Brazil but also elsewhere. The book will be of interest to teachers, researchers and students in economics, sociology, labour and development; public officials and policy-makers; the international development community; and the general public interested in Latin American affairs. They will find in the book an original and systematic analysis of the factors underlying unequal development and how they respond to different policy regimes and suggestions about the issues that need to be addressed in the future.

Gerry Rodgers has a DPhil in Economic Development from the University of Sussex (1972) and an MA (Cantab) in Economics and Mathematics. He worked at the International Labour Organization in a variety of research and management positions, including Director of the International Institute for Labour Studies. He has mainly worked on poverty, inequality and employment, especially in India and in Latin America, and has published widely on these issues. Presently he is a collaborator of the Laboratory for Studies and Research on Labour and Public Policy at the Federal University of Paraíba in João Pessoa, and is also Visiting Professor at the Institute for Human Development, New Delhi.

Roberto Véras de Oliveira has a doctorate in Sociology from the University of São Paulo (2002) and undertook post-doctoral work during 2015–2016 at the UCLA Institute for Research on Labor and Employment (Los Angeles). He is presently Full Professor at the Federal University of Paraíba, João Pessoa. His research is concerned with the Sociology of Labour, Political Sociology and Economic Sociology. He is a Scholar of the Brazilian National Council for Scientific and Technological Development and a member of its Social Sciences Advisory Committee, and a member of the Coordinating Group of the Network for Studies and Interdisciplinary Monitoring of the Labour Reform.

Janine Rodgers has a Degree in Economics from Paris (1966), an MA in Development Economics from the University of Sussex (1969) and a Certificate in Political Science from the Graduate Institute of International and Development Studies, Geneva (1982). She worked for the International Labour Organization on labour market inequalities, on gender issues and on crises. She has been Deputy Executive Secretary of the European Association of Development Research and Training Institutes (EADI). She is currently a collaborator of the Laboratory for Studies and Research on Labour and Public Policy at the Federal University of Paraíba, João Pessoa, and a Visiting Senior Research Fellow at the Institute for Human Development, New Delhi.

Routledge Inequality Studies

Inequality Studies from the Global South
Edited by Edward Webster, Imraan Valodia and David Francis

Unequal Development and Labour in Brazil
Gerry Rodgers, Roberto Véras de Oliveira and Janine Rodgers

For more information about this series, please visit: www.routledge.com/Routledge-Inequality-Studies/book-series/RIQS

Unequal Development and Labour in Brazil

Gerry Rodgers,
Roberto Véras de Oliveira and
Janine Rodgers

Routledge
Taylor & Francis Group
LONDON AND NEW YORK

Designed cover image: © Getty Images

First published 2023
by Routledge
4 Park Square, Milton Park, Abingdon, Oxon OX14 4RN

and by Routledge
605 Third Avenue, New York, NY 10158

Routledge is an imprint of the Taylor & Francis Group, an informa business

British Library Cataloguing-in-Publication Data
A catalogue record for this book is available from the British Library

Library of Congress Cataloging-in-Publication Data
Names: Rodgers, Gerry, author. | Oliveira, Roberto Véras de, author. | Rodgers, Janine, author.
Title: Unequal development and labour in Brazil / Gerry Rodgers, Roberto Véras de Oliveira, Janine Rodgers.
Description: Milton Park, Abingdon, Oxon ; New York, NY : Routledge, 2023.
| Series: Routledge inequality studies | Includes bibliographical references and index. |
Identifiers: LCCN 2022046608 (print) | LCCN 2022046609 (ebook) | ISBN 9781032353906 (hardback) | ISBN 9781032353920 (paperback) | ISBN 9781003326670 (ebook)
Subjects: LCSH: Labor productivity—Brazil. | Brazil—Economic conditions—21st century. | Economic development—Brazil. | Equality—Brazil.
Classification: LCC HC190.L3 R64 2023 (print) | LCC HC190.L3 (ebook) | DDC 331.120981—dc23/eng/20220930
LC record available at https://lccn.loc.gov/2022046608
LC ebook record available at https://lccn.loc.gov/2022046609

ISBN: 978-1-032-35390-6 (hbk)
ISBN: 978-1-032-35392-0 (pbk)
ISBN: 978-1-003-32667-0 (ebk)

DOI: 10.4324/9781003326670

Typeset in Times New Roman
by codeMantra

Contents

Figures

Tables

Preface

This book is about the economic and social development of the Brazilian Northeast, with a particular emphasis on labour, employment and inequality. In the course of Brazil's history, marked by periods of rapid economic growth but also by repeated economic and political crises, and subject to diverse and contradictory political regimes, this region of the country has suffered persistent disadvantage. Our aim is to document this disadvantage and how it has evolved, and to contribute to reflection on how it might be overcome. To this end, we consider both the history of Brazil's development and the social and economic patterns that we observe today, setting the trajectory of the Northeast within that of Brazil as a whole; and we bring together an analysis of macro-level patterns and trends with detailed empirical studies within the region.

The book draws on and consolidates work that has been carried out under several research projects based at universities within the Northeast region. The main source is a project entitled *A Reprodução das Desigualdades no Nordeste do Brasil: Regimes de Trabalho e Desenvolvimento* (The Reproduction of Inequalities in Northeast Brazil: Labour and Development Regimes), which brings together studies carried out over a decade by research groups within two universities: the Laboratory for Studies and Research on Labour and Public Policy (LAEPT) at the Federal University of Paraíba, João Pessoa, Paraíba (UFPB), and the research group on Labour, Development and Public Policies (TDEPP) at the Federal University of Campina Grande, Paraíba (UFCG). The authors are, respectively, director (Véras de Oliveira) and collaborators (Gerry and Janine Rodgers) of these groups. The book also draws on long-standing collaborations with researchers in other universities of the region, notably the Federal University of Pernambuco (UFPE), and on participation in a national project on *Configurações do Desenvolvimento, Trabalho e Ação Coletiva* (Configurations of Development, Labour and Collective Action) co-ordinated by José Ricardo Ramalho of the Federal University of Rio de Janeiro (UFRJ), Marcelo Carneiro of the Federal University of Maranhão (UFMA) and Roberto Véras de Oliveira.

Much of the research under the former project has been reported in detail in a book published in 2022 in Portuguese by Annablume Editora, São Paulo, entitled *Desenvolvimento e Regime de Trabalho: A Trajetória do*

Nordeste do Brasil (Development and Labour Regime: The Trajectory of the Northeast of Brazil), edited by two of the authors of the present book. The present English language publication draws on this material along with other sources, synthesizing, extending and complementing it within an integrated approach. The goal is to identify, examine and document key issues in the development of the region, in particular the labour arrangements and the sources of inequality both within the region and between the Northeast and the rest of Brazil, and so to contribute to the wider literature on unequal development in Brazil, as well as to regional studies more generally.

There have been many contributors to the analysis and debate embodied in this book. First, there are the participants in the research groups, whose names are listed at the end of this preface. They have undertaken many detailed empirical studies, which provided material that has been summarized in Chapter 4, and which has informed the book as a whole. Second, we would like to thank Alexandre de Freitas Barbosa of the University of São Paulo for his substantive contribution to the project, including his analysis of the long-term transformation of the economy of the Northeast. We are also grateful to him and to José Ricardo Ramalho for their participation in discussions on the project and the individual research studies and for their helpful comments. We would like to thank Roseli de Fátima Corteletti and Mario Henrique Guedes Ladosky, who head the TDEPP, and whose efforts were fundamental for the development of this project. We would also like to thank Jorge Alves and Pedro Alves for their valuable assistance in data processing. Finally, we would like to thank the *Conselho Nacional de Desenvolvimento Científico e Tecnológico* (CNPQ) and the *Coordenação de Aperfeiçoamento de Pessoal de Nível Superior* (CAPES), federal agencies to promote research and higher education, which provided support to this project through a grant to Roberto Véras de Oliveira.

Gerry Rodgers
Roberto Véras de Oliveira
Janine Rodgers
João Pessoa, Paraíba, June 2022

Participants in the project on The Reproduction of Inequalities in Northeast Brazil: Labour and Development Regimes, associated with the LAEPT (UFPB) and the TDEPP (UFCG), are as follows:

Ana Carmen Navarro de Moraes, Ana Márcia Batista Almeida Pereira, Anderson Matias Cardozo, Bruno Mota Braga, Camilla de Almeida Silva, Cláudia Freire, Eduardo Donato, Eugenio Vital Pereira Neto, Gerry Rodgers, Guilherme José Mota Silva, Janine Rodgers, José Aderivaldo Silva da Nóbrega, José Cleyton Neves Lopes, Kerilin Laine Andrade Chang, Luciana Waclawovsky, Maressa Fauzia Pessoa Dantas, Maria Clara Lima de Menezes, Mario Henrique Guedes Ladosky, Maurício Rombaldi, Rejane Gomes Carvalho, Roberto Véras de Oliveira, Roseli de Fátima Corteletti, Victor de Oliveira Rodrigues and Wanderleya dos Santos Farias.

Acronyms

ADENE	*Agência do Desenvolvimento do Nordeste* – Northeast Development Agency
BNB	*Banco do Nordeste do Brasil* – Regional Development Bank for the Northeast of Brazil
BNDES	*Banco Nacional de Desenvolvimento Econômico e Social* – National Bank for Economic and Social Development
CAGED	*Cadastro Geral de Empregados e Desempregados* – General Employment Register
CGEE	*Centro de Gestão e Estudos Estratégicos* – Centre for Management and Strategic Studies
CLT	*Consolidação das Leis do Trabalho* – Consolidation of Labour Laws
CNPJ	*Cadastro Nacional da Pessoa Jurídica* – National Registry of Legal Entities
CUT	*Central Única dos Trabalhadores* – United Workers' Central
DIESSE	*Departamento Intersindical de Estatística e Estudos Socioeconômicos* – Inter-Union Department of Statistics and Socioeconomic Studies
EAP	Economically Active Population
EAS	Shipyard "Estaleiro Atlântico Sul"
ECLAC	United Nations Economic Commission for Latin America and the Caribbean
FCA	Fiat Chrysler Automobiles
FINOR	*Fundo de Investimentos do Nordeste* – Northeast Investment Fund
GDP	Gross Domestic Product
GRP	Gross Regional Product
GVC	Global Value Chain
IBGE	*Instituto Brasileiro de Geografia e Estatística* – Brazilian Institute of Geography and Statistics
ICT	Information and Communication Technology

IDB	Inter-American Development Bank
INPC	*Índice Nacional de Preços ao Consumidor* – National Consumer Price Index
IT	Information Technology
MST	*Movimento dos Trabalhadores Rurais Sem Terra* – Landless Workers Movement
PAC	*Programa de Aceleração do Crescimento* – Growth Acceleration Programme
PNAD	*Pesquisa Nacional por Amostra de Domicílios* – National Household Sample Survey
PNADC	*Pesquisa Nacional por Amostra de Domicílios Contínua* – Continuous National Household Sample Survey
POF	*Pesquisa de Orçamentos Familiares* – Consumer Expenditure Survey
PPP	Public–Private Partnerships
PREALC (ILO)	*Programa Regional del Empleo para América Latina y el Caribe* – Regional Employment Programme for Latin America and the Caribbean
PT	*Partido dos Trabalhadores* – Workers' Party
RAIS	*Relação Anual de Informações Sociais* – Annual Social Information Report
SEBRAE	*Serviço Brasileiro de Apoio às Micro e Pequenas Empresas* – Brazilian Micro and Small Business Support Service
SENAC	*Serviço Nacional de Aprendizagem Comercial* – National Service of Commercial Training
SENAI	*Serviço Nacional de Aprendizagem Industrial* – National Service of Industrial Training
SINDMETAL-PE	*Sindicato dos Trabalhadores Metalúrgicos de Pernambuco* – Union of Workers in the Metallurgical Industries of Pernambuco
SINE	*Sistema Nacional de Emprego* – National Employment Service
SUDENE	*Superintendência do Desenvolvimento do Nordeste* – Superintendency for the Development of the Northeast
UFCG	*Universidade Federal de Campina Grande* – Federal University of Campina Grande, Paraíba
UFPB	*Universidade Federal da Paraíba* – Federal University of Paraíba, João Pessoa
UNDP	United Nations Development Programme

1 A focus on the Northeast

Não há idéias do passado nem do presente. Há idéias certas e erradas
(Celso Furtado)[1]

1 The regional question in Brazil

The pattern of development in Brazil has always been unequal, with a regional concentration of economic and political power that changed over time. The Northeast of the country was the heart of colonial Brazil from the arrival of the Portuguese in 1500 until the 1700s, but was displaced both economically and politically by the South and Southeast of the country in the nineteenth century. In the second half of the twentieth century, there was an expansion into the new agricultural frontier of the Centre-West, especially after the building of Brasilia, which was intended to shift the country's economic and political centre of gravity towards the interior, but this did not undermine the dominance of the Southeast. Meanwhile, the vast and lightly populated territory of the Amazon Basin in the North remained largely peripheral to the economic development of the country.

One result of this history has been a long-standing concern with regional inequality, for there is considerable economic and social variation across the country. At present, Brazil is officially made up of five large regions, distinguishing parts of the country with different geographies, economic bases and socio-cultural traditions. Figure 1.1 shows the corresponding administrative divisions. The Southeast, including the major cities of São Paulo, Rio de Janeiro and Belo Horizonte, has the largest share of population and economic activity, and along with the South the highest incomes. The Centre-West, with Brasilia at its eastern edge, includes both extensive commercial agriculture and undeveloped natural regions. The North includes the cities of Manaus and Belem as well as the Amazon forest and river system. And the Northeast is a diverse region, including a well-watered coast with several large cities, and a largely dry interior. These regions are not homogenous, and their borders are to some degree arbitrary. In addition, federal Brazil is built on states, of which there are 26, rather than regions, so that each region is made up of a number of states, from three in the South to nine in

DOI: 10.4324/9781003326670-1

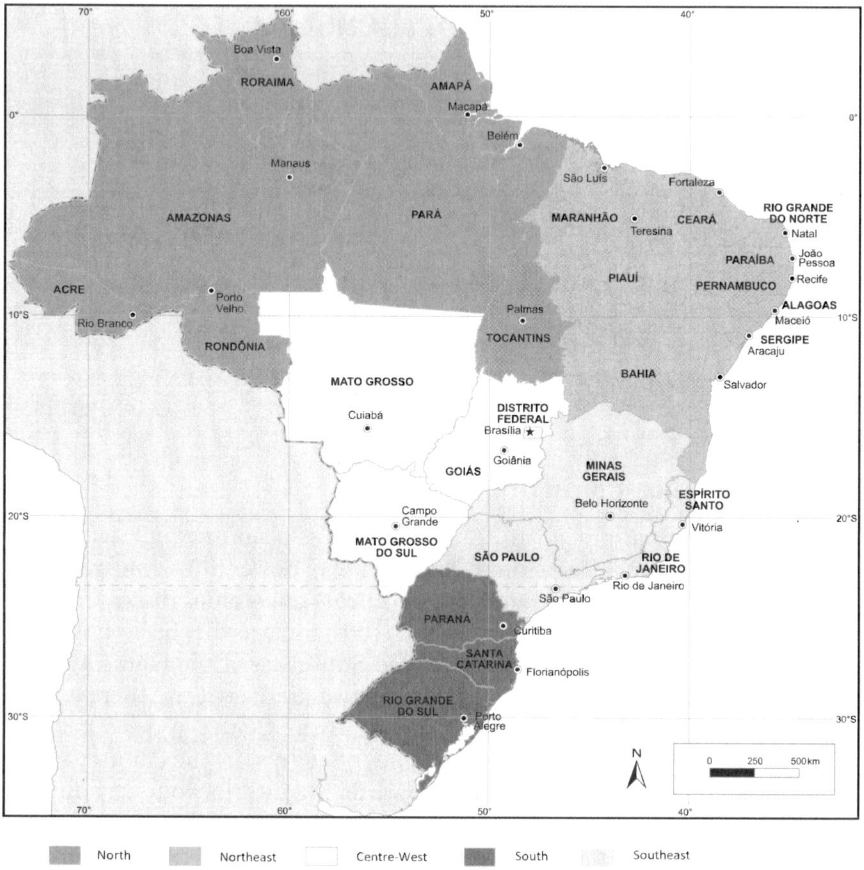

Figure 1.1 Brazil, states and major regions.
Source: Brazilian Institute of Geography and Statistics (IBGE).

the Northeast. Political and administrative authority is concentrated at the level of the states, and even more so at the Federal Level, rather than at the level of the region. Nevertheless, the differences between the regions are real and important, and they have become embedded in popular perception and political action. Each region has its own character, reflecting elements that are shared among the states of which it is composed. Above all, the regions have played diverse roles in the political and economic development of the country and have benefitted from that development in very different ways.

This book is about the development of the Northeast of Brazil, and, in particular, how that development has been both conditioned by, and determinant of, the patterns of work and employment in the region. The economic development of the region is intimately related to that of the country as a whole, but what marks out the trajectory of the Northeast is its persistent disadvantage compared with other parts of Brazil. That disadvantage can readily be seen by comparing economic and social indicators for the different regions.

Table 1.1 shows the overall population size of each region, its share in GDP, the sectoral distribution of output and the average level of labour income. The Northeast accounts for 27% of Brazil's population, but only 14% of its GDP. Only the North, among other regions, has a similar deficit, and the dominance of the Southeast, with 42% of the population and 53% of GDP, is clear. Income differences broadly reflect GDP per capita, only half as high in the Northeast as in the Southeast. These differences in output and income are in part the consequence of differences in the production structure. The Northeast has less industry, and a low share of private modern and business services, which are concentrated in the Southeast. The Northeast, like the North and the Centre-West, is much more dependent on the public sector and also has a high share of trade and of personal services. The share of agriculture was high until the end of the twentieth century and was still over 10% in the early 2000s, though it is now not much higher than the national average. But the broad economic structure is less important than differences in productivity, much lower in the Northeast, and in the organization of production.

Table 1.1 Basic economic indicators, Brazil and major regions

Indicators	*North*	*Northeast*	*Centre-West*	*Southeast*	*South*	*Brazil*
Population 2021 (million)	18.9	57.7	16.7	89.6	30.4	213.3
Share of national GDP 2019 (%)	5.7	14.3	9.9	53.0	17.2	100
Sectoral distribution of output 2019 (%)						
– Agriculture	8.8	6.5	10.1	2.0	7.8	4.9
– Industry	27.6	18.5	13.8	22.6	24.8	21.8
– Trade and personal services	15.5	17.7	14.6	16.4	17.8	16.6
– Modern services and transport	22.3	31.4	33.5	45.8	35.4	39.3
– Public services	25.7	25.9	28.1	13.1	14.2	17.4
Median household income per person, 2019 (R$)	511	506	998	1,012	1,141	861

Sources: IBGE (Brazilian Institute of Geography and Statistics), Regional Accounts (https://www.ibge.gov.br/en/statistics/economic/national-accounts/16855-regional-accounts-of-brazil.html?=&t=resultados);

Population estimates from IBGE, *Diretoria de Pesquisas, Coordenação de População e Indicadores Sociais.*

Household income from IBGE, *Pesquisa Nacional por Amostra de Domicílios Contínua* (PNADC), 2019.

Table 1.2 Basic social and labour market indicators, Brazil and major regions

Indicators	*North*	*Northeast*	*Centre-West*	*Southeast*	*South*	*Brazil*
Illiteracy rate 2019 (%) – population aged 15+*	7.6	13.9	4.9	3.3	3.3	6.6
Population aged 25+ with less than complete fundamental schooling 2019 (%)*	43	49	37	33	38	39
Infant mortality per 1,000 live births 2020***	16.6	15.2	13.0	11.9	10.2	13.3
Households with bathroom and sewage system, 2019 (%)**	21	43	55	89	68	66
Unemployment 1st qtr 2020 (%)*	12.1	15.8	10.7	12.5	7.7	12.4
Informality in the labour market (%)§, 2019*	62	57	41	35	29	42
Real wage in principal employment, 1st qtr 2020 (R$)*	1,879	1,743	2,917	2,782	2,769	2,541
Gini coefficient of household labour income per capita, 2019*	0.537	0.559	0.507	0.527	0.467	0.54[illegible]
Human development index 2010****	0.667	0.663	0.757	0.766	0.754	0.727

Sources: * IBGE, PNADC (annual and quarterly), 2019 or 2020.
** IBGE, *Pesquisa Nacional de Saúde* (National Health Survey), 2019.
*** Ministry of Health (https://www.gov.br/saude/pt-br/centrais-de-conteudo/publicacoes/boletin boletins-epidemiologicos/edicoes/2021/boletim_epidemiologico_svs_37_v2.pdf).
**** UNDP (2016).

Notes: § Includes wage employees and domestic workers without signed labour card, self-employed an employers not contributing to social security, and family workers; discussed further in Chapters and 3.

Table 1.2 presents a number of social and labour market indicators. Here we see the particularly high levels of illiteracy and low levels of schooling in the Northeast, relatively high levels of infant mortality, poorer sanitary facilities, and, in the labour market, higher levels of unemployment and informality. It is also striking that inequality of labour income is highest in the Northeast, and the human development index is lowest.

We explore some of the reasons for these differences in this book, including history, politics and social institutions. Regional inequality is just one aspect of structural inequality within Brazil, and there are many other dimensions, with respect to gender and race, between different groups of workers, between labour and capital. These inequalities intersect, making Brazil one of the most income-unequal countries in the world.[2] This pattern has been built up over a long period, is deeply rooted, and many of the historical factors and forces concerned remain powerful today.

In many respects, there is a sharp divide between the South, Southeast and Centre-West of Brazil on the one hand, and the North and Northeast, on the other. The latter two regions share poor economic and social indicators. But the historical and geographical origins of the relative backwardness of the North and Northeast are different. The North is much larger than the Northeast in area, but much smaller in population, of which a substantial part is indigenous. Dominated by the Amazon, both the river and the forest, it has a very different economic character and history, and has never been integrated into the Brazilian economy to the same extent, or in the same way. The story of the North is fascinating, and it presents major environmental, developmental and human rights challenges. But in this book our focus is on the Northeast.

The Northeast lost its political and economic pre-eminence in the eighteenth and nineteenth centuries, but the roots of today's regional inequalities lie more in the unbalanced process of industrial growth in the first half of the twentieth century. During this period there was a concentration of capital accumulation in the Southeast, associated with an inflow of European migrant workers, and a growing dependence of other regions on their commercial relations with this economic pole (Araújo, 2000). A stereotype emerged in which the Southeast was viewed as the fount of economic dynamism, while in the Northeast archaic production relations persisted and the economy stagnated. This image was in large measure socially and politically constructed, a "historical invention" (Muniz de Albuquerque, 2014, p.12), but it had real economic consequences, as the country became increasingly polarized. Investment and industrial development were concentrated in the Southeast, where migrants from the Northeast provided unskilled labour, but were often despised and discriminated against, sometimes in semi-racist terms. The image of backwardness in the Northeast was reinforced by the novels of authors such as Graciliano Ramos and Jorge Amado in the 1930s,[3] which painted a picture of exploitation and misery (Rodgers, 2020). Recurrent drought in the Northeast widened the economic gap. There was also a countermovement, built around the reinforcement of regional identity, exemplified in the writings of Gilberto Freyre (e.g. 1937), which stressed the distinctive nature of Northeastern society, and its strong social and cultural traditions. But at the same time, these traditions served the interests of the landed oligarchy, who had little interest in accelerated economic development.

After the Second World War, the process of economic development in Brazil thus found the Northeast in a disadvantaged position. The goal of the State[4] was to make Brazil an industrialized country, and policies to this effect were built on the existing capitalist dynamic in the Southeast of the country, rather than on attempts to change the regional balance. Polarization intensified. Initially, the "regional question" in the Northeast was seen as one of recurrent droughts, leading to crop failures and distress migration from rural areas, and government action concentrated on the management of water resources. But under the impetus of the leading economist of the time, Celso Furtado, a view emerged that there was a need for the State to combat the structural economic and social relationships that hindered development in the region, and the Superintendency for the Development of the Northeast (Sudene) was created in 1959 under his leadership, with a mandate to promote investment and modernization. In the 1960s, as development studies emerged as an academic discipline in the universities of Europe and North America, and gave rise to widespread efforts to promote economic growth in developing countries, the Northeast of Brazil offered an example of how a State-led drive for development might overcome regional backwardness.

But Furtado's efforts ended with the military coup in 1964. And while there has been much effort by the State and by regional actors to overcome economic backwardness since that time, the gap between the Northeast and the rest of the country has hardly diminished. Poverty remains greater in the Northeast, economic productivity is lower, economic segmentation is more accentuated, working conditions are poorer and informality is more widespread.

Why does this situation persist? Some of the problems of the Northeast lie within the region, in an unequal social structure, an outdated productive base, inadequate infrastructure, an under-skilled workforce, ill-adapted economic institutions and weak collective organization of workers. But these deficiencies are not an accident. The roots of the problem lie in the structural characteristics of the national and the international economy, in which the Northeast plays a dependent and subordinate role. The process of capitalist accumulation in Brazil, as elsewhere, tends to polarize, as investment is concentrated in those regions, especially the Southeast, where markets and financial institutions are more developed, where a pool of skilled labour is available and where ownership and management of companies is located. At the same time, the core production system is able to take advantage of lower costs in other regions through subcontracting or outsourcing of intermediate inputs, or through segmenting the production process and the labour market. As a result, the Brazilian economy concentrates opportunities and incomes among a fraction of the population, both within and across regions.

But Brazil is, of course, part of the global economy, and there are both direct and indirect effects on the Northeast. Despite the existence of a substantial manufacturing sector, Brazil's exports are still dominated by commodities, while imports are dominated by manufactures, capital goods and oil. This makes Brazil's connection with globalization heavily dependent on agroindustry and mining, so that fluctuations in global markets have a direct impact on the national economy. High commodity prices contributed to high growth in the 2000s; a slump in commodity prices has played an important role in the recession since 2015. There is a direct effect on employment in agroindustry and mining, but while these sectors are the main source of exports, they account for only a small share of the labour market, and most of the impact is indirect, through multiplier effects on the rest of the economy.

These connections with the global economy are conditioned by the structural heterogeneity of the Brazilian economy. Technologically advanced manufacturing and services and extensive commercial agricultural production coexist with a large sector of small-scale, low-productivity activities. Over half of employment is informal, in the sense that it consists either of unprotected wage work (without signed labour card – *carteira assinada*, discussed in Chapter 3), or self-employment. It is mainly the larger scale, often more capital-intensive enterprises that are most connected with the global economy, able to take advantage of global markets and attract investment from abroad. Productivity levels in this stratum of the economy are 20 times higher than in informal production; it accounts for 69% of output but only 18% of employment (Infante, 2015). Most of the enterprises concerned are subject to high levels of competitive pressure from the global economy, which makes it essential to keep costs down. This leads not only to pressure on wages but also to a great deal of outsourcing to small firms or to the informal economy. However, direct employment in the large, capital-intensive firms is much more likely to be regular and protected (91% of employment in firms with over 50 workers was with carteira assinada in 2019, against 57% in firms with six to ten workers[5]). This is a mechanism which perpetuates heterogeneity. This pattern is found in agriculture as well as industry. Productivity levels in export-oriented agroindustry are much higher than in small-scale family farms, although the latter account for the bulk of agricultural employment, and there are corresponding differences in incomes. These structural differences within the economy play an important role in overall inequality.

What are the implications for the Northeast? Many of these factors affect the Northeast, but in distinct ways because of its particular characteristics, and because of the position of the Northeast within the Brazilian economy. For if the Brazilian economy in many ways needs to be considered as part of the periphery of the global economy, then the Northeast is a periphery within a periphery – even more so than Brazil in the global economy, for there are no barriers to trade and labour mobility between the Northeast and the rest of Brazil, and its autonomy in relation to the rest of the Brazilian economy is limited. It constitutes, in reality, a relatively low-wage and labour-intensive sector of the national economy, dependent on the core of the production system in São Paulo and the Southeast, and on national policy choices.

As such, some of the problems faced by the Brazilian economy within the global market are faced by the Northeast vis-à-vis Brazil. First of all, the region depends heavily on the rest of Brazil, and to a lesser extent the rest of the world, for finance and investment. The autonomy of the region with respect to capital accumulation is therefore circumscribed. Second, it tends to compete, within Brazil, on the basis of low labour costs, in part within the informal economy. Labour is less well protected in the Northeast than elsewhere in the country, because the proportion of wage workers with a formal contract is lower, the labour laws are less well enforced and trade unions are weaker. Third, a part of the Northeast's production is destined for the local market, but many of the larger companies form part of national production chains – notably in automobiles, shoes, ethanol, beer production and other large-scale capital-intensive activities. In these chains, the routine, lower skill parts of the production process are often located in the Northeast, while management and research and development activities are concentrated in the Southeast – just as in global value chains, these functions remain in the Global North. Fourth, these more advanced production sectors form a much smaller part of the Northeastern economy than of the Southeast. Structural heterogeneity concerns the Brazilian economy as a whole, but it is even more deeply embedded in the Northeast. The size of the informal economy undermines the bargaining power of workers in larger firms, and labour market opportunities are more restricted.

The book examines the development of the Northeast at these different levels and tries to connect them. The goal is to identify and document relationships and mechanisms that underlie underdevelopment, economic insecurity, unemployment and inequality in the region. This calls for a historical perspective, for development possibilities and labour regimes today are strongly influenced by the historical trajectory, from the colonial period through to the international integration of the Brazil economy in the era of neoliberal globalization.

This history is told in the next chapter. Guimarães Neto (1997) identifies three principal phases in the history of the Northeastern economy. In the colonial era, and up to the middle of the nineteenth century, an economic system was built around the production for export of sugar (and later on, of cotton, tobacco, cocoa, etc.), based on slave labour and complemented by extensive cattle-raising and subsistence agriculture. From the middle of the nineteenth century to the middle of the twentieth, this economy was increasingly articulated with other regions of Brazil, together forming a national domestic market, but on an unequal basis. The development of the Northeast was narrowly based, since it continued to depend on both commercial (monoculture) and subsistence agriculture, and increasingly lost competitiveness in relation to the South and Southeast of the country. Then, from the 1950s onwards, as awareness grew of the increasing gap between the Northeastern economy and the thriving industrial system that had developed on the axis São Paulo-Rio de Janeiro, attempts were made to solve the problem through a transfer of productive capital, both public and private, towards the peripheral regions of the country. The conditions were thereby created for the productive integration of the Northeast into the national economy.

As a result the regional economy underwent profound transformations during the period of high growth under military rule in the second half of the 1960s and throughout the 1970s, but the production structure remained unbalanced. In the new regional division of labour, the Northeast was a producer of commodities and of intermediate inputs for industry in the more developed regions, a consumer of their industrial products and a supplier of low-wage labour. Meanwhile, the inheritance of slavery and an unequal agrarian structure based on large estates, combined with slow growth of regular wage employment and excess labour supply, facilitated exploitative and informal labour relations and low wages (Guimarães Neto, 1997).

The "Brazilian miracle" of high growth, based on import substitution and close collaboration between the State and both domestic and foreign capital, collapsed in the 1980s, in the face of rising indebtedness and global recession, while at the same time there emerged widespread popular resistance to the military regime followed by a return to democracy. But investment, industrial production and real wages fell dramatically, and inflation accelerated (Baer, 2014; Barbosa et al., 2017). The Northeast followed this movement, and real incomes fell, though paradoxically the region was to some degree protected by its relatively low level of industrialization.

This was the prelude to liberalization and deregulation in the 1990s. A series of reforms opened up the Brazilian economy through tariff reductions, liberalization of international capital flows and privatizations. But growth remained slow and erratic, and successive international financial crises in the 1990s led to massive capital flight and debt crisis. Open unemployment and informal work increased, while real wages stagnated (Barbosa et al., 2017, p.153). One consequence of the neoliberal economic policies of the 1990s was less state intervention in favour of the Northeast, and interregional inequalities persisted or grew at a time of worsening labour market conditions in the country as a whole (Gomes and Vergolino, 1995). While the disadvantage of the Northeast up to the 1980s can largely be understood in terms of the nature of the national development path, liberalization in the 1990s meant that regional development was increasingly influenced by the integration of Brazil in the global economy.

The Workers' Party (PT) came to power in the 2002 elections in the wake of the deep economic crisis at the turn of the century. Chapter 2 discusses how the Northeast benefitted from national economic growth, public sector investment and progressive social policies in the subsequent decade. But the region continued to be socially differentiated, with high levels of inequality and poverty.

This period of social and economic progress came to an end in 2015, when the Brazilian economy went into deep recession. The PT was evicted from power in 2016 and the new government tried to revert to the formulas from the neoliberal period, with privatizations, labour market reform, cuts in public spending and trade liberalization, but it was trying to open Brazilian markets at a time when industrialized countries were closing theirs (Salama, 2019). The Northeast was disproportionately affected, and many of the gains of the previous decade were reversed. In the region investment dried up and the labour market deteriorated, with rising unemployment, increasing informality and declining real wages, even more so than in the country as a whole. By 2020 the income gap between the Northeast and the rest of the country was much the same as in the 1960s.

The starting point for our analysis is to consider the Northeast as subordinate to the national growth regime, a periphery within the national economy. However, this is only part of the story, because there are many aspects of economy and society that are particular to the Northeast. There are production sectors in the Northeast with direct access to global markets – grapes and mangoes in the fruit-growing zone of Pernambuco and Bahia, sandals in Paraíba – and important sectors serving regional markets – textiles and apparel in Pernambuco and Ceará, for example. The Northeast (along with the North) has a much larger informal economy than other regions of Brazil. This includes, on the one hand, unregistered and often marginal self-employed workers, either autonomous or dependent on subcontracts from larger firms, and on the other, informal wage workers who lack regular legal protection and social security. This pattern is also observed elsewhere in Brazil, but is more pronounced in the Northeast. Partly as a result, inequality is greater in the region than in other parts of Brazil. There are also economic structures with their own distinctive forms of social organization and governance, such as collaborative networks of small producers. The rural Northeast has a very different character from the rest of Brazil, and this influences the pattern of agricultural production and employment. These differences have persisted over time. There is also a racial and colonial history, of which traces still linger today. A variety of historical and institutional factors intervene in labour market relations and influence the connections between society and economy. To understand the pattern of employment, production and inequality in the region, we need to explore how these regional characteristics and relationships interact with a changing national and global economy to generate a distinct development path, and the economic, social and political institutions on which it is built.

2 Theoretical reference points

To analyse the pattern of development and change in the Northeast, this book draws mainly on four theoretical traditions, which consider production, work, and distribution in the context of persistent economic structures and social institutions.

The first is the structuralist approach initially developed at the UN Economic Commission for Latin America (now ECLAC) under the leadership of Raúl Prebisch, in the late 1940s and the 1950s. Prebisch highlighted the peripheral nature of capitalist development in Latin America (a condition that was later addressed by dependency theorists such as Andre Gunder Frank and Fernando Henrique Cardoso, among others, as a matter of economic and political dependence). In this perspective, underdevelopment had its roots in an asymmetric participation in international trade, since the countries of the region were mainly exporters of primary products and importers of manufactures from the countries of the Northern Hemisphere. This diagnosis was the basis for Celso Furtado's analysis of the formation of the Brazilian economy (1963, 1964). Overcoming this disadvantage would require State intervention to modify the pattern of growth, giving priority to industrialization, largely based on import substitution. This conclusion also informed Furtado's efforts to accelerate the development of the Northeast. Backwardness in the Northeast was not due to climatic disadvantages or other natural reasons, but because of its structurally disadvantaged insertion in the Brazilian economy (Araújo, 2000).

A central concept, which remains pertinent today, was structural heterogeneity. Large disparities in productivity and income between individuals, sectors and regions persisted or widened in much of Latin America because they had structural origins, in inherited historical conditions and in the functioning of both capital and labour markets. Investment was inadequate and capital-intensive, and created employment only for a fraction of the abundant labour supply (Bielschowsky, 2009). The result was the coexistence of high-productivity capitalist production and low-productivity production in small businesses and informal activities. This was one of the main reasons for the high levels of inequality in Latin America, because the heterogeneity of the production system gave rise to corresponding disparities in opportunities and incomes. It was not just a question of a low-productivity segment of the economy that would ultimately be absorbed by the modern sector. On the contrary, following Oliveira (1972), this heterogeneity was embedded in the economy, as the capitalist sector took advantage of the informal economy as a reserve of labour and a source of low-cost wage goods and inputs for production.

The ECLAC approach evolved in the era of neoliberal globalization, but the structuralist underpinnings remained. Heterogeneity was still present, notably visible in the technological differences between a globalized, capital-intensive sector and the rest of the economy. The "neo-structuralist" approach that developed in ECLAC work from the 1990s onwards introduced a Schumpeterian focus on knowledge and innovation and the dynamics of the production structure, responding to the concern that capital accumulation was slow, while "the region's technical progress has been limited to enclaves that have few effects on the economy at large, which has fostered structural heterogeneity, informal labour activity, low wages, poverty and a concentration of income and wealth" (Bielschowsky, 2009, p.181). If this problem has not been overcome today in Brazil (commodities still account for half of Brazilian exports, and the Northeast remains disadvantaged), it is therefore not only because of the hegemony of neoliberal globalization, although global market forces certainly promote concentration, but also because the structural heterogeneity of the Brazilian economy conditions its connections with the global economy.

This structural view of the economy connects to a structural view of the labour market. In Latin America, the work of the ILO Regional Employment Programme for Latin America and the Caribbean (PREALC) incorporated the "informal sector" into an understanding of the functioning of the productive system and the labour market (Tokman, 1992). The notion of the informal sector became popular in the 1970s to describe the existence of a non-capitalist, small scale production sector alongside larger scale, capitalist firms. But the word "sector" was contested, since it suggested a separation between the formal and informal (Oliveira, 1972; Portes et al., 1989; among others). The PREALC work treated the informal sector as an aspect of labour market differentiation, reflecting the unequal forms of job creation in a capitalist development process. Different groups of workers had different opportunities, with only limited mobility between segments of the labour market, so that the growth of the formal sector did not absorb workers from informal activities. On the contrary, new forms of informal employment were created, including in the formal sector.

PREALC's approach is related to a second theoretical tradition that informs our work, namely labour market segmentation theory, which emerged from research into dual labour markets in industrialized countries, where "primary" and "secondary" workers faced different conditions of work and terms of employment (Doeringer and Piore, 1971). Subsequent research on labour market segmentation investigated a more general tendency for differentiation between social groups (women and men, racial groups) in opportunities and incomes (Wilkinson, 1981). The logic of segmentation was one of labour control, in which the differentiation reduced the bargaining power of workers, and permitted overall labour costs to be reduced and the profit rate increased by restricting higher wages to more qualified or better organized groups of workers, while discriminating against other groups of workers whose market position was weaker. Production systems adapted accordingly, so the patterns of segmentation and of production were intertwined (Burchell et al., 2003). It is possible to distinguish vertical segmentation, in which more than one group of workers participates in the same production process, with different terms and conditions; from horizontal segmentation, where different production processes exist side by side, with different labour conditions. These concepts are of obvious relevance for the analysis of heterogeneous production systems in Brazil, and their consequences for labour and distribution, provided they are adapted to the Latin American and Brazilian reality. Segmentation theory is consistent with the ECLAC work on structural heterogeneity because only a fraction of the economy involves high-productivity mass production. And the heterogeneous character of the production structure is reflected in the constitution of the labour market.

The literature on labour market segmentation is closely related to more recent writings on labour regimes (e.g. Baglioni et al., 2022), which also attempt to analyse labour use and the power relations that surround it within the social and institutional context of capitalist production systems and relations. We treat the labour regime within the framework of Régulation theory, discussed below.

The third broad theoretical approach on which we draw concerns the organization of global production systems, and their relationship with capital accumulation, economic growth and distribution. A large literature on "Fordism" in industrialized countries in the decades after the Second World War explored the relationship between mass production in a competitive market, mass consumption, regular and protected wage labour, a degree of coordination between capital and labour, and Keynesian demand management by the State. This model expanded towards the periphery of the global economy (Lipietz, 1989) in the search for competitiveness and economies of scale – including in Brazil during the phase of industrial growth in the 1960s and 1970s, but more particularly in East Asia. The process developed in a variety of ways in different parts of the world, but typically it was labour-intensive sectors and parts of the production process that spread to lower income countries, while the more advanced technological capabilities remained in the North, so replicating the core-periphery differentiation that was at the heart of ECLAC's earlier analysis. But these relationships also underpinned industrial growth in a number of middle-income countries, based on a growing integration of part of their economies in the global market.

In some countries this process gave rise to a real social transformation, with the development of a working class, middle classes and modern industrial capital, but there were limits to Fordist expansion (Lipietz, 1989). In some situations, there was a "relocation" of limited productive segments (especially textiles and electronics), intensive in labour, to peripheral countries, where local workers were subjected to high rates of exploitation (in terms of wages, and the duration and intensity of work), with the products being re-exported mainly to the centre ("primitive Taylorism"). This strategy was widely implemented, starting in the 1960s in the free economic zones of Korea and Taiwan, Singapore and Hong Kong. However, in certain countries (such as Brazil and Mexico) "peripheral Fordism" emerged in the 1970s on the basis of import substitution, involving autonomous local capital, a relatively large urban middle class and an embryonic skilled working class. But the best jobs, higher-skilled production, and above all, technological development remained largely outside these countries.

Peripheral Fordism has not disappeared in the era of neoliberal globalization, but the dominant model has changed. A large literature has analysed the growth of global value chains (GVCs), based on an international division of labour in production within the global economy. According to the World Bank (2020), the share of GVCs in global trade rose from 37% in 1970 to over 50% in 2008, before falling back after the Global Financial Crisis. Some of these chains involve a division of manufacturing processes across countries; others are based on the production of commodities, as inputs into a manufacturing or trading system in which surplus is extracted in the periphery, and concentrated in the centre.

The structure of Brazil's participation in GVCs reflects the high share of commodities in the country's pattern of international trade, noted above. Brazil is mainly an upstream supplier of raw inputs to GVCs, rather than participating intensively in the creation of value added. Only Russia, among major economies, has less backward linkages generating value added in the national economy (even before the current crisis) (OECD, 2013; Callegari et al., 2018). There are important exceptions, including automobiles, where Brazilian producers within the global chain produce for export to Latin American markets, and the small but advanced aerospace industry. In addition, for a significant number of products, final assembly, and the production of some intermediate parts, takes place in Brazil. But most Brazilian manufacturing exports are medium or low technology – food products, beverages, textiles and shoes. Sturgeon et al. (2013) argue that industrial policy in Brazil has been focused on building integrated national industries, and as a result has not taken advantage of global opportunities. Foreign Direct Investment tends to aim at the low-hanging fruit in agroindustry and mining, or in services. So Brazil's integration in GVCs is much more limited than that of countries in East Asia. Nevertheless, the manufacturing sector serves a substantial national market, and this has created a pool of skilled labour within Brazil, mainly in the Southeast. It has also generated a large, advanced service economy, some of it serving international markets.

In all these processes the logic of the global system is one of reducing costs and increasing competitiveness. Much of the literature concentrates on the organization and governance of such systems, but labour processes are key, since the principal mechanism for reducing costs is to offshore jobs to locations where wages are lower and workers more compliant (Gereffi, 2005; Selwyn, 2012). It is important to consider that participation in GVCs directly affects the pattern of employment and the conditions of work in countries such as Brazil. Specifications for products are set in industrialized country markets, and this has implications for labour use and the intensity of work. Models of labour organization may be imported directly from abroad, involving resistance among employers to local organization and bargaining. The pattern of employment may be set by external forces, and lead to the creation of labour hierarchies and increased segmentation.

We draw on this theoretical framework not only vis-à-vis Brazil's position in global production, but also with respect to the position of the Northeast in relation to the industrial centre of Brazil, since, as we noted above, some of the mechanisms are similar.

A fourth, broader theoretical schema, which in some ways encompasses the preceding three approaches, is provided by the Ecole de la Régulation. This theoretical framework was originally developed in Europe in an attempt to make sense of the long-term dynamics of the capitalist economies of Europe and North America (Aglietta, 1976; Boyer and Mistral, 1978). Its application to the relatively harmonious growth of European economies in the period after the Second World War was an important contribution to understanding why and how the instabilities and recessions of the interwar period were overcome, and why this "golden age" came to an end in the 1970s. By virtue of its origins, most empirical work within this framework has concerned industrialized countries. But it has also been applied in Latin America (including Lipietz, 1989; Boyer, 1994, 2015; Marques-Pereira and Theret, 2001; Aboites et al., 2002), and we have found that it can help frame the economic and social dynamics of the Northeast of Brazil as well.

The basic premise of the Régulation School is that capitalism takes many forms, and the characteristics and stability of each form depend on an underlying configuration of social and economic institutions, which determines the organization of production, the pace of capital accumulation, the functioning of markets and the pattern of distribution (Boyer, 2015). Boyer and others highlighted five institutional forms at the national level that play a central role in the pattern of production and distribution in Europe and North America:

- The monetary regime, notably the set of rules that governs credit and payments
- Forms of competition, which, unlike in conventional economics, depend on the relations among participants in the market and not on an invisible hand
- The nature of integration in the international economy, which limits the degrees of freedom within each country
- The wage labour nexus, or more broadly the nature of the employment relationship and the relations between labour and capital
- Last but not least, the State and the role it plays in managing and regulating economic activity

Under each of these headings, the institutions concerned reflect the social and economic character and history of each society, and so vary across space and time. They include both organizations and associations – trade unions, training organizations, enterprises, tribunals – and regularities of social and economic behaviour, resulting from regulations, rules and social norms. Institutions, especially in the latter category, can be either formal, in the sense that they are officially recognized, or informal, in the sense that even if not officially recognized they reflect socially accepted patterns. In the labour market, formal institutions include labour legislation and the employment contract; informal institutions include family networks, social hierarchy and unregistered employment. These institutions regulate the relations between capital and labour, between actors in the production system, between State and citizen. Unlike in a neoclassical model, economic outcomes do not reflect some market equilibrium between demand and supply, but rather the interactions among institutional forces, and the behaviour and power of the social and economic actors involved. Taken as a whole they establish the framework within which the capitalist market economy functions. In the Régulation literature the set of institutional mechanisms and their interaction is referred to as the mode of regulation.

This is a theory of dynamics, not of equilibrium. The mode of regulation gives rise to an "accumulation regime" and a particular development path or development regime. Whether this regime will be stable depends on the coherence of the institutional configuration which underpins it. Typically tensions among institutions grow even during a period of stable growth, so that ultimately conflicts and contradictions emerge, leading to a period of institutional reconfiguration before a new growth regime emerges. Régulation theory is thus a theory of crisis as much as of stability or growth. It seems particularly well adapted to the recurrent crises in the Brazilian economy.

This theoretical framework can be very useful for the study of the development path of the Northeast, its relation to the national economy, and its implications for labour relations. However, the key institutions of the mode of regulation in Brazil may differ from those in industrialized countries. In particular, we need to consider that the "accumulation regimes" in Brazil reflect the interaction and interdependence between capitalist and non-capitalist forms of productive organization (Oliveira, 1972). The corresponding "modes of regulation" are marked by overlaps and complementarities between formal and informal mechanisms, with implications for the monetary and credit regime, the forms of competition, the occupational pattern, the regulatory role of the State and the nature of international economic integration. We have made an effort to adapt the central categories suggested by the Régulation School to the Brazilian context. The use of the notions of "development regime" and "labour regime", in the following chapters, results from this effort.

We therefore set the socioeconomic situation of the Northeast within the overall *development regime* in Brazil – that is to say the organization of production and the distribution of its benefits, the process of capital accumulation, the role of the State and other actors and the social and economic institutions on which they rely. At the heart of these processes is the *labour regime*, which encompasses the level and structure of employment, the pattern of industrial relations, conditions of work and wages and the corresponding economic and social institutions. This includes the institutions of what Boyer (1994) calls the wage labour nexus, but it needs to be broader in the context of Northeast Brazil because there is also a diversity of forms of non-wage work that need to be taken into account, which play a key role in both production and distribution. Broadly, then, we consider the labour regime to refer to the institutions, structures and processes through which work is organized and governed. The labour regime directly affects productivity, and how it varies across different sectors of the economy. It also directly affects the pattern of inequality, through its consequences for the distribution of value added between capital and labour and between different categories of workers.

One advantage of this approach is its ability to bring together economic and social relations in a single analytical framework, which addresses both macro- and micro-levels. While institutional forms underlie a macroeconomic process – the development regime – they also condition the behaviour of economic and social actors at the micro-level, in the organization of production and the corresponding patterns of work. Coordination or contradiction between institutions, which are ultimately the source of stability or crisis in the development regime, are often visible within companies or in labour markets. At the same time, the type of organization of the production unit can, in turn, influence the macro-environment, with effects on investment, production and distribution. For instance, the informal network of small family businesses producing garments in the Agreste region of Pernambuco (discussed in Chapter 4), with a high level of coordination and cooperation, modifies the functioning of the regional market for labour; a similar phenomenon was observed in Italian industrial districts (Pyke et al., 1990). A single production process may draw on a variety of institutional forms, for example when activities are outsourced from a large company to small companies or individuals. To understand the general development regime and its consequences we also need to understand these institutional characteristics of production and distribution at the micro-level.

These four theoretical approaches provide a guide rather than a straitjacket. They are used in four ways in this book. First, they inform the historical analysis of growth and employment. The goal is not to try to test particular propositions, but rather to use these theoretical approaches as a source of insights about relationships and mechanisms, which can help us make sense of the patterns of production and distribution we observe in the Northeast, both historically, and today. Second, they help identify key institutions that need to be explored further, notably the labour institutions that govern work and employment, taking into account the different forms of segmentation to which they are subjected. Third, they help to interpret particular cases. The research reported in this book includes a series of detailed case studies of economic sectors and territories in the Northeast, which illustrate both the micro-level elements with which the overall development regime is constructed, and how the institutions of the overall development regime influence diverse forms of production and employment. Fourth, they permit us to explore the connections between structures of production and work in the region and national and international economic systems, notably through participation in national and global value chains.

3 Methodological approach

This book is part of and draws on a wider programme of empirical research on production systems, economic sectors, labour markets and local development processes in Northeast Brazil: "*A Reprodução das Desigualdades no Nordeste do Brasil: Regimes de Trabalho e Desenvolvimento*" (The Reproduction of Inequalities in the Northeast of Brazil: Labour Regimes and Development), co-ordinated by one of the authors (Véras de Oliveira).[6] This research has examined the socio-productive and institutional configuration of the region and the transformations it has undergone over time, especially as seen through the prism of work and employment, with a focus on the period since the 1990s and, spatially, on the states of Paraíba and Pernambuco. Studies under this programme have collected and analysed primary data, especially empirical material gathered in the course of case studies of enterprises and subregions, including semi-structured interviews, focus groups, small questionnaire-based surveys, documents and audio-visual material. Much of this material was collected during visits by researchers to factories, mines, production networks, trade unions and private and public institutions. The present book tries to connect the findings of specific studies in the region to the wider context of the development regime. In particular, Chapter 4 brings together material extracted from a number of empirical case studies, mainly in Pernambuco and Paraíba, to characterize and illustrate production systems in the region.

In addition to this case study material, and extensive use of the historical literature, a variety of secondary data sources have also been also used, including the censuses and household sample surveys carried out by IBGE, the Brazilian Institute of Geography and Statistics, monthly reports on industries and services and labour market registration records.[7]

The book seeks to draw lessons from historical experience, to dissect and document the nature of social and economic progress, and to emphasise the connections between the local, regional, national and international. A common hypothesis underlying this research, and which is also the theme of this book, is that employment relations in the Northeast have emerged and developed on a segmented and predominantly precarious base. The types of segmentation and of precariousness depend on the connections between the Northeast, the rest of Brazil and the international economy. They also depend on how economic, organizational and institutional initiatives have been integrated into the socio-productive fabric of the region: whether they are public or private in nature, the agents and enterprises involved, the roles of capital and of technology, and the ability of workers and political actors to defend social and labour rights. The persistence of regional disadvantage in the Northeast, under a variety of economic and political circumstances, suggests that new institutional arrangements and economic mechanisms will be needed if this disadvantage is to be overcome.

4 The organization of the book

The next three chapters of this book address the development of the Northeast from three different angles.

Chapter 2 expands the history that we have briefly summarized above. It examines the socioeconomic transformations of Brazil and the Northeast and their implications for work and employment. After the end of slavery in the latter part of the nineteenth century different labour market institutions emerged in the Northeast and the Southeast of Brazil, reflecting the dynamics of capitalist accumulation in the Southeast and the persistence of traditional agrarian relations in the Northeast, which reinforced regional differences. The dynamics of growth and employment are then examined in three periods: from the restructuring of the Northeastern economy that began at the end of the 1950s up to the neoliberal regime that prevailed in the 1990s; the period from 2003 until 2014, when neodevelopmentalist state policies dominated and regional inequalities declined; and the period of economic and political crisis since 2015, when a new economic, political and social environment emerged after the impeachment of President Dilma Rousseff in 2016. The effects of the economic crisis, a continuing process of deindustrialization, measures to deregulate labour relations and the weakening of social policies brought a deterioration of employment and income and an increase in unemployment which affected the whole country, but especially the Northeast.

Chapter 3 takes up the central question of the labour regime. First, it considers the main labour institutions, particularly state labour market regulation and the pattern of trade union membership and activity, how they have changed over time, and how they vary across different regions of Brazil. It highlights the importance of the informal economy for understanding the overall pattern of labour regulation. Second, it explores the nature of employment relationships, identifying a variety of wage labour statuses and types of self-employment, with different levels of employment quality, security, income and productivity, which are analysed empirically using household survey data. Third, the chapter examines the contribution of labour status to the overall pattern of inequality of income within the Northeast, and between the Northeast and the rest of Brazil. Fourth, it considers in more detail the impact of differentiation and discrimination in the labour market in terms of gender, race and their interaction, highlighting the distinctive features of the Northeastern labour market, and the role of these factors in overall inequality. Finally, it considers the trajectory and changing character of the labour regime, with particular attention to the crisis period since 2015.

Chapter 4 presents results from individual studies of local and sectoral production systems. It examines how patterns of production, labour relations, employment and income have evolved, and draws out implications for the structure of regional labour markets and the pattern of access to employment opportunities and livelihoods. The examples presented illustrate social and economic relations found at different levels – in large international companies that participate in global supply chains, in networks of small producers, in sectors where large and small companies coexist, in traditional sectors and in new economic activities subject to rapid technological changes, as well as exploring how different productive activities intersect in particular territories. The studies cover the production of sugar and fruit, mining, clusters of enterprises producing garments and shoes, construction, large-scale manufacturing including automobile production and ship-building, and some modern service sectors using advanced technology – call centres, information technology services and on-line taxi services.

Finally, Chapter 5 brings together the evidence and the arguments in the preceding chapters to give an overall assessment of the development and labour regimes in Northeast Brazil. The development of the region mirrors the story of Brazil as a whole, one of uneven growth, repeated crisis and high inequality. Returning to the theoretical framework presented in Chapter 1, the chapter summarizes the workings of the main institutional forms in the Brazilian economy, how they combine to generate a distinctive development regime in the Northeast, and their role in the persistence of regional inequality and disadvantage. In particular, the labour regime plays a central role in the long-term economic, social and political trajectory, through its influence on production, income and its distribution and social organization. The chapter concludes by identifying issues that will need to be addressed if there is to be a successful and egalitarian recovery not only from the long-drawn-out economic and political crisis in Brazil since 2015, but also from the devastating effects of the Covid-19 pandemic.

Notes

1 *Ideas are neither of the past nor of the present. Ideas are correct or mistaken.* From a poster in the street in João Pessoa, Paraíba.

2 The World Inequality Database https://wid.world gives an estimate of the Gini coefficient of 0.68 in 2021. This includes both labour and capital income, which explains why it is higher than the figure in Table 1.2, which only refers to labour income. Only South Africa, among major economies, has a higher income Gini coefficient. The figure for Chile and Mexico is similar to that for Brazil.

3 E.g. Ramos (1938) and Amado (1934).

4 The word "State" can refer both to the national institutions of governance, as in this case, and to the individual provinces (states) within the Brazilian Federation, as shown in the map of the country. We write "State" with an initial capital letter in the former use, and also when it is part of the name of a specific state (e.g., São Paulo State; but the state of São Paulo). When used as an adjective ("state policies"), we do not capitalize.

5 Source: IBGE, PNADC, 2019, third quarter, own calculations from micro-data. These figures are for Brazil as a whole, but the same pattern is observed in the Northeast, with somewhat lower shares of wage work with carteira, especially in small firms (88% and 47%).

6 This research was undertaken by research groups at the Federal University of Paraíba, João Pessoa (UFPB), and the Federal University of Campina Grande, Paraíba (UFCG); more details are given the preface to this book. Results of some of these studies were included in a detailed publication in Portuguese (Véras de Oliveira and Rodgers, 2022), and in earlier publications (Véras de Oliveira and Santana, 2013; Véras de Oliveira, 2014; Cavalcanti et al., 2018; Ramalho et al., 2021; among others).

7 Data used from IBGE included the National Household Sample Survey (*Pesquisa Nacional por Amostra de Domicílios* – PNAD), carried out annually until 2014, and its successor, the Continuous National Household Sample Survey (*Pesquisa Nacional por Amostra de Domicílios Contínua* – PNADC); the Family Budget Survey, 2002–2003, 2008–2009 and 2017–2018 (*Pesquisa de Orçamentos Familiares* – POF); the Demographic Census 2010; the Monthly Surveys of Services (*Pesquisa Mensal de Serviços* – PMS) and Industry (*Pesquisa Industrial Mensal* – PIM), and the Municipal Agricultural Survey (*Pesquisa Agricola Municipal* – PAM). Employment registration data were used from the Annual Social Information Report (*Relação Anual de Informações Sociais* – RAIS) and the General Employment Register (*Cadastro Geral de Empregados e Desempregados* – CAGED), both maintained by the Labour and Social Security Secretariat of the Economics Ministry (formerly the Labour Ministry). We have reprocessed micro-data from the PNADC and the RAIS, in order to explore particular aspects of work and employment relationships in greater depth.

References

Aboites, Jaime, Luis Miotti and Carlos Quenan. 2002. "Regulationist approaches and accumulation in Latin America" in Robert Boyer and Yves Saillard (eds.): *Régulation theory: The state of the art* (pp. 280–288). London and New York: Routledge.

Aglietta, Michel. 1982 (1976). *Régulation et crises du capitalisme.* Paris: Calmann-Levy.

Amado, Jorge. 2010 (1934). *Cacau.* São Paulo: Companhia das Letras.

Araújo, Tânia Bacelar de. 2000. "A 'Questão Regional' e a 'Questão Nordestina'" in Maria da Conceição Tavares (ed.): *Celso Furtado e o Brasil* (pp. 71–92). São Paulo: Editora Fundação Perseu Abramo.

Baer, Werner. 2014. *The Brazilian economy* (7th ed.). Boulder, CO: Lynne Rienner.

Baglioni, Elena, Liam Campling, Neil Coe and Adrian Smith (eds.). 2022. *Labour regimes and global production.* Newcastle Upon Tyne: Agenda Publishing.

Barbosa, Alexandre de Freitas, Maria Cristina Cacciamali and Gerry Rodgers. 2017. *Growth and inequality: The contrasting trajectories of India and Brazil.* New Delhi: Cambridge University Press.

Bielschowsky, Ricardo. 2009. "Sixty years of ECLAC: Structuralism and neo-structuralism". *CEPAL Review*, 97: 171–192.

Boyer, Robert. 1994. "Do labour institutions matter for economic development? A 'Regulation' approach for the OECD and Latin America with an extension to Asia" in Gerry Rodgers (ed.): *Workers, institutions and economic growth in Asia* (pp. 25–112). Geneva: International Institute for Labour Studies.

———. 2015. *Economie politique des capitalismes: Théorie de la régulation et des crises.* Paris: La Découverte.

Boyer, Robert and Jacques Mistral. 1978. *Accumulation, inflation, crises.* Paris: Presses Universitaires de France.

Burchell, Brendan, Simon Deakin, Jonathan Michie and Jill Rubery (eds.). 2003. *Systems of production: Markets, organisations and performance.* London: Routledge.

Callegari, Julia, Tatiana Massaroli Melo and Carlos Ferreira de Carvalho. 2018. "The peculiar insertion of Brazil into global value chains". *Review of Development Economics*, 22(3): 1321–1342.

Cavalcanti, Helenilda, Maria Ângela Souza and Roberto Véras de Oliveira. 2018. *Suape: Desenvolvimento em questão. Impactos do complexo industrial portuário de Suape (CIPS): Migração, trabalho, condições de moradia, identidade e novas territorialidades*. Recife: Massangana.

Doeringer, Peter and Michael Piore. 1971. *Internal labor markets and manpower analysis*. Lexington, MA: Heath.

Freyre, Gilberto. 2003 (1937). *Nordeste*. São Paulo: Global Editora.

Furtado, Celso. 1963. *The economic growth of Brazil: A survey from colonial to modern times*. Los Angeles: University of California Press. (Original publication: *Formação econômica do Brasil*. Rio de Janeiro: Fundo de Cultura, 1959).

———. 1964. *Development and underdevelopment*. Los Angeles: University of California Press. (Original publication: *Desenvolvimento e subdesenvolvimento*. Rio de Janeiro: Fundo de Cultura, 1961).

Gereffi, Gary. 2005. *The new offshoring of jobs and global development*. ILO Social Policy Lectures, Jamaica. Geneva: International Institute for Labour Studies.

Gomes, Gustavo Maio and José Raimundo Vergolino. 1995. *A macroeconomia do desenvolvimento nordestino: 1960/1994*. Texto para Discussão, no. 372. Brasília, DF: IPEA.

Guimarães Neto, Leonardo. 1997. "Trajetória econômica de uma região periférica". *Estudos Avançados*, 11(29), January/April. São Paulo.

IBGE (Instituto Brasileiro de Geografia e Estatística). Various dates. PNADC (*Pesquisa Nacional por Amostra de Domicílios Contínua*). Rio de Janeiro.

Infante, Ricardo. 2015. "Brasil no umbral do desenvolvimento. Um exercício de convergência produtiva" in Ricardo Infante, Carlos Mussi and Mauro Oddo (eds.): *Por um desenvolvimento inclusivo: O caso do Brasil* (pp. 301–341). Santiago: CEPAL.

Lipietz, Alain. 1989. "Fordismo, fordismo periférico e metropolização". *Ensaios Fundação de Economia e Estatística*, 10(2): 303–335.

Marques-Pereira, Jaime and Bruno Theret. 2001. "Régimes politiques, médiations sociales de la Régulation et dynamiques macroéconomiques. Quelques enseignements pour la théorie du développement d'une comparaison de caractères nationaux distinctifs du Brésil et du Mexique à l'époque des régimes d'industrialisation par substitution des importations". *L'Année de la Régulation*, 5: 105–143.

Muniz de Albuquerque, Durval. 2014. *The invention of the Brazilian Northeast*. Durham, NC: Duke University Press. Translated by Jerry Dennis Metz from the original: *A invenção do Nordeste e outras artes*. São Paulo: Cortez Editora, 1999.

OECD (Organization for Economic Cooperation and Development). 2013. *Global value chains: Brazil*. Paris. https://www.oecd.org/sti/ind/GVCs%20-%20BRAZIL.pdf

Oliveira, Francisco de. 2003 (1972). *Crítica à razão dualista: O ornitorrinco*. São Paulo: Boitempo.

Portes, Alejandro, Manuel Castells and Lauren A. Benton (eds.). 1989. *The informal economy. Studies in advanced and less developed countries*. Baltimore, MD: Johns Hopkins University Press.

Pyke, Frank, Giacomo Becattini and Werner Sengenberger (eds.). 1990. *Industrial districts and inter-firm co-operation in Italy*. Geneva: International Institute for Labour Studies.

Ramalho, José Ricardo, Marcelo Carneiro and Roberto Véras de Oliveira. 2021. *Configurações do desenvolvimento, trabalho e ação coletiva*. São Paulo: Annablume.

Ramos, Graciliano. 2016 (1938). *Vidas secas*. Rio de Janeiro: Editora Record, 131th edition. English translation by Ralph Edward Dimmick: *Barren lives*. Austin: University of Texas Press, 1965.

Rodgers, Gerry. 2020. "Thwarted desires: Life and exploitation in the Northeast of Brazil in the 1930s". *Review of Agrarian Studies*, 10(1), January–June. http://www.ras.org.in/thwarted_desires.

Salama, Pierre. 2019. "O Brasil em retrocesso?". *Cadernos do Desenvolvimento*, 14(-24): 177–203.

Selwyn, Ben, 2012. *Workers, state and development in Brazil: Powers of labour, chains of value*. Manchester: Manchester University Press.

Sturgeon, Timothy, Gary Gereffi, Andrew Guinn and Ezequiel Zylberberg. 2013. *Brazilian manufacturing in international perspective: A global value chain analysis of Brazil's aerospace, medical devices, and electronics industries*. Oxford: Said Business School.

Tokman, V. (ed.). 1992. *Beyond regulation: The informal economy in Latin America*. Boulder, CO: Lynne Rienner.

UNDP (United Nations Development Programme). 2016. *Desenvolvimento humano nas macrorregiões brasileiras*. Brasilia: UNDP. https://www.br.undp.org/content/dam/brazil/docs/IDH/undp-br-macrorregioesbrasileiras-2016.pdf, accessed 22-06-2022.

Véras de Oliveira, Roberto. 2014. *Dinâmicas atuais do trabalho na Paraíba: Leituras sociológicas*. Campina Grande: Eduepb.

Véras de Oliveira, Roberto and Gerry Rodgers (eds.). 2022. *Desenvolvimento e regime de trabalho: A trajetória do Nordeste do Brasil*. São Paulo: Annablume.

Véras de Oliveira, Roberto and Marco Aurélio Santana. 2013. *Trabalho em territórios produtivos reconfigurados no Brasil*. João Pessoa: Editora Universitária da UFPB.

Wilkinson, Frank. 1981. *The dynamics of labour market segmentation*. London: Academic Press.

World Bank. 2020. *World Development Report 2020: Trading for development in the age of global value chains*. Washington, DC.

World Inequality Database. https://wid.world, accessed 03-11-2021.

2 The historical trajectory

1 Introduction

This chapter provides a historical overview of the development regime in Northeast Brazil, considering patterns of economic growth and recession, modes of state intervention and fluctuations in levels of employment and income. We start, briefly, with the long-term historical context, but focus on the period that began with the creation of the Superintendency for the Development of the Northeast (Sudene) in 1959, and, in particular, the period since the 1990s.

We referred in the last chapter to Guimarães Neto's (1997) identification of three main phases in the economic history of the Northeast: the constitution of an economic system in the region during the colonial period; the articulation of this system with other economic structures which were established in Brazil, especially after the middle of the nineteenth century, when a national domestic market developed; and the emergence, especially from the 1950s onwards, of a "regional question" in the country, resulting from the economic backwardness of the Northeast compared with the rapid industrialization of the Rio de Janeiro-São Paulo area, and the beginning of a process of economic integration of all regions (and, in particular, the Northeast) under the dominance of the South and Centre of the country.

The colonization of the Brazilian territory, which began in what today comprises the Northeast, basically took two forms. On the coast, where sugarcane plantations developed, slave labour predominated (coexisting with various forms of "free" non-wage work, but which were of secondary importance). Inland, an economy was established that was initially focused on supplying agricultural and livestock products to the sugarcane region. As colonization extended further into the interior, there developed a production system built around extensive livestock and subsistence agriculture, where slave labour was practically non-existent (Andrade, 1963).

Revisiting Brazilian economic and social history through the prism of the constitution of the "labour market", Barbosa also identified three main periods:[1] the first, during the colonial period, dominated by "non-labour market" work, since there was no space for the emergence of market employment

DOI: 10.4324/9781003326670-2

relations because of the dominance of slavery; a second, between 1850 and 1930, when the foundations for the construction of a "labour market" were laid, notably through state initiatives to promote the replacement of slave labour by wage work when the former was abolished in the latter part of the nineteenth century; and a third, with the beginning of industrialization and the establishment of a (partial) framework of state regulation of labour relations (between 1930 and 1980), when there was an expansion of the "labour market" at the national level, but in a selective and segmented process.

In the Northeast, the transition to "free labour" and the growth of an urban proletariat was slower and less complete than in the economic centre around São Paulo. A major factor was the modernization of sugarcane cultivation and sugar production, which began in the early twentieth century, when the artisanal sugar mills began to be replaced by industrial factories (Andrade, 1963). Cotton cultivation, which gained momentum in the second half of the nineteenth century in the Agreste region, an intermediate region between the coast (Zona da Mata) and the semiarid interior (Sertão) of the Northeast, was already mainly using non-slave labour. However, as Barbosa (2022) notes, the nature of the transition away from slavery in the Northeast was in fact connected with the region's growing economic backwardness in relation to the South and Centre of the country. Even in the more dynamic sectors, such as the sugarcane and cotton agroindustries, it mainly took the form of "semi-wage labour relations" (Andrade, 1963) after slave labour ended. The worker remained as a resident (*morador*) of the large farm, and provided the owner with labour for his plantation, at low wages; in addition, the *morador* had the right to cultivate a small area of land for his sustenance and that of his family.

> The gradual nature of this transition reflected historical contingencies – loss of the stock of slaves, availability of a huge population and limited demand for labour – which allowed estate owners to maintain control over an emerging rural proletariat that was only marginally inserted in and subordinated to the market economy. This slowness can be seen as both cause and effect of an economy that lacked dynamism, driven by the logic of commercial capital, and characterized by horizontal expansion with little social differentiation (Barbosa, 2022, p.76).[2]

For Barbosa, until the first decades of the twentieth century regional inequalities reflected differences in international economic connections, which had their origins in the colonial economy. The country's industrialization process along the Rio-São Paulo axis resulted in a growing gap with the economy of the Northeast. In the latter region, the prevalent labour relations (predominantly non-capitalist), and a lack of export dynamism hampered the emergence of a high-productivity industrial sector. Oliveira (1981) argued that the regime of capitalist accumulation that was established from the 1930s onwards was anchored in a new regional division of labour.

In São Paulo, increasingly industrialized, there was an expansion of capitalist forms of production and labour relations; in the Northeast, the maintenance of non-capitalist and semi-wage labour relations (in the sugar and cotton-livestock sectors) kept the region's economy trapped and dependent on earlier forms of reproduction of capital, rendering infeasible industrialization at the pace and on the scale of São Paulo (Barbosa, 2022).

The full economic integration of the Northeast into the national economy only started to occur after the 1950s, at a time when regional differentiation had become a key issue in the country's political agenda. However, it was, as we will see, a form of integration that was subordinate to capital from São Paulo and, in a broader sense, subordinate to the economy of the Southeast of the country (Oliveira, 1981).

2 From Sudene to the "fiscal war"

2.1 Sudene, the restructuring of the regional economy and the transformation of work

The present-day character of the Northeast, in terms of both socioeconomic environment and patterns of work, has roots not only in the historical formation of the region, as we saw briefly above, but also in the transformations brought about by the Superintendency for the Development of the Northeast, Sudene. Sudene was created in 1959 as an organ of the Federal Government, based in Recife, Pernambuco, with the main objective of coordinating development policies in the Northeast, including the nine states of the region and the north of the State of Minas Gerais.[3] Sudene and the *Banco do Nordeste* (Bank of the Northeast) – which had already been created in 1952 – established the foundations of a developmental policy for the region.

According to Oliveira (1981), until the military coup in 1964, the Sudene project was under intense political dispute among the actors concerned: the São Paulo bourgeoisie (in turn, associated with international capital), the Northeastern industrial bourgeoisie, the local agrarian oligarchy with interests in cotton and livestock, and popular forces that emerged at that time, especially the Peasant Leagues[4] and trade unions in both urban and rural areas.

Starting from a traditional and technically outdated industrial base producing non-durable consumer goods (textiles, footwear, clothing, food), a new industrial sector was established in the region with the support of Sudene, producing intermediate goods (mainly in Bahia) and durable consumer goods (especially in Pernambuco). This development was promoted by tax incentives, investment by state-owned companies (Petrobras and Vale do Rio Doce, in particular) and public sector credit, mainly from BNDES (the National Bank for Economic and Social Development), and the *Banco do Nordeste*. There was also some modernization of old agricultural areas through the extension of irrigation, and a development of urban services, mainly in metropolitan centres. Nevertheless, in the semiarid region subsistence agriculture and extensive livestock farming persisted, and in the cities the informal economy expanded (Guimarães Neto, 1997).

In the assessments of Oliveira (1981) and Araújo (2004), the result of this process was a *dependent* economic integration; the industrial expansion of the Northeast, from 1960 to 1980, was essentially based on capital investment originating in the Centre-South. In the new regional division of labour, the Northeast, broadly speaking, played the role of producer of inputs for the industry of the more developed regions, but also of consumer of final goods produced in these regions, and – through a significant flow of migrants – supplier of a large contingent of low-wage workers to these regions, mainly São Paulo.

In the new Northeastern economic space, Gomes and Vergolino (1995) identified four main sub-regions: (a) the metropolitan areas of Salvador (Bahia), Recife (Pernambuco) and Fortaleza (Ceará), where most of the large industrial projects were concentrated (the Camaçari Industrial Complex in Bahia, spinning and weaving, metalworking, chemical, paper and cellulose industries in Pernambuco and the textile and garment pole in Ceará); (b) the Zona da Mata, including the coastal regions and most of Maranhão, with emphasis on the sugar and alcohol agribusiness in Pernambuco and Alagoas, cocoa in Bahia, and babassu palm and wood in Maranhão, in addition to tourism and some industry and services in non-metropolitan state capitals; (c) the semiarid region of the interior, where historically a low-productivity economy was based on extensive livestock and subsistence agriculture, subject to cyclical droughts; (d) the main irrigated zones, where modern agroindustry emerged, producing for national and international markets, including the Açu area in Rio Grande do Norte, and areas irrigated from the São Francisco river in Bahia and Pernambuco.

Investment was concentrated in large industrial, agricultural and service projects, which modified the links between the regional economy and external capital and markets, with dynamic areas beginning to coexist with large stagnant sub-regions (Guimarães Neto, 1997). In general, this investment involved both public and private capital, some of the latter locally based, but mainly national and international. As shown by Araújo et al. (1997), from then on economic "poles" were established, distinguished and differentiated from traditional activities, but with a limited capacity to spread more widely.

Manufacturing industry acquired a new character. According to Oliveira (1981), the "traditional" industries (textiles, in particular), which in 1959 accounted for 70% of industrial value added (IVA), had fallen to only 30% of IVA at the end of the 1970s. The opposite occurred with the "dynamic" industries (especially metalworking).[5] For Araújo (2004), based on data from Sudene, between 1967 and 1989, while agriculture shrank from 27.4% to 12.1% of Gross Regional Product, industry increased from 22.6% to 29.3%. The service sector also grew, from 49.9% to 58.6% of GRP.

Overall, from the beginning of the 1960s onwards, the region began to track the growth of the Brazilian economy and its conjunctural fluctuations, sometimes a little above and sometimes a little below (Araújo, 2017). According to the calculations of Gomes and Vergolino (1995), between 1960 and 1993, the average rates of growth were very close: 5.5% in the Northeast and 5.6% in Brazil. However, traditional production patterns continued to resist change. For Araújo (2004, pp.12–13),

> While various parts of the Northeast were modernizing, others were more resistant to socioeconomic change, particularly in the traditional cacao- and sugar-producing areas and in the semiarid interior. Modernization in these areas, when it occurred at all, was restricted and selective, helping to maintain a dominant traditional system.

In addition, according to Oliveira (1981, p.45), the investment model adopted by Sudene, in which tax incentives were the main instrument for promoting industrialization and economic modernization, had a "highly concentrating" effect, primarily benefiting large national conglomerates and international capital, which further strengthened a historically unequal economic system.

Growth was especially concentrated in the cities, particularly in the metropolitan regions of Salvador, Recife and Fortaleza, and to a lesser degree the other Northeastern capitals. With the modernization of transport, medium-sized cities such as Campina Grande, Feira de Santana, Caruaru, Juazeiro and Petrolina, among others, which had previously served as distribution centres for goods to the interior, were adversely affected (Guimarães Neto, 1985).

In the Northeast as a whole, GNP tripled between 1970 and 1993 (from US$20.8 billion to US$65.3 billion, measured at 1993 prices), while per capita production doubled in the same period (from US$740 to US$1,486) (Araújo, 2004, pp.33–34). According to Ablas and Pinto (2009), GDP (at constant prices) of the Northeast accounted for 11.7% of national GDP in 1970, 12% in 1980, and 12.7% in 1990. According to Silva (2005), GDP per capita in the Northeast was 42.9% of GDP per capita in Brazil in 1974, rising to 56.3% in 1986. That is, in the period considered, both indicators grew faster in the region than at the national level. These gains were to some extent reflected in incomes. According to PNAD[6] data from 1981 and 1992, the median monthly household income per capita[7] in the Northeast remained around half of that of Brazil, but the gap diminished slightly: in 1981 it was 50.4% and in 1992, 55.5%. But in the end, the development brought by Sudene not only did not overcome inequality but also brought new disparities and imbalances.

The socioeconomic transformations that occurred in the Northeast under the umbrella of Sudene had a substantial impact on the structure of the workforce and the pattern of labour relations. However, the legacy of slave labour and an agrarian structure based on large estates, along with a slow and partial expansion of wage labour and an abundant labour supply, facilitated the persistence of exploitative labour relations and low remuneration levels, despite economic modernization (Guimarães Neto, 1997).

By prioritizing investment in capital-intensive sectors, Sudene contributed to the expansion of a well-defined but small segment of relatively skilled and well-paid workers, coexisting with a much larger contingent of low-skilled, low-wage workers. An emblematic case could be found in Bahia. In a study originally published in 1987, Oliveira (2003) analysed how the labour process developed in that state, starting with the installation of the national petroleum company Petrobras in the 1950s and, subsequently with the establishment of the Camaçari Industrial Complex in the 1970s. The result was a new class configuration. A modern bourgeoisie was constituted, capturing part of the space in the power structure previously occupied by the old agrarian and financial oligarchies. New "middle classes" emerged with the incorporation, in the emerging production system, of technicians, engineers, chemists, managers, administrators, planners, etc. At the same time, the combination of an abundant supply of labour (the "industrial reserve army") and a capital-intensive technical system that "deskilled" workers (dominated by assembly operations) produced a polarized employment structure: on the one hand, a minority of workers with relatively high wages and good working conditions; on the other, the bulk of workers, many of them with insecure jobs, subject to high job turnover, low wages and long working hours. Alongside this modern sector, there continued to exist a heterogeneous set of non-capitalist activities. The "informal sector", as it was called in the literature of the time, involving street trading, personal services, repair services, and other urban activities, but also subsistence agriculture, had already been analysed by Oliveira (1972). For this author, far from constituting a separate reality, these segments, although very different in nature from large scale capitalist production, had a dialectical relationship with the accumulation process that underlay Brazilian industrialization.

Overall, according to Araújo (2004), there was an expansion of wage employment in the region, primarily in urban areas (with the development of industry and services), but also in rural areas (both in existing production sectors, such as the sugarcane plantations, and in new areas of agroindustrial investment).

Using the IBGE Monthly Employment Survey, Araújo et al. (1997) showed that from 1982 to 1994 open unemployment rates in the metropolitan regions of Recife and Salvador were well above those in the other metropolitan regions of the country then covered by the survey (Belo Horizonte, Rio de Janeiro, São Paulo and Porto Alegre). According to the 1991 Census, only 26.9% of employed persons in the Northeast had a formal contract (*carteira assinada*, signed labour card, discussed in more detail in Chapter 3), much lower than the figure for Brazil as a whole, 41.7%. Overall, the extent of informality in the Northeast, in the sense of workers outside wage employment or in wage employment without a formal contract, was much greater than the Brazilian average.

Migration to other regions was a "way out" found by millions of Northeasterners, especially in times of drought and economic crisis. Araújo (2004) states that between 1960 and 1980, some 4 million people left the region, out of a total population in 1980 of around 35 million (IBGE/Census, 1980). At the same time, migration within the region increased, especially from rural areas and small municipalities towards the medium-sized and larger Northeastern cities, notably the major metropolises.

2.2 The neoliberal wave, the end of Sudene and the "fiscal war"

The contest between Fernando Collor and Lula da Silva in the presidential election of 1989 opposed two very different projects: the first was neoliberal in nature, in line with the global trends of convergence towards the Washington Consensus; the second was social in orientation, an expression of the accumulation of popular struggles throughout the 1980s. The former project won, and from then on a frankly pro-market policy was put in place. Even after Collor's impeachment in 1992, and his replacement first by Vice-President Itamar Franco, and then by his successor Fernando Henrique Cardoso, who was in office for two terms, the political agenda was characterized by economic restructuring, the privatization of state-owned companies and public services, a weakening and flexibilization of state regulation of labour relations and the administrative (managerial) reform of the State; the outcome was higher unemployment, informalization and a growth of precarious work (Pochmann, 2008).

From the point of view of economic performance, investment had been falling in Brazil since the 1980s (Cano, 2017). This process intensified in the 1990s, with the shrinking role of the State in the economy.[8] One of its consequences was the development of the so-called "fiscal war", a policy of "salve-se quem puder" (everyone for themselves) between subnational governments (mainly state, but also municipal), as all attempted to attract or retain private investment in their territories (Dulci, 2002).

This situation had even greater repercussions in the Northeast than elsewhere, since the State's participation in the economy had become a decisive factor in the region, directly (through investment in infrastructure and state-owned companies) and indirectly (through incentives to private capital, the generation of demand and the creation of employment), in line with the policies of Sudene and, at the federal level, the National Development Plans I and II (applied in the 1970s and 1980s). Sudene and its regional development policies were increasingly eroded until it was shut down in 2001. In its place, the Northeast Development Agency (ADENE) was created, with much more modest functions.[9]

According to Monteiro Neto et al. (2017), adding together all government investment expenditure in the three spheres (municipal, state and federal) and also including investment by state-owned companies, in 1970 this represented 17%, 11% and 15.6% of GDP in the North, Northeast and Centre-West, respectively. At the beginning of the 2000s, in contrast, these figures had fallen to 6.2%, 4.5% and 7.7%. During this period overall economic growth fell from a peak of 9.4% on average in the 1970s, to 4.3% in the 1980s and 2.6% in the 1990s (Carvalho, 1986; Guimarães Neto, 1997). Between 1995 to 2002, during the two presidential terms of Fernando Henrique Cardoso, the national economy grew just 14.9% in eight years and the Northeast, 15.5% (BNB, 2013).

During this period (1995–2002) there was little change in the sectoral distribution of production. At the national level the share of agriculture fell from 10.7% in 1995 to 8.8% in 2002; that of industry grew from 22.3% to 24.5%; that of services hardly changed (66.9% to 66.8%) (BNB, 2013). As for the share of the Northeast in Brazil for each sector of activity, the same study showed that value added in agriculture in the region as a percentage of national production in the sector fell from 22.9% to 17.1%. Meanwhile, the Northeast's share of industry and services grew from 10.0% to 12.0% and from 12.4% to 14.3%, respectively. Overall, according to the IBGE's Regional Accounts for Brazil, between 1992 and 2002, the share of the Northeast in the country's GDP fluctuated around 13%, with a slight increase in the last year of the series.

The most dynamic industrial areas in the Northeast felt the effects of this new economic and political context. The Camaçari zone, the most important industrial complex in the region, was subject to privatization, internationalization and the incorporation of new technological and management standards; this was associated with corporate restructuring, involving mergers and acquisitions, the elimination of positions and levels of management, and the widespread adoption of outsourcing (Druck, 1999). The level of employment in this industrial zone fell in the late 1990s to about one third of the level reached in the 1980s (Almeida, 2008), resulting in an increase in unemployment.

However, there was new investment in the garments sector in this period (the 1990s), especially in Ceará. This sector, despite technological innovations, remained labour-intensive. In order to meet growing international competition, economic restructuring involved increased subcontracting and the relocation of factories to regions with lower production costs, especially cheaper labour, less market regulation and the absence of union organization. This is what happened to the textile/clothing and footwear industry of São Paulo and the South, with the displacement of several factories to the Northeast, taking advantage of the "fiscal war," and with Ceará the main destination (Saboia, 2001). Starting in 1986 and throughout the first half of the following decade, the government of Ceará offered advantages in infrastructure, tax incentives, training of workers, etc., in order to attract new investment. Between 1990 and 1995, according to Araújo et al. (1997), while Bahia had an average annual output growth of 2.2%, Pernambuco, 1.5%, Maranhão, 2.9%, the Northeast, 2.6% and Brazil, 2.7%, Ceará's growth rate was 5.3%. The footwear sector also made strategic use of the "fiscal war," involving, in addition to Ceará, the states of Paraíba, Rio Grande do Norte and Pernambuco (Lima, 2002). Lima argued that, for the local populations – historically faced with scarce employment opportunities and low levels of remuneration – the new investment in the Northeast provided opportunities that had not existed before.

At the same time, another front of new investment emerged with the growth of the tourism industry. From the first half of the 1990s on, tourism began to be perceived as a sector with growing economic potential. In the case of Brazil, even in a context of reduction of state intervention in the economy, policies of the federal government and subnational governments aimed to support the expansion of the sector, especially through financing and infrastructure works for transport, energy and urban facilities (Alban, 2006). In the case of the Northeast, an important stimulus occurred with the creation, in 1991, of the Tourism Development Programme in the Northeast (Prodetur/NE), based on a consortium of Sudene and the Brazilian Tourism Company (Embratur), with contributions from the Inter-American Development Bank (IDB), the BNB and the BNDES (Paiva, 2010). This was conceived as a programme of public investment in infrastructure in areas considered to have high tourist potential in the region, in order to leverage private investment in the sector. According to data from the BNB (2005), the number of tourists in the capitals of the Northeast rose from 5 million in 1996 to just over 10 million in 2004, an average annual growth of 10%. The number of foreign tourists in the region, accounting for 15.6% of all foreign tourists in the country in 1996, jumped to 30.6% in 2004. However, these results were unevenly distributed within the region. According to Dantas e Silva (2009), the states most favoured by the programme between 1995 and 2003 were Bahia and Ceará, which together accounted for 51% of the resources invested in the sector. Labour incomes in the sector were on average low, with only 6.1% of those employed receiving incomes of five or more minimum wages, and 6.3% in the range of three to five minimum wages.

Araújo (2017, p.49) summarized the implications for the Northeast's economy in the 1990s, at the level of individual states, as follows:

> Ceará's "conservative modernization" was driven by the local business community, based on labour-intensive production sectors (textile/garments and modern retail), which promoted a local mobilization (of large and small enterprises, but also of workers), more than in Pernambuco, where the traditional business community progressively lost territory and the capacity to direct the economic dynamics, leading to, above all, the closure of textile factories and sugar mills. In Bahia, where economic restructuring was heavily based on the production of intermediate goods, destined as inputs to industry, there was an increase in production without a corresponding growth of job creation. The states of Rio Grande do Norte and Sergipe developed a different dynamic, strongly influenced by investment in the oil and gas industry;

while the development of Maranhão and Piauí was linked to the expansion of the agricultural frontier and, in the case of Maranhão, to exports and processing of iron ore from Pará.[10]

In general, we can say that, throughout the decade, the Northeast reproduced the weak performance of the Brazilian economy. At the same time, the pattern of development in the region reflected its historical character (including the results of Sudene's interventions). New and old economic and social imbalances and inequalities, both within the region and in relation to other parts of the country, continued to be visible. Below we illustrate this with some social indicators.

First, the distribution of household income per capita, between 1992 and 2002, shows that the large differences between the Northeast and Brazil as a whole remained. As noted above, according to PNAD data, in 1992 the median monthly household income in the Northeast was 55.5% of the average for Brazil, and in 2002 it had hardly changed, at 56.5%. The Gini coefficient of the distribution of per capita household income showed a slight downward trend during the 1990s (from 0.575, in 1992, to 0.571, in 2001, in the case of Brazil, and from 0.591 to 0.574 for the Northeast), but high levels of income concentration persisted in both regions, even higher in the Northeast than in Brazil as a whole, though converging at the end of the period.

Second, the unemployment rate (unemployed persons as a percentage of the economically active population) rose sharply in the 1990s both in the Northeast and in the country as a whole, with unemployment in the Northeast generally below national levels (Table 2.1).

Third, another important indicator of labour market conditions is the distribution of workers across different types of employment relationship. This is analysed in more detail in the next chapter using data for the most recent period. Here we consider an indicator of informality in employment, aggregating the labour status categories used in the PNAD at that time. We treat the following categories as formal: "wage workers with a formal contract (carteira assinada)", "military", "statutory civil servants", "domestic workers with carteira assinada" and "employers"; and the following as informal: "other wage workers without a formal contract (without carteira assinada)", "domestic workers without carteira assinada", "own account workers", "workers in production for their own consumption", "workers in construction for their own use" and "unpaid workers".[11] On this admittedly

Table 2.1 Unemployment rate, Brazil and the Northeast, 1992–2002 (%)

	1992	*1993*	*1995*	*1996*	*1997*	*1998*	*1999*	*2001*	*2002*
Brazil	6.5	6.2	6.1	7.0	7.8	9.0	9.6	9.4	9.2
Northeast	6.2	6.2	5.3	6.0	6.7	7.1	8.0	8.8	8.3

Source: IBGE, *Pesquisa Nacional por Amostra de Domicílios* (PNAD), 1992–2002.

simplified and approximate basis, for Brazil as a whole the informality rate fluctuated, from 60% in 1993, to 59% in 1996, 60% in 1999, and 58.1% in 2002, while for the Northeast the corresponding estimates were 76.6%, 74.6%, 76.3% and 74%, respectively. It can be seen that there was little change in informality during the period (a small drop at the end of the period), but a large difference between the Northeast and the rest of Brazil.

In this period, regular, protected wage work increased slightly as a share of all employment, but unprotected wage work (without carteira) increased more, in both the Northeast and the rest of Brazil. There was a corresponding decrease in self-employment, especially subsistence self-employment. Overall there was little sign of improvement in labour market conditions, and some sign of deterioration.

3 The period of neodevelopmentalist policies

3.1 The reactivation of the economy of the Northeast

In 2002 the Presidential election was won by the Workers' Party candidate, Lula da Silva, and from then onward the Federal Governments were led by the Workers' Party continuously until 2016, under Lula's presidency until 2010, and then under Dilma Roussef. During this period, developmentalist policies returned to the agenda. In 2003, economic recovery began, with a positive impact on employment. Despite the 2008 global financial crisis and its effects on GDP growth, employment indicators continued to improve until 2014. A new developmentalist discourse, emphasizing the commitment to job and income generation and macroeconomic stability (Pêgo and Campos Neto, 2008), set the political agenda, especially from 2006. Its emblematic core, the Growth Acceleration Programme (PAC), was launched in 2007.

The PAC aimed, through public and private investment, mainly in infrastructure, to increase the productivity of companies, stimulate private investment, generate employment and income, and reduce regional inequalities. Priority was given to the sectors of energy, transport, housing, sanitation and water resources, as well as social impact programmes such as *Minha Casa Minha Vida* (housing) and *Luz para Todos* (electricity distribution). With the PAC, the share of total investment in GDP rose from 16.4% in 2006 to 18.4% in 2010 (Brazil, 2010). The government's strategy to mobilize resources for these infrastructure investments relied on public-private partnerships (PPP), instituted through Law no. 11079 of 2004, with the BNDES (via Treasury funds) as the main financing agency (Jardim e Silva, 2015).

> The PPP law, associated with other previous laws, such as the concession law[12] and, later, the entry of BNDES as a guarantee fund,[13] served as a legal and financial framework which permitted the PAC to be created and put into practice (ibid., p.62).

Between 2007 and 2010, the Brazilian government invested of the order of R$503.9 billion (about US$300 billion at the December 2010 exchange rate) in infrastructure within the framework of the PAC, 43.5% of which came from state-owned and mixed economy companies (29.5% from Petrobras, a mixed economy company), 13.5% from the fiscal budget of the Union and the remaining 43% directly from the private sector, especially companies, pension funds and financial market funds (Brazil, 2010).

In 2010, PAC 2 was launched, to run from 2011 to 2014, reaffirming the previous priorities (Brazil, 2012), with an investment forecast of R$1 trillion (US$595 billion at the December 2010 exchange rate). It was conceived as part of the government's reaction to the global economic crisis. According to Araújo (2017, p.53),

> The national economy shrank in 2009, but resumed growth in 2010 following the adoption of counter-cyclical measures. One of the main measures adopted was the implementation of a second stage of the PAC, which … included new social and urban infrastructure projects, as a way of 'facing' the problems of large Brazilian cities and boosting the economy through the expansion of investment, public and private, which would be the main engine for a continuous increase in national economic activity.[14]

This renewed interventionist role of the State in the economy was associated with a series of social policies aimed at dealing with popular demands and needs, such as the *Bolsa Família* Programme, the policy of a rising minimum wage, the *Minha Casa Minha Vida* and *Luz para Todos* programmes mentioned above, One Million Cisterns, and others. In addition, a government stance in favour of social negotiation led to the creation of the National Labour Forum (FNT), aimed at promoting negotiations on labour and trade union legislation, the National Council for Economic and Social Development (CDES), the National Bureau of Collective Bargaining for federal civil servants, and the National Social Security Forum. Over the years, numerous ministerial conferences were held, with broad social participation, in the areas of work and employment, health, education, environment and cities, among others.

The improvement in economic and social indicators from 2004 onwards can be credited to both the new economic dynamism and the new political conditions, including a certain reactivation of wage and trade union struggles (Baltar and Krein, 2013).

This new context favoured the resumption of economic growth. The policies that were adopted helped increase the general level of demand in the economy and, with it, economic activity as a whole. Moreover, since they had a disproportionate effect on the purchasing power of low-income groups, they helped raise the consumption demand of the poorest. As a result, and helped by the global commodity boom during this period, there was a substantial acceleration of economic growth, especially in the period 2003–2008, and less consistently from 2010 to 2013.

The Northeast broadly followed the national pattern. But according to the Regional Accounts of Brazil[15] for the years 2003 to 2015, on the whole the Northeastern economy did better than the national average, both in the period of higher growth between 2003 and 2008 and in the more uneven period from 2009 to 2015, after the global financial crisis of 2008. In the former period, the region's annual average growth was 4.5%, slightly higher than the national average of 4.2%. In the second period, an abrupt drop in growth after 2008 was followed by a rapid recovery, but this was in turn was followed by a second recession. In this period the region's average growth was 2.5%, much lower than the previous period, but again above the average national growth rate of 1.9%. As a result, the region's share of the country's GDP increased from 12.8% in 2003 to 14.2% in 2015. In the same period, per capita GDP in the region rose from 45.4% to 51.1% of the national average, a distinct improvement, though the gap remained large.

This outcome, however, did not result from an explicitly regional developmental policy, as had been the case during the heydays of Sudene. The latter, despite having been re-established in 2007, no longer played a prominent role in the promotion and coordination of development policies in the region. During this period, among the transfers of federal resources to the Northeast, only a small part concerned funds specifically aimed at regional development. As observed by Monteiro Neto et al. (2017), even in the 1960s and 1980s, when regional policy played a key role in economic modernization of the North and Northeast regions, national sectoral policies were also important, especially with respect to infrastructure for transport, energy, communications and housing, as promoted by the National Development Plans I and II. This was even more so in the period after 2003, when investment in the poorest regions relied mainly on national sectoral policies, and only to a much lesser extent on regional policy as such.

One exception concerned the constitutional funds for regional development (see footnote 8). These had been tightly constrained during the 1990s. Their budget allocations were increased from 2007 onwards,[16] but they played a smaller role in promoting regional development than disbursements from the BNDES (aimed at financing national sectoral policy) and resources from social programmes. Even so, the overall volume of federal resources invested in the Northeast increased 2.5 times between the periods 2000–2006 and 2007–2012 (with similar increases in the North and the Midwest).

The recovery of the Northeastern economy actually resulted from a broader combination of factors. On the one hand, there was a significant increase in the consumption capacity of families, favoured by the increase in federal monetary transfers to the region, proportionately greater than the national average, as well as by the policy of raising the minimum wage and by wage readjustments above inflation for many occupational categories.

In January 2007, the Northeast accounted for 49.9% of the 10,908,452 families benefiting from the *Bolsa Família* Programme in the country, and in January 2016, 50.3% of 13,969,391 families (in comparison the region accounted for 27.8% of the country's population, according to Census data for 2010). As Araújo (2014, p.8) observed, since rural poverty is concentrated in the region, especially in small municipalities in the semiarid region, and considering that the productive base of these municipalities is very fragile, "the new and systematic flow of income not only provided social coverage to the direct beneficiaries, but also supported shops, pharmacies, bakeries and weekly fairs." As for the Continuing Provision Benefit (BPC), from the National Social Security Institute (INSS), the Northeast accounted, in January 2007, for 35.8% of a total of 2,489,025 beneficiaries, rising to 36.3%, in January 2016, out of 4,251,134.[17] Falvo (2013) also calculated that the share of the Northeast in the number of beneficiaries of Rural Social Security (social security linked to the INSS, aimed at formal and informal rural workers) was 47.2% in 2004. And in relation to the rising minimum wage,[18] Falvo (2013, p.54) comments: "the relative contribution of this increase was greater for Northeastern workers than for Brazilians, in general, given that 14% of the former, as against 10% of the latter, received exactly the minimum wage in 2007." All this, however, as observed by Lavinas (2010, p.138), did not prevent the proportion of poor people in the Northeast from remaining much higher than in the rest of Brazil: "The biggest problem continues to be that of employment opportunities and occupations for northeasterners ... 26 million people are poor in the Northeast because of labour market problems and low occupational incomes."

On the other hand, there was a significant increase in public and private investment, both in production sectors and in infrastructure. Private investment reflected increasing incomes in the region, according to Araújo (2014, p.8):

> It will not be possible to understand the recent changes in the economic life of the Northeast without examining this other component [private investment]. Food and beverage and durable goods industries, for example, sought to establish themselves or to expand production in the region, especially in the medium-sized cities. Large supermarket chains and shopping centres also multiplied in these locations, in order to compete for new consumers.[19]

Public investment, especially at the federal level, fell largely under the PAC, involving public–private partnerships, with emphasis on large infrastructure works (Araújo, 2017) in transport and water supply (see the discussion of the construction sector in Chapter 4). Other investments were aimed at the intermediate goods sector (such as the installation of the Abreu e Lima Refinery and Suape Petrochemicals, both located in the Suape Industrial Port Complex, Pernambuco) or the production of final goods, targeting the national or even international market (such as the automotive hub led by Fiat Chrysler Automobiles (FCA), in Pernambuco, as well as the naval shipyards installed in Suape, also discussed in Chapter 4).

Credit policy (for enterprises and individuals) was also important (Guimarães Neto, 2010). Investment credit in the Northeast (provided by BNDES) jumped tenfold from an average around R$200 million per year in the period 2006–2008 to R$2,000 million per year in 2009–2012.

With regard to foreign trade, despite the good performance of the regional economy, Galvão (2014) observed that, between 2000 and 2013, the share of the Northeast in the value of Brazilian exports fell from 7.6% to 7.1%. The author also added that there was no important change in the composition of exports in this period; they remained dominated by raw sugar, cellulose, raw aluminium or alumina, raw soybeans, iron ore and oil. The main new item was, from 2002, the export of Ford automobiles from Camaçari.[20]

In sum, the regional economy benefited, to a greater extent than the national average, from the new economic dynamism of the country.

3.2 Sectoral and spatial differences

The Centre for Management and Strategic Studies (CGEE) (2014, p.24) summarized the changes that were occurring in the region's production system as follows:

> Loss of relative importance of old traditional bases (livestock/cotton/multi-cropping, and the sugar-alcohol complex) and significant expansion of the tertiary sector (education, health and modern commerce, business services), of industry (manufacturing and construction) and of agribusiness (focused on grain and fruit production).[21]

The new economic momentum modified the productive structure of the region, producing shifts in the sectoral shares in value added (Table 2.2). Agriculture continued its downward trajectory, from 7.2% of value added in the Northeast in 2003 to 5.0% in 2015. Industry, which reached a maximum in 2005 (28.5%), began a gradual downward trajectory, interrupted briefly in 2011, but accelerating thereafter. The largest change concerned manufacturing industry, which fell from 16.9% in 2003 to 12.2% in 2015. Services were initially stable, around 66% and 68%, but started to gain after 2013, reaching 72.5% in 2015.

The decrease in the importance of agriculture in relation to industry and, above all, in relation to services, reflects the growing urbanization of the country and the region. The Northeast, however, maintained and continues to maintain a much higher proportion of rural population than the national average. According to the 2010 Census, while in Brazil 15.6% of the population was rural, in the Northeast this proportion was 26.9%.

Table 2.2 Share of economic sectors in Gross Value Added (%), Northeast, 2003–2015

	2003	*2005*	*2007*	*2009*	*2011*	*2013*	*2015*
Agriculture and livestock	7.2	5.5	5.2	5.2	5.1	5.3	5.0
Industry	27.0	28.5	27.1	25.6	27.2	24.9	22.5
Mining	2.2	3.1	3.0	2.2	4.4	4.2	2.1
Manufacturing	16.9	17.4	16.6	15.3	13.9	12.3	12.2
Public utilities	3.3	3.4	3.0	2.7	2.7	2.0	2.4
Construction	4.6	4.6	4.6	5.4	6.3	6.4	5.7
Services	65.8	66.0	67.7	69.2	67.7	69.9	72.5
Total	100.0	100.0	100.0	100.0	100.0	100.0	100.0

Source: Reworked from Trovão et al. (2019).

The CGEE report (2014) identifies as the main transformations in agriculture, from the early 2000s to the early 2010s: improvements in family farming, due to government programmes such as the construction of water tanks; the relative decline of typical family farming products, such as cassava (concentrated in Bahia and Maranhão) and beans (grown mainly in Bahia, and increasingly an agribusiness item); a drop in the share of traditional sugarcane monoculture (historically concentrated in Pernambuco and Alagoas); an increase in the importance of soybean production (undergoing rapid expansion in western Bahia and southern Maranhão and Piauí), maize (increasingly an agribusiness crop, especially in Bahia, Sergipe, Maranhão and Piauí), cotton (mainly grown commercially in the savannahs of Bahia and the south of Maranhão) and other irrigated crops, such as grapes and mangoes (notably in the fruit-growing pole of Juazeiro and Petrolina). Livestock is concentrated in Bahia, Pernambuco and Ceará (cattle, goats, sheep and chickens), Maranhão (cattle) and Piauí (goats and sheep). During the 2000s, the Northeast performed better (in terms of production growth) than the Brazilian average in sheep and beef raising (data from the IBGE Municipal Livestock Survey).

But these changes in Brazilian and Northeastern agriculture have not been accompanied by democratization of access to land and of the conditions for its use. On the contrary, the model is one of "conservative modernization" (a term coined by Guimarães, 1997), now under the aegis of agribusiness, with increasing repercussions in the Northeast. Elias and Pequeno (2007, pp.30–31) summarize the impacts of the expansion of agribusiness in vast areas of the Northeast, especially with respect to fruit cultivation and soya production:

> Among the negative impacts of this process, we would highlight: the destructuring of subsistence agriculture and the increase in the share of commercial enterprises in agricultural and livestock production; the expansion of monoculture and, consequently, a decrease in biodiversity

> and an increase in genetic erosion; the change in agricultural technical systems, with the dissemination of a technological package dominated by oligopolistic production and often inappropriate for regional environmental conditions, destroying historically constructed knowledge and practices. And also: the increase in land concentration, with the expropriation of farmers who do not own the land; the expansion of the land market, which has seen prices increasing, undermining aspirations for agrarian reform; the privatization of water, with development of new forms of regulation of its use, leading to the emergence of hydrobusiness; the establishment of a formal agricultural labour market, with the expansion of wage work, whether manual or specialized; the fragmentation of the agrarian system, increasingly differentiating the spaces of production and creating local production arrangements; the increase of the urban economy and of small and medium cities; the disorderly growth of some cities, with the consequent expansion of urban peripheries and infrastructure deficits.[22]

The performance of industry, in terms of output growth, varied from one subsector to another. According to Trovão et al. (2019), using official data sources, mining showed the lowest growth, averaging 0.1% per year between 2003 and 2008 and 0.3% between 2009 and 2015. The growth of construction was close to regional GDP growth, slightly lower between 2003 and 2008 (4.1% against 4.5%), slightly higher between 2009 and 2015 (3.1% compared to 2.5%). Manufacturing industry grew at an average annual rate of 5.6% between 2003 and 2008, but only 0.1% between 2009 and 2015. Public utilities was the only subsector that exceeded the average growth of regional GDP in both periods, 5.1% up to 2008 and 4.3% after 2009. The average growth rates for the second period were all affected by the recession from 2014 on, with negative growth in 2015.

There were substantial differences between states within the region in their participation in this growth; Pernambuco increased its share of regional industrial production from 12.2% to 18% between 2007 and 2015, and most other states showed some increase, at the expense of Bahia, whose share dropped from 51.9% to 41.4%.[23]

Despite some decentralization, the three main metropolitan regions (Salvador, Recife and Fortaleza) continued to account for almost half of the output of the sector, although, as shown by Araújo (2017, pp.89–90), their performances differed:

> Only the Recife Metropolitan Region achieved an increase in industrial output equal to the regional average (3.7% per year), as a result of investment in the Suape Port and Industrial Complex, but, above all, reflecting the dynamism of construction activities for the establishment of these industries and for the real estate market. (...) The Metropolitan Region of Fortaleza expanded 3.3% per year in the period from 2000

> to 2010 (…) The Metropolitan Region of Salvador had the smallest increase in industrial activity, only 2.7% per year, but it remains the main regional industrial hub, accounting for 22.9% of regional industrial value added in 2010.[24]

The service sector, despite great heterogeneity and much fluctuation over the period, generally performed better than industry and agriculture. Trovão et al. (2019) found that the following subsectors grew faster than regional GDP between 2003 and 2008: "financial activities, insurance and related services" (7.8%), "sale and repair of motor vehicles and motorcycles" (6.0%), "business services" (5.1%), "real estate" (5.0%), "transport, storage and communications" (4.7%) and "hotels and restaurants" (4.6%). During the period 2009–2015, the majority of service sector activities grew faster than or close to the growth of regional GDP, with the notable exception of public services (administration, education, health, public research and development, defence, social security), whose slow growth was partly due to cuts in public spending in 2014–2015. Public services had also grown more slowly than GDP during the 2003–2008 period. However, "financial activities, insurance and related services" continued to grow particularly fast after 2009 (annual average growth 6.4% between 2009 and 2015), reflecting within the Northeast the growing centrality of financial activities in the national economy. To sum up, two general trends stand out in the service sector: financialization of the regional economy and, especially in the last years of the period, deceleration in the growth of the public sector.

Araújo and Favareto (2020) also call attention to other structural changes that affected the Northeast during this period, highlighting the expansion of medium-sized cities in the interior of each state, with respect to health services and, even more so, higher education, science and technology (through expansion in the interior of the networks of public and private universities and technology institutes). In these areas there was an expansion of public services and job opportunities. It is worth underlining the expansion of higher education. Between 2009 and 2015, enrolment in higher education grew by 49.1% in the Northeast, compared with 34.8% for Brazil.[25] Moreover, within states the growth in enrolment in higher education was higher in medium-sized cities in the interior than in the capitals: 44.3% against 24.6% in Bahia; 45.9% against 34.4% in Pernambuco; 104% against 74.3% in Ceará; and 98.4% against 66.1% in Paraíba. This expansion of federal higher and technical education had repercussions far beyond the educational indicators, including, according to Máximo (2020, p.2), economic and urban dimensions such as:

> increased demand for urban mobility, due to the need for travel to educational campuses, often located far from the high-density residential areas; growth in the local real estate market, with the construction of new buildings intended for rental, especially for students; increase in commercial and local services aimed at this new population; and also

> the flexibilization of urban legislation, with the expansion of the urban perimeter and the inclusion of these new campuses in areas previously considered to be rural, which also contributed to the creation of new residential estates.[26]

Overall, the Northeast was particularly benefited by these economic changes and policies, which affected much of the production system of the region. However, some previous economic characteristics continued to have an influence, notably the old agrarian structure and the importance of rural occupations, even as urbanization increased. The Northeast accounts for almost half of Brazil's agricultural workforce, according to the last IBGE Agricultural Census. And a large gap in social indicators persists between the Northeast and the richer regions of the country. For example, the illiteracy rate, while falling, remains much higher in the Northeast: 9.0% (of those aged 10 or more) in Brazil in 2010, but 17.6% in the Northeast. And in the rural Northeast, the rate was still almost 30% in 2010 (Araújo, 2014, p.18).

Thus, not only did some aspects of heterogeneity within the region persist (especially the contrasts between traditional and modern, rural and urban, and formal and informal), but there was also a diversification and complexification of the socioeconomic subsystems that made up this reality. Araújo and Favareto (2020, p.14) proposed that the regional issue be addressed at another level, "very different from the one in which classical approaches and known patterns of organization of public policies for planning in the Northeast were formulated." At the same time, as we have seen above, the factors that stimulate the regional economy and affect its territorial and sectoral patterns have changed, while remaining dependent on both national and foreign capital from outside the region.

3.3 Implications for employment and income

Despite the fluctuations in the performance of the regional economy in this period, as well as the varying effects on areas and economic sectors, labour market indicators improved, in many respects more so in the Northeast than in the country as a whole. However, favourable aspects of demographic changes that affected the country and the region should not be overlooked.

Between 2003 and 2015, the population grew, according to IBGE, 15.6% for Brazil and 15.8% for the Northeast. In the same period, the population of working age grew 21.9% in Brazil and 19.1% in the Northeast, in both cases faster than overall population growth. This difference reflects the "demographic dividend", which arises when the base of the age pyramid narrows because of falling fertility, increasing the share of the population of working age, while lower dependency rates of both young and old favour entry into the labour force of those of working age. However, to take advantage of this situation, the economy needs to generate jobs faster than the growth of the total working-age population.

If we divide the period from 2003 to 2015 into the same two sub-periods discussed above, then between 2003 and 2008, for Brazil, the population of working age (PWA) increased by 11.3%, and the economically active population (EAP) by 12.4%; while, between 2009 and 2015, the growth was much smaller, respectively, 7.9% and 3.2%. In the Northeast, the growth was 8.8% (PWA) and 8.9% (EAP) in the first period and 7.8% and 0.2% in the second. This implies that between 2003 and 2008 labour force participation rose in both Brazil and (slightly) the Northeast; but between 2009 and 2015 the labour force participation rate dropped, quite sharply in the Northeast. In the case of Brazil, the rate dropped from 62.1% in the first period to 60.4% in the second period; in the case of the Northeast, from 60.6% to 57.2.[27]

Considering only the Metropolitan Regions (MR), using data from the IBGE Monthly Employment Survey (Figure 2.1), it can be seen that for the MRs of Recife and Salvador, between 2002 and 2015 unemployment rates were consistently above the average for all MRs in the country, although converging to the same level in 2012, in a context of a general decline that started in 2003. After 2012, Recife and Salvador again started to show a gap in unemployment compared with the rest of the country, as unemployment started to rise again.

Using data for 2002–2015 from the PNAD on labour status in the main occupation, we can examine the distribution of workers between formal and informal employment situations. Based on the same proxy as we used for the

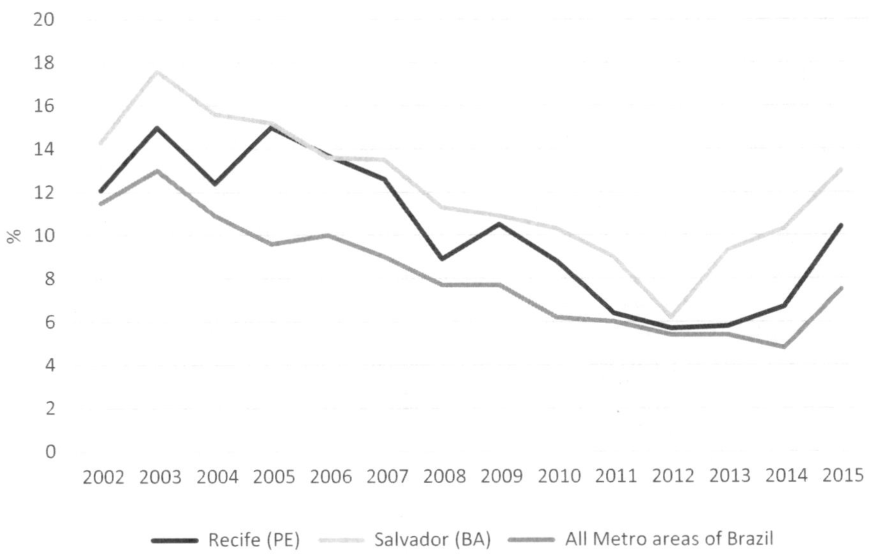

Figure 2.1 Unemployment rate (%), Recife, Salvador and all Metropolitan Regions of Brazil, 2002–2015 (September).

Source: Own calculations based on IBGE, Monthly Employment Survey (2003–2015).

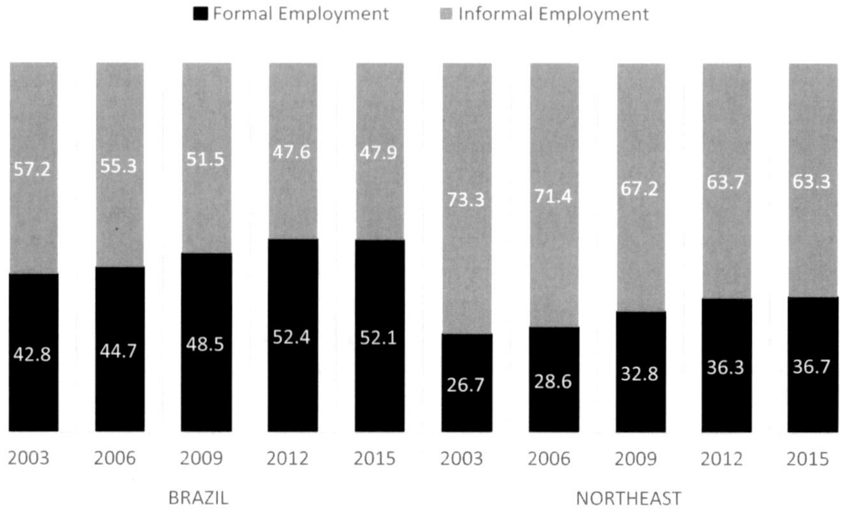

Figure 2.2 Formal and informal employment (% distribution), Brazil and the Northeast, 2003–2015 (selected years).

Source: Own calculations based on IBGE, *Pesquisa Nacional por Amostra de Domicílios* (PNAD), 2003–2015.

1990s, above, we can see (in Figure 2.2) a trend of increasing formalization of occupations in both the Northeast and Brazil, although at the end of the series this trend stabilized. From 2003 to 2015, there was an increase of around 10% in the proportion of formal occupations in both regions. However, the share of informal employment was more than 15% points higher in the Northeast, and this gap hardly changed over time.

Figure 2.3 breaks down the pattern of employment in more detail, for the Northeast and the rest of Brazil (this figure, like several figures in Chapter 3, shows the rest of Brazil excluding the Northeast). The figure includes data from 1995, for comparison with the period 2003–2015. Four labour status categories are identified: the formal wage labour market, consisting of wage work with carteira and regular public sector employment; informal wage work, without carteira; self-employment and employers; and subsistence and unpaid work. In 1995, in the Northeast these groups were of a comparable size (21%, 24%, 31% and 24%, respectively); in the rest of Brazil the formal labour market was larger, around 40%, and there was much less subsistence and unpaid work (about 11%).

Then in the period from 2002 to 2014, wage work with carteira shot up, while the share of wage work without carteira declined. So the labour market formalized throughout the country in this period, slightly more in the Northeast, where the share of self-employment declined more sharply. A part of this change was due to a fall in the share of agricultural employment, especially in the Northeast, but only a part.

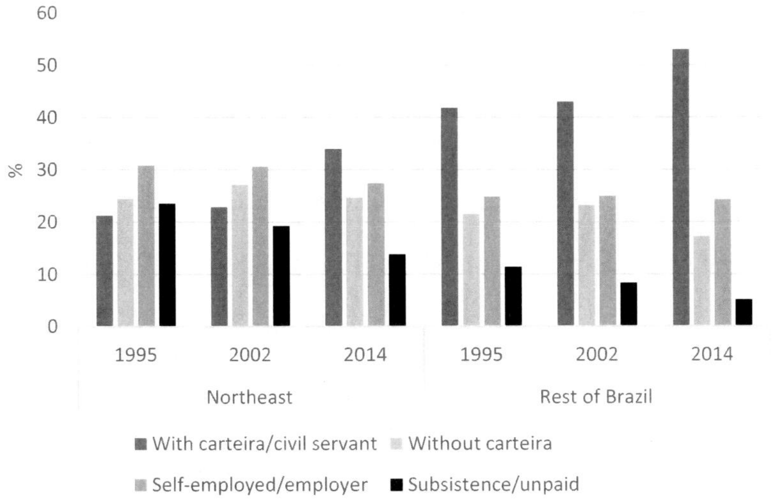

Figure 2.3 Trends in labour status, Northeast and Rest of Brazil, 1995–2014 (% distribution).
Source: IBGE, PNAD, 1995, 2002, 2014 (https://www.sidra.ibge.gov.br).

Overall there was a clear process of proletarianization throughout the period, with significant improvements in labour rights and protection for a minority of workers after 2002. Nevertheless, the gap between the Northeast and the rest of Brazil was not reduced, and the share of wage work without carteira in the Northeast was much the same in 2014 as in 1995, though it declined in the rest of the country.

All gender and racial groups benefited from the growth of protected wage work, though not all to the same extent. In 1995 a smaller proportion of black workers than white[28] were in wage work with carteira both in the Northeast and in the rest of Brazil. This gap hardly changed in the period up to 2014, although both groups gained. There was less difference between men and women in the Northeast, and this too hardly changed. However, the position of white women improved in the rest of Brazil. By 2014 almost 60% of working white women in the rest of Brazil were in protected wage work, and over 50% of black women, in both cases about 20 percentage points higher than in the Northeast, and significantly higher than for men. So the formalization of the labour market benefited women, both black and white, but more in the rest of Brazil than in the Northeast. Nevertheless, the changes were relatively small, and there was little sign of structural transformation in the labour market with respect to either gender or race.

Nevertheless, between 2002 and 2014 there were significant reductions in both gender and regional income inequality. PNAD data indicates that average monthly income in the Northeast, which was 57% of the national average in 2002, rose to 64% in 2014. And the average monthly income of women, which was 50% of that of men in Brazil in 2002, rose to 61% in 2014; while in the Northeast it rose from 56% to 68%.

So in the period up to 2014 there was significant progress in labour market outcomes, and the gains were widely spread across gender and racial categories. Black men and white women did relatively well, and there was some reduction in income disparities, but structural inequalities in employment were not much reduced; in particular, the gaps between the Northeast and the rest of Brazil persisted.

Looking specifically at formal employment relationships, using data on registered employment from the official Annual Social Information Report (RAIS), in Brazil the share of industry in all formal employment fell from 23.6% in 2002 to 22.2% in 2015; for the Northeast, these percentages were 19.5% and 18.6%, respectively. The share of services, in the same years, rose from 72.6% to 74.6% in Brazil; and in the Northeast, from 76.6% to 78.5%. With regard to agriculture, in these years, there was a drop from 4% to 3.1%, in Brazil, and from 4% to 2.7%, in the Northeast. It is clear that services were the main source of growth of formal employment in the period. There was little difference between the Northeast and the rest of Brazil in this respect.

As for income, based on PNAD data, comparing the Northeast and Brazil in the same period, three main observations stand out (Table 2.3). The first concerns the change between 2003 and 2015. Taking the median income by labour status in the principal occupation (expressed in constant 2015 prices), for Brazil and the Northeast, there is a rise in income between 2003

Table 2.3 Median monthly income (R$ at constant 2015 prices*) in principal occupation by labour status category, Brazil and the Northeast, 2003, 2012 and 2015

	Brazil			*Northeast*		
	2003	*2012*	*2015*	*2003*	*2012*	*2015*
Private sector wage worker with carteira assinada	1,060	1,325	1,300	706	1,034	950
Military	2,208	2,650	2,600	1,766	2,253	2,400
Statutory civil servant	1,810	2,347	2,300	1,302	1,723	1,800
Private sector wage workers without carteira assinada	552	876	800	441	795	750
Domestic worker with carteira assinada	662	994	950	530	824	788
Domestic worker without carteira assinada	442	729	700	265	504	500
Self-employed	839	1,325	1,188	530	824	788
Employer	3,311	3,975	3,500	2,185	2,650	2,500

Source: Own calculations based on IBGE, PNAD, 2003–2015.
* Deflated by the official retail price index, INPC.

and 2012 for all categories, followed by a second period up to 2015 when income falls predominated (mainly due to the economic crisis that began in 2015), although incomes remained above the levels of 2003. In Brazil as a whole, between 2012 and 2015, there was a loss in median incomes in all categories, though for "wage workers with carteira assinada", "military" and "statutory public servants", these losses were small (evidence that these categories were relatively protected). As for the Northeast, in this period, incomes fell for all categories except for "military" and "statutory public servant", but the changes were smaller than in the rest of Brazil.

A second observation refers to the differences between the Northeast and Brazil as a whole, both in the initial rise in incomes and in the subsequent fall, as well as in the median incomes in the three years considered. In 2003, taking the three categories with the highest shares in employment, wage worker with carteira assinada (29.3%), wage worker without carteira assinada (18.5%) and self-employed worker (22.3%), the median incomes for the Northeast were, respectively, 66.7%, 80.0% and 63.2% of those in the country as a whole. In 2012 these proportions were 78.0%, 90.8% and 62.2%, and in 2015 73.1%, 93.7% and 71.4%. That is, during the period there was some tendency for the income gap between the Northeast and the rest of Brazil to decline, but substantial discrepancies still persisted at the end of the period.

The third observation relates to the difference in income levels, in the case of the Northeast, between formal and informal occupations. In the three years considered, the median incomes of informal occupations were lower than those of formal occupations – with the exception of domestic workers with carteira assinada (a very small category). The median income of wage workers without carteira assinada was 62% of that of wage workers with carteira assinada in 2003, rising to 79% in 2015. There was a similar change, but smaller, in the figure for Brazil, which rose from 52% to 61%. Thus, during this period precarious wage workers in the private sector gained in terms of income in comparison with regular workers, but in the Northeast they gained relatively more.

During the period analysed in this section, there was a general reduction in indicators of structural poverty. A study by Silva et al. (2017) on multidimensional poverty[29] in the Brazilian Northeast, based on the PNAD database, supports this conclusion. The following dimensions were considered: food and water; communication and information; education; housing conditions; health; work and demography. Analysing deprivation in each dimension, the authors estimated the gaps (the distance of poor individuals from a poverty threshold), showing that the incidence of deprivation fell on all indicators for Brazil and the Northeast during the period 2009–2015. Based on these gaps, the study computed the extent of multidimensional poverty by region. Multidimensional poverty was higher in the Northeast than in Brazil as a whole, but declining in both – from 25.8% to 23.8% in the Northeast between 2009 and 2015, and from 22.6% to 20.9% in Brazil as a whole. Among the dimensions considered in the study with the greatest impact on poverty, the following were highlighted: education, work and demography, communication and information and health.

4 Regional implications of Brazil's economic and social setbacks, 2015–2019

In this section we examine the repercussions, in the region, of the political, economic and social shift that the country underwent after the impeachment of President Dilma Rousseff in 2016, with the return of neoliberal economic policies (in a more radical version than in the 1990s), accompanied by a dismantling of social rights and of policies for income redistribution and social protection.

4.1 Changes in the national scenario and its repercussions on the economy of the Northeast

As we have seen, there were significant economic and social achievements as a result of the neodevelopmentalist policies of the PT-led governments, especially from the perspective of the most economically and socially vulnerable segments. There was a drop in unemployment levels, increased formalization of labour relations, greater respect for labour rights, an increase in the real value of the minimum wage, an expansion of income transfer policies, and a fall in poverty. It is certainly true that these advances were insufficient to overcome the structural weaknesses of the labour market, which continued to be characterized by segmentation, inequality, surplus labour, flexibility and high turnover, widespread violation of labour laws and a high level of informality (Krein et al., 2013). But despite the limitations, there was evident economic and social progress. Nevertheless, the development regime was showing clear signs of exhaustion by 2015–2016, and this was both cause and consequence of instability and political crisis.

A sequence of political, social and economic factors contributed to the crisis. Among them, the following stand out:

- the first signs of a slowdown in the Brazilian economy (from 2012), mainly due to the fall in international commodity prices, and subsequently, the decreasing effectiveness of the mechanisms adopted by the government to boost domestic income and consumption;
- the political attrition of the government and the spread of public demonstrations, with support from conservative segments of the middle class, especially after the June 2013 protests;[30]
- the 2014 presidential election, which, although it resulted in the fourth consecutive victory for a PT candidate (twice with Lula and twice with Dilma), was won by a very small margin, in a highly polarized and tense environment;

- the *Operação Lava Jato* (Car Wash operation), conducted by the Federal Public Ministry of Paraná with the declared objective of combating corruption in Petrobras, which made the government and leaders of the PT priority targets of its investigations – this being one of the factors which triggered Dilma's impeachment, in 2016, and which prevented Lula from being a candidate in the 2018 presidential elections (Milla, 2020);
- the adoption, by the Dilma government, at the beginning of her second term (2015), of an inconsistent macroeconomic policy, marked, on the one hand, by the maintenance of social policies and tax relief measures in some sectors of the economy and, on the other hand, by the adoption of deflationary fiscal measures;
- the spread of a conservative, market-driven, anti-democratic perspective in public opinion, the media, the business community and in key State institutions (legislative, judiciary, Public Ministry, etc.).

Increasing political instability and economic recession culminated in the impeachment of Dilma in 2016. The economy stagnated and unemployment exploded. Pressures from the "market" grew for more fiscal austerity, for the privatization of public assets and for labour, social security and tax reforms. The parliamentary faction that constituted the lobby in favour of impeachment also increased their demands, which included a larger share of the federal budget for the local projects of members of Congress and the implementation of a regressive social, political, environmental and cultural agenda. Pressures from the forces that took power after the impeachment led to numerous measures to deregulate labour and civic rights, and, in particular, to the labour reform of 2017, which we discuss in the next chapter.[31]

At the same time both the economy and the world of work were affected by deindustrialization. This was the continuation of a process that started much earlier. According to Cano (2012), the causes of the country's deindustrialization date back to the early 1990s. With the neodevelopmentalist governments from 2003 to 2015, and especially with the investments of the PAC (discussed above) and the increase in domestic demand (resulting from the increase in family consumption and government spending), the process of industrial decline slowed. However, higher economic growth during this period was also in part due to the commodities boom until 2008.

With the global financial crisis of 2008, and subsequent global recession, international demand for commodities fell and international competition in the production of manufactured goods intensified. As we have seen, despite counter-cyclical measures, Brazil was not able to maintain the same growth rate between 2009 and 2015 as during the period 2003–2008. This was despite some recovery in the investment rate, which, after remaining low since the 1980s, started to recover after 2005, reaching 17% in 2008 and 19% in 2010 and 2011, before falling again. At no point did Brazil reach the investment level of the 1970s, around 25% of GDP (Cano, 2012, p.837). One of the consequences of this process was the reversion of the country's export agenda to dependence on primary products (as we already noted in the case of the Northeast) – with manufactured goods falling from a proportion of 60% of total exports in 2000 to 37% in 2011.

With regard to work and employment, the economic crisis not only affected the level of employment in manufacturing industry, but also the remuneration and the quality of these jobs (Krein et al., 2020). We have seen how, in the case of the Northeast, the recovery of formal employment in the period 2003–2015 mainly came from the service sector. The crisis that began in 2015 involved a series of negative factors: the effects of the *Lava Jato* anti-corruption operation on the country's production base (in the oil and gas industry, civil construction, shipbuilding and others), the adoption of restrictions on public expenditure, the abandonment of national development policy, the loss of Latin American markets for the export of manufactured goods, and a fall in household consumption, all of which reinforced the deindustrialization process. This was combined with increasing tertiarization of production and employment, and the growing precariousness of work.

Under the Temer (2016–2018) and Bolsonaro (2019–2022) governments, the country entered an era of clear social regression. In the field of labour regulation, the biggest changes came with the tertiarization law and the labour reform, both in 2017. In addition to the liberalization of outsourcing in the tertiarization law, negotiated agreements were given primacy over legislated rules (at the same time as the space for collective bargaining was systematically restricted), the CLT (labour legislation) was weakened (more than 100 of its articles were changed), different types of atypical and precarious contracts were legalized, and the roles of the Labour Court and of trade unions were weakened (Cesit, 2017). For Pochmann (2019, p.98),

> The substantial changes in the world of work reflect both the early process of deindustrialization, seen in the way in which Brazil participated in capitalist globalization since the 1990s, as well as the more recent deconstruction of the regulatory framework of the labour market imposed by neoliberal reforms. The result of all this has been massive open unemployment, accompanied by a growing underutilization of the workforce and the generalization of precarious employment. The growing polarization within society can be seen not only in the destruction of middle-class jobs, but also in the expansion of higher-paying self-employed jobs without access to social and labour protection.

The year 2016 marks, for the country as a whole and for the Northeast, in particular, a shift towards an economic and social model which was in sharp contrast to the previous period. The progressive development regime was undermined and displaced, but a coherent alternative has not yet been established. Between 2015 and 2019, Brazil's GDP fell, by an average of 0.6% per year, and the Northeast closely followed this track, doing slightly worse, falling at 1.0% per year, while continuing to account for just over 14% of national GDP (BNB, 2020). There is a striking contrast with the 2003–2014 period, when the Northeast grew faster than Brazil (BNB, 2019).

There were large differences between economic sectors in this performance. With respect to agriculture, the Northeast lost ground compared with the rest of the country, its share of output falling from 12.2% in 2015 to 11.8% in 2019,[32] and its share of cropped area from 15.2% in 2015 to 13.2% in 2019. Sugarcane monoculture continued its downward trajectory, with the region's share of national production falling from 18.9% in 2015 to 13.6% in 2019.[33] The production of crops typical of family farming, such as cassava and beans, also fell sharply. The crops that did best in the Northeast were the most important agribusiness products: soya, corn, herbaceous cotton, mangoes and grapes. In general, they are cultivated in the cerrado (west of Bahia and south of Piauí and Maranhão) or in irrigated areas, particularly in the fruit-growing pole of Juazeiro and Petrolina. There was also some increase in production of livestock and in poultry. In general, the costs of the downturn in agriculture fell on family farms, which had benefited from public policies in the previous period, but which after 2015 began to suffer from the disarticulation of these policies (Araújo and Favareto, 2020). In particular, the National Programme for the Strengthening of Family Agriculture, PRONAF, created in the 1990s to provide access to credit for family farms, and which had its budget multiplied tenfold between 2000 and 2015, was drastically affected in the following years.[34] Given the relatively greater weight of family farming in the Northeast, compared to the rest of Brazil, the consequences of these ruptures and discontinuities were clearly more drastic for the Northeast than for the rest of the country.

According to data from the Monthly Industrial Survey (2020), after growing until 2013 Brazilian industrial production declined sharply in the period 2014 to 2016 (Table 2.4), and hardly recovered thereafter. The Northeast

Table 2.4 Industrial production: Percentage change in volume of output over previous 12 months, Brazil and Northeast, December each year, 2010–2019

	Brazil	*Northeast*
2010	10.2	8.6
2011	0.4	–4.6
2012	–2.3	1.6
2013	2.1	3.4
2014	–3.0	0.2
2015	–8.3	–3.0
2016	–6.4	–2.8
2017	2.5	–0.3
2018	1.0	0.2
2019	–1.1	–2.8

Source: Own calculations based on IBGE, Monthly Industrial Survey (2020).

followed a similar pattern, with a smaller initial impact, but a more persistent decline.

However, there were large differences between subsectors. Mining was more adversely affected in the Northeast than in the rest of Brazil. According to Barroso (2019, p.134), almost half of industrial production in the Northeast in 2017 was concentrated in four activities: 17.7% in food products, 13.0% in coke, petroleum derivatives and biofuels, 10.4% in chemical products and 8.2% in mining. Within manufacturing industry there has been a fall in the importance of metalworking, and an increase in the relative importance of the leather and footwear and pulp and paper segments. One factor that prevented industrial output from falling further in the Northeast was the coming on stream of large automobile plants, notably the Ford Troller factory in Ceará, in 2014 and the Fiat Chrysler Jeep factory in Pernambuco, in 2015. Taking the capacity to generate employment as a reference, rather than output, the sectors that stood out in 2017, according to the same study, in addition to the food industry (responsible for 27.5% of the total in 2017), were: leather and footwear (11.3%), clothing (10.6%), non-metallic mineral products (7.6%) and textiles (4.2%). Together, these sectors accounted for 61.2% of total industrial employment in that year.

Construction was particularly hard hit by the recession. Between 2015 and 2018 output fell by 6.5% per year in the Northeast, according to the Annual Survey of Construction, but even so this was slightly less than the decline in Brazil as a whole (7.7%).

The *Lava Jato* anti-corruption operation played a significant role in the economic crisis, because it targeted specific sectors, all of which were disproportionately affected: oil and gas, shipbuilding, metalworking and construction sectors (Paula and Moura, 2019). With respect to construction, there were large falls in the gross revenues of companies in the sector and in their employment capacity, along with sale of assets to foreign groups. But the authors considered that:

> the oil and gas segment was the spearhead of the process of economic disruption ... The disruption of these two sectors – civil construction and oil and gas – contributed greatly, on the one hand, to the deepening of the economic crisis as of 2015, from which we have not yet recovered; on the other hand, to disrupting some of the few sectors in which national capital was strong and internationally competitive.

The service sector, which accounted for almost three-quarters of GDP in 2016 in both Brazil as a whole and in the Northeast (Valente Junior and Silva, 2019), continued to grow in Brazil between 2015 and 2019, but at only 0.5% per year; while the Northeast did worse, with negative growth (–2.5%).[35] This sector, in a broader sense (including commerce, education, health, finance, security, among other activities), is markedly dualistic in

Brazil, and even more so in the Northeast, with a sharp contrast between a high productivity segment (dominated by large commercial enterprises in business services, tourism, logistics, communications and information, and finance) and a low productivity segment with a high level of informality (especially street commerce, personal services, and a variety of other service activities). Between 2014 and 2018, the share in income of the more modern and formal parts of the sector fell, and that of more traditional and informal activities rose: information and communication services, and professional and administrative services, which together accounted for 50.5% of the sector in 2014, fell to 45.9% in 2018, while services to households, transport and related services rose from 41.5% to 45.7%.

In terms of foreign trade, a study by Freire (2019) for the BNB shows that between 2002 and 2009, imports into the Northeast varied between 8.4% and 9.7% of all Brazilian imports, increasing thereafter to a maximum of 12.9% in 2017, falling to 12.0% in 2018. In 2018 intermediate goods (such as chemicals, petroleum products and parts and accessories for motor vehicles) accounted for 55.8% of imports, capital goods (such as vehicles, machinery and equipment, etc.), 7.8%, consumer goods 7%, and fuels and lubricants 29.4%. Consumer goods were a very small share of imports into the region.

The share of the Northeast in all Brazilian exports fluctuated around 7% to 8%, but the share of unprocessed commodities in exports rose from 18% to 29% between 2000 and 2018 (largely due to an increase in soya exports), with a corresponding decline in the share of manufactures. Products with a relatively low level of processing, such as pulp, iron and steel, varied, between 2010 and 2018, around 30%, with a downward trend. Other products with a higher degree of processing, such as aluminium oxides and hydroxides and passenger cars, varied around 40%, with a tendency to rise.

In summary, the evidence shows that the economic crisis hit the Northeast even harder than Brazil as a whole. This was due not only to greater weaknesses in the region's economic structure but also to a reduction in public sector investment. Vidal (2019) shows that inflows of federal public investment into the region, as a percentage of all federal public investment, fell from 19.3% in 2011 to 3.3% in 2018. One of the main factors in this drop was the privatization of the oil and gas sector in the region. Such a fall has greater consequences for a region, like the Northeast, which depends more on federal public resources than more developed regions. At the same time, the importance of the service sector in relation to industry and agriculture has been growing; the contrasts between the modern and traditional sectors of the regional economy are increasing; family farming has declined and the importance of agribusiness in regional agriculture has grown; and in industry, the importance of metalworking has declined and that of more traditional products like leather and footwear and pulp and paper has grown.

4.2 The worsening of social and labour indicators has widened the gap between the Northeast and the rest of Brazil

According to data from the PNADC, between the third quarters of 2014 and 2019, the population of the Northeast grew by 2.8%, while that of Brazil grew by 4.1%, the difference in part reflecting migration flows out of the region. In the same period, the population aged 14 or over (considered of working age) rose by 5.4% in the Northeast, and by 5.7% in Brazil. As a result, the share of the population of working age in the Northeast rose from 78.2% to 80.2%, slightly below, but converging towards the Brazilian average. In contrast, the labour force (sum of employed and unemployed) in the Northeast grew by 1.1%, against 7.5% in the country as a whole. The labour force participation rate, already lower in the Northeast, therefore declined further, from 56.8% to 54.5%, while it rose for Brazil as a whole, from 60.9% to 61.9%.

The difference between the Northeast and the rest of Brazil mainly concerns younger workers. Between 2014 and 2019, in the Northeast the percentage of the adult population in the labour force fell by eight percentage points for those aged less than 35, but rose by ten percentage points for those aged 35 or more. In contrast, in Brazil as a whole, the percentage of the population in the labour force fell by only one percentage point for those aged less than 35, but rose by 15 percentage points for those aged 35 or more. An increase in the proportion of people of working age outside the workforce is a potential indicator of labour market discouragement. Of course, there are other possible causes – illness, family responsibilities, education. But in this case the changes are clearly related to the economic crisis. It is worth noting that the largest falls in employment rates were found in the 14–19 year age group, suggesting that there was some return to schooling in the face of lack of jobs.

In both the Northeast and Brazil the population of working age grew faster than the population as a whole, which indicates that the "window of opportunity" provided by the "demographic dividend" has not yet come to an end. But from another angle, this growth of the labour force is a source of pressure on the labour market, if the growth of employment is too slow to absorb the new demand for jobs. This was notably the case during the recession that started in 2015, but with different adjustments in the Northeast and the rest of Brazil.

In Brazil as a whole, there was a small increase in employment between 2014 and 2019 (2.3%), but not enough to absorb the growing labour force, so there was also a spectacular increase in unemployment (66.5%). In the Northeast, in contrast, the labour force grew well below the growth rate of the working-age population, but the fall in employment was larger (4.7%), so there was again an increase in unemployment of 81.5%, even larger than in Brazil as a whole. In the Northeast, a larger proportion of the working-age population abandoned the search for employment or were discouraged from seeking entry to the labour market, an indication that the adverse effect on labour market opportunities was greater in the region.

The unemployment rate is traditionally one of the main indicators of labour market conditions. Table 2.5 shows that between the fourth quarters of 2014 and 2019 there was a substantial increase in unemployment both in Brazil as a whole and in the Northeast, peaking in 2016 and hardly declining thereafter. Unemployment in the Northeast was always higher than in the rest of the country, with a gap that widened during the recession.

The PNADC (which replaced the PNAD as from 2014) provides additional indicators, which permit a finer assessment of the labour market situation, including the underemployment rate due to insufficient hours worked, the percentage of the population in the potential workforce and the composite rate of underutilization of the labour force.

The underemployment rate due to insufficient hours worked (those who in the reference week usually worked less than 40 hours and would like to work more hours) is an important indicator of employment availability and quality. Table 2.6 shows a rise in this rate between 2015 and 2018, for both the Northeast and Brazil, followed by a slight decrease. The difference between the Northeast and Brazil as a whole for this indicator is even higher than that for unemployment.

In addition to the unemployed and underemployed, there are those who are potentially part of the labour force. Basically, these consist of two groups: people who looked for work, but were not available to work in the

Table 2.5 Unemployment rate in the reference week, population aged 14 or more, 4th quarter, 2014–2019, Brazil and Northeast (%)

	2014.4	*2015.4*	*2016.4*	*2017.4*	*2018.4*	*2019.4*
Brazil	6.5	8.9	12.0	11.8	11.6	11.0
Northeast	8.2	10.4	14.3	13.8	14.3	13.6

Source: Own calculations based on IBGE, Pesquisa Nacional por Amostra de Domicílios Continua (PNADC), 2014–2019.

Table 2.6 Rate of underemployment due to insufficient hours worked, in the reference week, population aged 14 or more, 4th quarter, 2015–2019, Brazil and Northeast (%)

	2015.4	*2016.4*	*2017.4*	*2018.4*	*2019.4*
Brazil	4.4	5.8	7	7.4	7.2
Northeast	8.4	11.1	12.7	13.2	12.6

Source: Own calculations based on IBGE, PNADC, 2015–2019.
Note: As of the 4th quarter of 2015 there was a change in the methodology of calculating hours of work and measuring underemployment, so this table starts from that date.

reference week; and those who did not search for work (dropouts due to discouragement), but would like to have a job and were available to work in the reference week. Table 2.7 shows the percentage of people in the potential workforce in relation to the population of working age outside the workforce. In this case, like for underemployment, the trend is upward until 2018 and then declines slightly, in both Brazil and the Northeast. There is a large and rising gap between the Northeast and the rest of Brazil in this respect.

The large difference between the Northeast and the rest of Brazil in these patterns suggests that the social and economic response was different in the Northeast. In their analysis of labour force discouragement in Brazil, Peruchetti and Richter (2020) indicated that in 2019, around 60% of discouraged workers in Brazil were found in the Northeast and the main reported reasons for abandoning job search were "there is no work in the area" (63%) and "could not find an adequate job" (19.5%).

Table 2.8 adds these three variables together (unemployment, underemployment and potential labour force) in a composite indicator of the underutilization of the labour force, using as denominator the sum of the labour force and the potential labour force. This is a broader and more representative indicator of the degree of lack of access to employment. This rate rose monotonically for both the Northeast and Brazil up to 2019, with a large and rising gap to the disadvantage of the Northeast, increasing from 9.1 percentage points in 2015 to 11.9 in 2019. This table shows how the labour market deteriorated during the crisis; by 2019 almost a quarter of workers were affected in Brazil as a whole, and more than one third in the Northeast, showing the greater impact of the crisis on the labour market in the region.

Table 2.7 Percentage of the population of working age outside the labour force who are in the potential labour force in the reference week, 4th quarter, 2014–2019, Brazil and Northeast

	2014.4	*2015.4*	*2016.4*	*2017.4*	*2018.4*	*2019.4*
Brazil	6.7	8.3	10.3	11.8	12	11.8
Northeast	11.7	13.4	16.7	18.2	18.9	18.8

Source: Own calculations based on IBGE, PNADC, 2014–2019.

Table 2.8 Composite rate of underutilization of the workforce (%), in the reference week, 4th quarter, 2015 –2019, Brazil and Northeast

	2015.4	*2016.4*	*2017.4*	*2018.4*	*2019.4*
Brazil	14.9	17.3	22.2	23.5	23.8
Northeast	24.0	25.6	33.0	34.6	35.7

Source: Own calculations based on IBGE, PNADC, 2015–2019.
Note: Starting from 2015; see note to Table 2.5.

Table 2.9 Changes in the proportion of the population aged 14+ outside the labour force, Brazil and Northeast, 2014–2019 (percentage points)

	Brazil		*Northeast*	
	2014–2017	2017–2019	2014–2017	2017–2019
Men				
White	−0.6	+0.7	+3.0	+2.2
Black	+1.2	−0.1	+4.1	+0.6
Women				
White	−1.9	−0.6	+0.6	−0.8
Black	−2.2	−1.0	+0.4	−0.6
Total	−0.9	−0.3	+2.1	0.0

Source: Own calculations using micro-data from IBGE, PNADC, third quarter, 2014, 2017, 2019.

There was a strong gender and race pattern to these changes. Table 2.9 shows the changes in the proportion of the population of working age that was outside the labour force in the periods 2014–2017 and 2017–2019. For all gender-race groups the observed discouragement was greater in the Northeast in the early part of the crisis. Men were more affected than women, indeed in Brazil as a whole the participation rates for women increased, while they fell slightly in the Northeast. Black men were more affected than whites up to 2017 but this was reversed thereafter, and overall the differences between racial groups were smaller than those between men and women.

Overall the crisis led to a deterioration in the labour market and a rise in unemployment for all groups. In Brazil as a whole this led not to dropout but to an increase in labour force participation, especially among women, in many cases no doubt attempting to compensate for higher unemployment among other family members. But in the Northeast, particularly among men, and among younger adults aged less than 35, the result was labour market dropout, as people abandoned the search for jobs in a bleak labour market.

Turning our attention to the employed and focusing on labour status in the principal occupation, Figure 2.4 gives the distribution of formal and informal occupations for Brazil and the Northeast from 2014 to 2019 (fourth quarter of each year). Since this figure uses the PNADC, the proxy for informality differs from that used for earlier periods, based on the PNAD.[36] The general tendency in both Brazil and the Northeast was for informality to increase during this period, somewhat more in Brazil as a whole than in the Northeast, but the level of informality remained much higher in the Northeast throughout the period.

Combining this evidence on informalization and the previous discussion on the underutilization of the workforce, it can be said that, in the

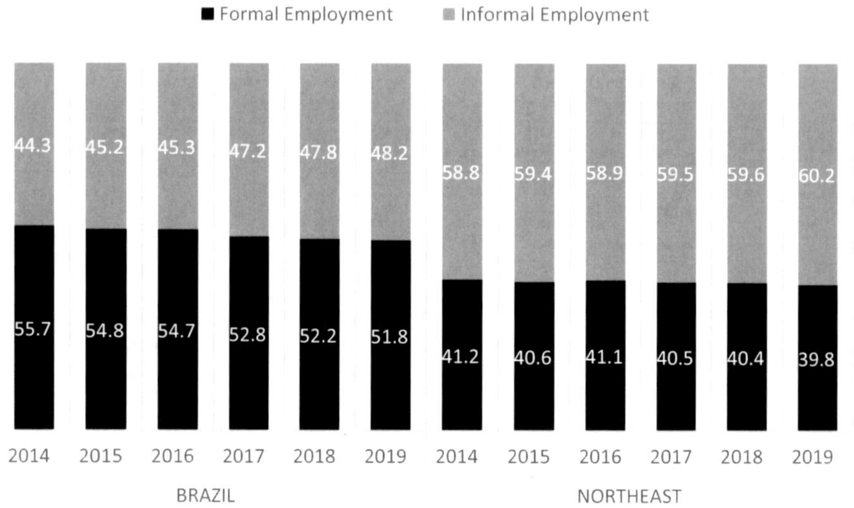

Figure 2.4 Formal and informal employment (% distribution), Brazil and the Northeast, fourth quarter 2014 to fourth quarter 2019.
Source: Own calculations based on IBGE, PNADC, 2014–2019.

Northeast, the bulk of the impact of the crisis that hit the region from 2015 onwards was felt through growth in unemployment, underemployment and exclusion from the labour force, while for Brazil as a whole there was greater growth in informality. Perhaps the space for greater informalization in the Northeast is limited, because informality is already so extensive, so that the crisis above all excluded workers from the labour market.

Turning to income, between 2014 and 2019, despite the deterioration in social and labour indicators, changes in real monthly income were mixed. Some categories of workers suffered declining real incomes, including some private sector wage workers both with and without carteira assinada, domestic workers without carteira and own account workers, in both Brazil and the Northeast. However, public sector employees obtained higher real incomes. It should be noted that when unemployment rises, and those with low wages are more vulnerable to job loss, then there can be an artificial rise in average wages.

At the same time, in this period the income gap between the Northeast and Brazil remained large. Table 2.10 shows the average real monthly income in the Northeast as a percentage of the average for Brazil, in the fourth quarter of 2014 and the fourth quarter of 2019, for selected categories of workers.

It can be seen that there was a general tendency for the gap to widen for private sector wage workers, but not for public sector workers or the self-employed, and changes were fairly small. In general, incomes in informal

Table 2.10 The income gap between the Northeast and Brazil, 2014 and 2019 (fourth quarter). Northeastern incomes as a percentage of the Brazilian average, selected labour status categories

	2014	*2019*
Private sector wage workers with carteira	76.5	75.2
Private sector wage workers without carteira	65.8	61.9
Public sector employees	78.2	79.4
Domestic workers	67.4	66.3
Own account workers	57.9	59.3

Source: Own calculations based on IBGE, PNADC, 2014–2019.

labour statuses were lower than in formal employment. Income changes are discussed in more detail in Chapter 3.

If we look specifically at formal employment relationships (using the RAIS), we observe that the potential of the industrial sector for generating formal jobs continued to decline, while the service sector continued to expand and agriculture stabilized. Industry accounted for 22.2% of formal jobs in Brazil in 2015, falling to 20.8% in 2019; for the Northeast, these percentages were 18.6% and 16.7%, respectively, another indicator of deindustrialization in both cases. In this sector, the largest change concerned the construction sector, which for Brazil fell from 5% to 4.2% of formal employment, and in the Northeast from 5.6% to 4.4%, reversing the rising trend in formal employment creation between 2002 and 2015, when investment under the PAC played a major role in the country and especially in the Northeast.

The share of services in formal employment increased during this period, from 74.6% to 76% in Brazil, and from 78.5% to 80.3%, in the Northeast. Within this sector there was increased formal employment in both Brazil and the Northeast in a variety of activities, including wholesale trade, real estate, medical services and teaching, while there was a loss of employment share in restaurants, hotels and repair services, among others. Some activities grew in importance in Brazil but not in the Northeast, including financial activities and public administration. It is a worth noting that this last category continued to be the largest single employer in both Brazil and the Northeast, representing 19% of formal employment in the former and 28% in the latter. The dynamics of this sector are complex. For example, as modern services expand (segments of retail and wholesale trade, hotel chains, information and communication technology, financial systems, etc.), their capacity to create formal jobs grows; but this occurs to a very variable extent from one segment to another, and can be unstable (demand for labour may expand and contract rapidly with changing commercial conditions, which can be seen, for example, in the case of call centres, discussed in Chapter 4).

Most formal jobs in the Northeast continued to be concentrated in the metropolitan regions, especially Salvador, Recife and Fortaleza. In these cases, the proportion of formal jobs in the metropolis, within their respective states (Bahia, Pernambuco and Ceará), fell between 2015 and 2019, respectively, from 47.5% to 43.9%, from 65.2% to 62.3% and from 68.5% to 66.9%. No doubt this was because the recession hit formal jobs, concentrated in metropolitan regions, particularly hard. In 1992, the share of formal employment in these three metropolitan areas had been higher – 62.6%, 69.9% and 76.5%, respectively. Since that date there seems to have been some degree of decentralization, especially in the case of Bahia. This is consistent with the evidence presented above about the trend, in recent decades, for industrial activities and modern services to expand in medium-sized cities in the region.

5 Concluding remarks

Taking a historical perspective, in this chapter we have sought to highlight the most important contrasts between the Northeast and Brazil, in terms of their socioeconomic transformations and the more general implications for work and employment, as well as differences within the Northeast between territories and sectors of activity.

The productive base of the Northeast underwent significant transformations, especially as a result of the actions of Sudene, from the 1960s, when the region was increasingly integrated into the dynamics of the national economy, though in a complementary and dependent position in relation to the more developed regions of the country. Since then, its economic performance, measured by GDP growth, has sometimes been a little above, and sometimes a little below the national average, generally gaining during periods when developmentalist policies prevailed, and losing ground during market-driven and liberal periods.

Major interventions in the region, whether by the State, private actors or mixed in nature, have contributed to technical and economic modernization, but at the same time have also contributed to the reproduction of existing social, sectoral and regional inequalities, as well as creating new segmentations. The dynamics of accumulation have been modernized, incorporating new technological, institutional and logistical components, but the tendency remains for the economic structures and mechanisms of the region to concentrate income and wealth.

In this trajectory, the territorial and/or sectoral configurations that have been established (in the form of poles, clusters, districts, local productive arrangements, etc.), aiming to promote economic dynamism, technological modernization and increases in employment and income, did not spread to the economy as a whole, remaining confined to restricted spaces. In some prominent cases the connections of these poles with national and international production chains have taken precedence over a stronger rooting in local economies.

All this has produced a web of forms and types of work relationships, which, despite their segmented and heterogeneous character, coexist and interact in the regional space. Alongside relatively well-paid and protected jobs, limited to specific areas and sectors, there exist large contingents of informal, semi-formalized and precarious workers, waged, semi-waged and self-employed, often involved in traditional forms of "autonomous work" (such as street vendors and artisans), or in "modern" forms of self-employment (such as on-line services), which may be based in urban peripheries and rural areas.

After the restructuring of the region's economic base resulting from the interventions of Sudene, and the later period of the "fiscal war", when development policy for the Northeast was completely disarticulated, the regional economy greatly benefited from the neo-developmental policies and investments of the administrations of Lula and Dilma. Between 2003 and 2015, the economic growth of the Northeast was, on average, above the average for Brazil, stimulated, on the one hand, by a greater increase in family income (due to growing employment and income levels, the formalization of employment, the increasing real minimum wage, social policies, consumer credit, etc.) and, on the other hand, by an increase in productive investment, especially stimulated by the PAC. With the resumption of the development agenda of the State, the reinforcement of social policies, the expansion of social dialogue and a fall in social inequality, the whole country participated in a dynamic feedback process, and the Northeast was particularly favoured.

Alongside these long-term transformations in the region's economy, certain historical features remained, such as the old and highly concentrated agrarian structure, and the enclave character of large investments. On the one hand, some aspects of heterogeneity within the region persisted, notably the contrasts between the traditional and the modern, the rural and the urban, and the formal and the informal. On the other hand, there was a diversification and complexification of the socioeconomic systems of the region. Traditional economic sectors have lost importance (especially those linked to the sugar-alcohol complex, the livestock/cotton system and the large areas devoted to subsistence agriculture), agribusiness has been expanding (especially in the production of foodgrains and fruits), new industrial investment has modified the manufacturing production base and many service activities have been modernized, including banking, telecommunications and transport (airports, ports, railways and highways). One significant development was the growing importance of medium-sized cities in the expansion and modernization of the socio-productive structure. In terms of output, the importance of agriculture and livestock production has fallen, as has that of industry (particularly manufacturing industry), while the share of services has increased.

In terms of employment and income, although there was some convergence between regional and national indicators, the gap between the Northeast and the rest of Brazil remained large. Illustrations of this double movement (of some convergence between the Northeast and Brazil, while large differences remained) can be found in the extent of informality in employment, and in average income levels. Another significant aspect of the socioeconomic transformations in the region lies in the persistence of social inequalities, to which we return in the next chapter.

This was the economic and social context, marked by major transformations, including advances, stagnation and setbacks, of the changes in the country and in the region from the mid-2010s onwards. A variety of factors led to the exhaustion of the neodevelopmentalist cycle, which had lasted more than a decade. The Brazilian economy began to show signs of loss of dynamism from 2014 onwards (in part a reflection of unfavourable international conditions after the 2008 global financial crisis) and social indicators began to deteriorate from 2015 onwards. A new economic, political and social environment emerged, especially from 2016, with the impeachment of President Dilma Roussef.

The economic and political phase that started in 2015–2016 was in striking contrast with the previous period of growth and social progress. The effects of the economic crisis, the continuing process of deindustrialization, government measures to deregulate labour relations and the weakening or abandonment of social policies brought a deterioration of indicators of employment and income which affected the whole country and even more so the Northeast, maintaining or widening the gaps between the region and the rest of the country.

The rates of unemployment and underemployment, as well as the informality rates and average levels of income, provide evidence of this deterioration, and of its greater impact in the Northeast. One consequence was that inequality has increased again. According to data from the PNADC (IBGE, 2020, p.52) for 2019, while the Gini index of per capita household income inequality in Brazil was 0.543, for the Northeast this index was 0.559, and in both regions it had risen since 2015, by 0.025 in the Northeast and 0.019 in Brazil. Based on the same data source, the *Diário Econômico ETENE* (BNB, 2020) highlighted the large increase in the income of the richest 1% in the Northeast (up 14.9%) between 2015 and 2019 and the income losses (–5.0%) of the region's poorest 10%, contributing to the increase in the concentration of income.[37]

This chapter gives a structural, historical view of the economic development of the Northeast in recent decades, with particular emphasis on indicators of production, work and employment. We sought to highlight the most relevant economic patterns, their spatial distribution and their implications for employment and incomes, in order to identify, on the one hand, important contrasts between the region and the country as a whole and, on the other, the disparities and inequalities within the region. The following chapters take up some of these issues in more detail.

Notes

1 This section draws on Alexandre de Freitas Barbosa's chapter "Regimes de acumulação e trabalho no Brasil e as transformações do Nordeste, 1850–1980" in Véras de Oliveira and Rodgers (2022).
2 Authors' translation from original Portuguese.
3 This corresponds to an area of 1,650,000 sq. km. (18.4% of the national territory), which in 1980 was home to about 35 million inhabitants (30% of the Brazilian population).

4 This was a peasant movement that emerged in the mid-1950s in the sugarcane region of the Northeast, around the goal of agrarian reform. It gained considerable national influence and became one of the priority targets for political repression under the military regime from 1964 on. For an overview see, for example, Benevides (1985).
5 The new profile of industry from the time of Sudene was extensively documented and analysed by Oliveira (1981). A more detailed analysis of the case of Bahia can be found in Oliveira (2003). On the transition from the primacy of the textile industry to the metallurgical industry in the case of Pernambuco, see Lima (2002).
6 IBGE, *Pesquisa Nacional por Amostra de Domicílios* (National Household Sample Survey).
7 According to a technical note from IBGE, the monthly household income per capita is "the result of dividing the monthly household income by the number of members of the household, excluding pensioners, domestic employees or relatives of a domestic employee" (IBGE, *Síntese de Indicadores Sociais – Uma análise das condições de vida da população brasileira*. Available at: <https://biblioteca.ibge.gov.br/visualizacao/livros/liv66777.pdf>. Accessed on 25 February 2021).
8 This occurred despite the creation of the Constitutional Finance Funds in 1989, mandated by the 1988 Constitution, which sought to reduce regional inequalities in the country (there were separate funds for the North, the Northeast and the Midwest).
9 Sudene was closed during the Fernando Henrique Cardoso government, and was replaced by ADENE. This measure was reversed in 2007, at the beginning of the second term of Lula da Silva, and Sudene was re-established. However, it never had the same political support or influence as before.
10 Authors' translation from original Portuguese.
11 According to a PNAD document (IBGE, 2016, p.29),

> from the 1992 PNAD onwards, in order to capture certain groups of people involved in economic activity who were not previously included in the employed population, the concept of work became more comprehensive, including, in the identification of employed persons, workers in production for their own consumption and workers in construction for their own use.

In the first group were included people who worked "for at least one hour a week, in the production of goods including agriculture, forestry, livestock, plant extraction, fishing and fish farming, for their own consumption of at least one member of the household" and, in the second, people who worked "for at least one hour a week, in the construction of buildings, private roads, wells and other improvements (except works intended solely for renovation) for their own use of at least one member of the household". The first group (but also part of the second) mainly refers to activities in rural areas.

12 Provides for the concession and permission regime for the provision of public services by private companies.
13 In this case, provision by a public investment bank of guarantees for these partnerships.
14 Authors' translation from original Portuguese.
15 Regional series as revised in 2007, adopting 2002 as a base year (IBGE, 2008).
16 According to Monteiro Neto et al. (2017, p.42), the size of the *Fundo Constitucional de Financiamento do Nordeste* (Constitutional Fund for Financing of the Northeast) increased from 1.6% of GDP in 2005 to 2.1% in 2010 and 2.0% in 2012; and there were similar increases in other regions covered by similar funds.
17 Data from the website of the Ministry of Social Development. Available at: <https://aplicacoes.mds.gov.br/sagi/cecad20/agregado/index4.php>. Accessed on 15 January 2021.

18 The minimum wage increased 77.2% above inflation from 2002 to 2016, according to calculations by the Ministry of Labour (https://economia.uol.com.br/noticias/redacao/2016/05/01/salario-minimo-cresceu-77-desde-2002-diz-ministerio-do-trabalho.htm).
19 Authors' translation from original Portuguese.
20 The foreign trade performance of the Northeast was greatly influenced, in this period, by the relationship with China. According to Melo (2013, p.461):

> In the period 2003–2008, Northeastern exports to China grew, on average, 68% per year and imports registered an average annual growth of 64%. The share of this destination in Northeastern foreign trade has been increasingly important for the dynamics of foreign exchange in the region (...) The trade flow between the Northeast and China was, in 2010, 40% higher than that in 2008.

The author also notes that this relationship focuses

> on export sales of products from a small number of sectors, mainly minerals and agricultural commodities, and import purchases from this source with a reasonable level of diversification, including, in addition to consumer goods, increasingly intermediate and capital goods, a pattern that is not very different from that maintained by the region with the rest of the world.

21 Authors' translation from original Portuguese.
22 Authors' translation from original Portuguese.
23 Data from the IBGE Annual Survey of Industrial Production (refers to companies with 5 or more workers).
24 Authors' translation from original Portuguese.
25 Data from the Higher Education Census, carried out by the National Institute of Educational Studies and Research Anísio Teixeira (INEP).
26 Authors' translation from original Portuguese.
27 The displacement of part of the population of working age out of the labour force is largely the result of the phenomenon of "discouragement" in the face of an adverse labour market situation (in this case especially in 2015, when the Brazilian economy entered into recession). We discuss discouragement further in the next section, concerned with the period 2015–2019. It is particularly important in the Northeast. In addition the labour force participation rate is lower in the Northeast, particularly for women, due to a combination of social and economic factors, not all of which have been well studied.
28 The race/colour classification is discussed in Chapter 3, Section 5.
29 Which, in addition to income, considers basic human capabilities and needs (access to food, housing, clothing, medical care, school, basic sanitation, etc.).
30 Protests that started with the struggle of students against the increase in urban bus fares, but which turned into demonstrations with a strong presence of workers and prominent segments of the middle class, directed (with important media support) against the government of Dilma Rousseff. See, for example, Singer (2013).
31 See, for example, Krein, Véras de Oliveira and Filgueiras (2019).
32 Source: IBGE, *Pesquisa da Pecuária Municipal* (Livestock Survey), 2019.
33 Source: IBGE, *Produção Agrícola Municipal* (Municipal Agricultural Production), 2019.
34 Several other policies that were to a greater or lesser extent focused on this segment of the population, such as the *Programa de Aquisição de Alimentos* (Food Access Programme) and the *Territórios da Cidadania* (Territories of Citizenship, coordinated local development programmes) as well as social programmes, such as *Bolsa Família* (Family Allowance), *Um Milhão de Cisternas* (a million water tanks) and *Luz para Todos* (Light for All), suffered severely, after 2015,

from reduced budgets, cancellations and restructurings (Araújo and Favaretto, 2020, p.23).

35 Source: IBGE Monthly Services Survey, 2020. This survey includes information, communication, real estate, professional and administrative activities, accommodation and food, transportation, storage and postal services and other services.

36 The methodologies adopted by the PNAD and PNADC to identify labour status are different, which affects measured informality rates. Estimates of informality based on the PNAD were higher than those based on the PNADC, for both Brazil and the Northeast, notably because the latter excludes work for own consumption, a category that is larger in the Northeast. For the purposes of Figure 2.4 formal labour statuses were defined to include private sector wage employees and domestic workers with carteira assinada, public sector workers with carteira assinada, civil servants and military, and employers. Informal labour status included private sector wage employees, domestic workers and public sector workers without carteira assinada, own account workers and unpaid family workers. In Chapter 3 we examine the distribution of labour status in more detail.

37 Available at <https://www.bnb.gov.br/documents/1342439/7243032/71_15_06_2020.pdf/7c83bc0b-95ec-35da-dc31-4048fb0f1422>. Accessed on 25 February 2021.

References

Ablas, Luís Augusto de Queiroz and Rafael Fontana Pinto. 2009. "Nordeste Brasileiro: Crescimento e dinâmica espacial no período 1970–2008". *Revista Econômica do Nordeste*, 40(4): 821–832.

Alban, Marcus. 2006. "Turismo no Brasil: A estratégia de expansão espacial e seus problemas". *Turismo: Visão e Ação*, 8(2): 301–308.

Almeida, Paulo Henrique de. 2008. "A economia de Salvador e a formação de sua Região Metropolitana" in Inaiá Maria Moreira de Carvalho and Gilberto Corso Pereira (eds.): *Como anda Salvador e sua região metropolitan* (pp. 13–52). Salvador: EDUFBA.

Andrade, Manuel Correia de. 1963. *A terra e o homem no Nordeste*. São Paulo: Brasiliense.

Araújo, Juliana Bacelar de. 2017. *Mercado de trabalho e desigualdade: O Nordeste brasileiro nos anos 2000*. Thesis (Doutorado), Instituto de Economia/Universidade Estadual de Campinas (UNICAMP). Campinas-SP.

Araújo, Tânia Bacelar de. 2004. "Northeast, Northeasts: What Northeast". *Latin American Perspectives*, 31(2): 16–41.

———. 2014. "Nordeste: Desenvolvimento recente e perspectivas" in Paulo Ferraz Guimarães, Rodrigo Almeida de Aguiar, Helena Maria Martins Lastres and Marcela Machado da Silva (eds.): *Um olhar territorial para o desenvolvimento: Nordeste* (pp. 540–561). Rio de Janeiro: Banco Nacional de Desenvolvimento Econômico e Social.

Araújo, Tania Bacelar de and Arilson Favareto. 2020. "O papel da agricultura familiar para um novo desenvolvimento regional no Nordeste – uma homenagem a Celso Furtado". *Revista Econômica do Nordeste*, 51(suplemento especial, Agosto): 9–29.

Araújo, Tarcisio Patricio de, Aldemir do Vale Souza and Roberto Alves da Lima. 1997. "Nordeste: economia e mercado de trabalho". *Estudos Avançados*, 11(29): 55–77.

Baltar, Paulo Eduardo de Andrade and José Dari Krein. 2013. "A retomada do desenvolvimento e a regulação do mercado do trabalho no Brasil". *Caderno CRH*, 26(68): 273–292.

BNB (Banco do Nordeste do Brasil). 2005. *Relatório final do PRODETUR NE*. Brasília.

———. 2013. *A Região Nordeste nas Contas Regionais do Brasil – 1995–2010*. Fortaleza: BNB/ETENE.

———. 2019. *BNB Conjuntura Econômica*, 59 and 61. Fortaleza: BNB/ETENE.

———. 2020. *Diário Econômico Etene*, 3(11), 5 February. Fortaleza: BNB/ETENE.

Barbosa, Alexandre de Freitas. 2022. "Regimes de acumulação e trabalho no Brasil e as transformações do Nordeste, 1850–1980" in Roberto Véras de Oliveira and Gerry Rodgers (eds.): *Desenvolvimento e regime de trabalho: A trajetória do Nordeste do Brasil* (pp. 61–105). São Paulo: Annablume.

Barroso, Liliane Cordeiro. 2019. "Indústria Nordeste – 2002 a 2018". *BNB Conjuntura Econômica*, Edição Especial 15 Anos: 133–150. Fortaleza: BNB/ ETENE.

Benevides, Cezar. 1985. *Camponeses em marcha: Estudo das Ligas Camponesas paraibanas (1960–1964)*. Rio de Janeiro: Paz e Terra.

Brazil, Government of. 2010. *Programa de Aceleração do Crescimento: Balanço 4 anos (2007–2010)*. Brasília: Ministério do Planejamento.

———. 2012. *Programa de Aceleração do Crescimento 2*. Brasília: Ministério do Planejamento.

Campos, Pedro Henrique. 2019. "Os efeitos da crise econômica e da operação Lava Jato sobre a indústria da construção pesada no Brasil: Falências, desnacionalização e desestruturação produtiva". *Mediações*, 24(1): 127–153.

Cano, Wilson. 2012. "A desindustrialização no Brasil". *Economia e Sociedade*, 21 (Special issue): 831–851.

———. 2017. "Prefácio" in Aristides Monteiro Neto, César Nunes de Castro and Carlos Antonio Brandão (eds.): *Desenvolvimento regional no Brasil: Políticas, estratégias e perspectivas* (pp. 11–19). Rio de Janeiro: IPEA.

Cardoso, Adalberto Moreira. 2015. "Dimensões da crise do sindicalismo brasileiro". *Caderno CRH*, 28(75): 493–510.

Carvalho, Inaiá Maria Moreira de. 1986. "Urbanização, mercado de trabalho e pauperização no Nordeste Brasileiro: Uma resenha dos estudos recentes". *BIB-Revista Brasileira de Informação Bibliográfica em Ciências Sociais*, 22(2): 3–25.

Castro, Nadya Araujo and Marcia de Paula Leite. 1994. "A sociologia do trabalho industrial no Brasil: Desafios e interpretações". *BIB-Revista Brasileira de Informação Bibliográfica em Ciências Sociais*, 37(1): 39–59.

Cavalcanti, Clovis. 1978. *Viabilidade do setor informal: A demanda de pequenos serviços no Grande Recife*. Recife: Ministério da Educação e Cultura/SUDENE, Instituto Joaquim Nabuco de Pesquisas Sociais.

———. 1987. "O mercado do pequeno e a síndrome da informalidade: Atividades informais e população de baixa renda no Nordeste". *Cadernos de Estudos Sociais*, 3(1): 65–74.

Cavalcanti, Clovis and Renato Duarte. 1980a. *O setor informal de Salvador: Dimensões, natureza, significação*. Recife: SUDENE/Fundaj; Brasília: M.T.

———. 1980b. *A procura de espaço na economia urbana: O setor informal de Fortaleza*. Recife: SUDENE/Fundaj; Brasília: M.T.

CESIT (Centro de Estudos Sindicais e de Economia do Trabalho). 2017. *Contribuição crítica à reforma trabalhista*. IE/CESIT, Universidade Estadual de

Campinas (Unicamp). Campinas-SP. <https://www.eco.unicamp.br/images/arquivos/Dossie14set2017.pdf>, accessed 12-09-2020.

CGEE (Centro de Gestão e Estudos Estratégicos). 2014. *Plano de ciência, tecnologia e inovação para o desenvolvimento sustentável do Nordeste Brasileiro*. Documento Técnico No. 22. Brasília: CGEE.

Dantas, Eustógio Wanderley Correia and José Borzacchiello da Silva. 2009. "A formação histórica da metrópole e as principais tendências de desenvolvimento" in Luís Renato Pequeno (regional coord.): *Como anda Fortaleza*, Vol. 5, 'Como andam as regiões metropolitanas' Collection (pp. 1–39). Brasília: Ministério das Cidades. <https://www.observatoriodasmetropoles.net.br/wp-content/uploads/2020/11/vol5_Fortaleza.pdf>, accessed 10-05-2022.

DIEESE (Departamento Intersindical de Estatística e Estudos Socioeconômicos). 2012. "Balanço das greves em 2009 e 2010". *Estudos e Pesquisas 60*. São Paulo: DIEESE.

———2015. "Balanço das greves em 2013". *Estudos e Pesquisas 79*. São Paulo: DIEESE.

Druck, Maria da Graça. 1999. *Terceirização: (Des)fordizando a fábrica. Um estudo do complexo petroquímico*. Salvador: Edufba; São Paulo: Boitempo.

Dulci, Otávio Soares. 2002. "Guerra fiscal, desenvolvimento desigual e relações federativas no Brasil". *Revista de Sociologia e Política*, 18: 95–107.

Elias, Denise and Renato Pequeno. 2007. "Desigualdades socioespaciais nas cidades do agronegócio". *Revista Brasileira de Estudos Urbanos e Regionais*, 9(1): 25–39.

Falvo, Josiane Fachini. 2013. "A desigualdade social nas metrópoles de Salvador, Recife e Fortaleza" in Inez Silvia Batista Castro (ed.): *Novas interpretações desenvolvimentistas* (pp. 15–94). Rio de Janeiro: Centro Internacional Celso Furtado.

Faria, Vilmar Evangelista. 1980. "Divisão inter-regional do trabalho e pobreza urbana: O caso de Salvador" in Guaraci Adeodato Alves de Souza and Vilmar Faria (eds.): *Bahia de todos os pobres* (pp. 23–40). Petrópolis: Vozes.

Freire, Laura Lúcia Ramos. 2019. "Comércio exterio", *BNB Conjuntura Econômica*, Edição Especial 15 Anos: 205–225. Fortaleza: BNB/ETENE.

Fusco, Wilson. 2012. "Regiões metropolitanas do Nordeste: Origens, destinos e retornos de migrantes". *Revista Interdisciplinar de Mobilidade Humana*, 20(39): 101–116.

Galvão, Olimpio José de Arroxelas. 2014. "Inserção comercial da economia do Nordeste no exterior e no Brasil e proposição de políticas". *Análise temática dos estudos prospectivos sobre o desenvolvimento do Nordeste para o BNB* (pp. 6–103). Fortaleza: BNB/IICA.

Garcia Jr, Afrânio Raul. 1989. *O Sul: Caminho do roçado. Estratégias de reprodução camponesa e transformação social*. São Paulo: Marco Zero/CNPq/UNB.

Gomes, Gustavo Maia and José Raimundo Vergolino. 1995. *A macroeconomia do desenvolvimento nordestino: 1960/1994*. Texto para Discussão 372. Brasília: IPEA.

Gonçalves, Guilherme Quaresma, José Alberto Magno de Carvalho, Laura Lídia Rodríguez Wong and Cássio Maldonado Turra. 2019. "A transição da fecundidade no Brasil ao longo do século XX – uma perspectiva regional". *Revista Brasileira de Estudos da População*, 36: 1–34.

Grupo de Trabalho para o Desenvolvimento do Nordeste/GTDN. 1967. *Uma política de desenvolvimento econômico para o Nordeste*. Recife: SUDENE.

Guimarães Neto, Leonardo. 1985. *A gestão do trabalho urbano no Nordeste*. Recife, Fundação Joaquim Nabuco.

———. 1989. *Introdução à formação econômica do Nordeste*. Recife: Massangana.

———. 1997. "Trajetória econômica de uma região periférica". *Estudos Avançados*, 11(29): 37–54.

———. 2010. *Nota Técnica sobre as desigualdades regionais no Governo Lula, preparada para o estudo Brasil 2003–2010*. Brasília: CGEE.

Guimarães, Alberto Passos. 1976. "O complexo agroindustrial". *Reforma Agrária* 6(1–2): 2–12.

Guimarães, Paulo Ferraz, Fernando Castilhos de Araújo Galindo Félix, Rodrigo Almeida de Aguiar, Ana Carolina Varejão Lima Carvalhosa and Tagore Villarim de Siqueira. 2014. *Atuação do BNDES na região Nordeste*. Brasília: BNDES (Biblioteca Digital). <https://web.bndes.gov.br/bib/jspui/bitstream/1408/2982/1/Atua%C3%A7%C3%A3o do BNDES na regi%C3%A3o Nordeste_1_P.pdf >, accessed 10-05-2022.

Harvey, David. 1990. *The condition of postmodernity: An enquiry into the origins of cultural change*. Cambridge, MA; Oxford: Blackwell.

Heredia, Beatriz Maria Alásia de. 1979. *A morada da vida: Trabalho familiar entre pequenos produtores do Nordeste do Brasil*. Rio de Janeiro: Paz e Terra.

Hoffmann, Rodolfo. 2002. "A distribuição da renda no Brasil no período 1992–2001". *Economia e Sociedade*, 11(2): 213–235.

IBGE (Instituto Brasileiro de Geografia e Estatística). Various dates. *PNAD (Pesquisa Nacional por Amostra de Domicílios)*. Rio de Janeiro: IBGE.

———. Various dates. *PNADC (Pesquisa Nacional por Amostra de Domicílios Contínua)*. Rio de Janeiro: IBGE.

———. 2008. *Série relatórios metodológicos 37* (Contas Regionais do Brasil). Rio de Janeiro: IBGE.

———. 2012. *Contas Nacionais 38* (Contas Regionais do Brasil 2010). Rio de Janeiro: IBGE.

———. 2016. *Síntese de indicadores 2015*. Pesquisa Nacional por Amostra de Domicílios/PNAD (Coordenação de Trabalho e Rendimento). Rio de Janeiro: IBGE.

———. 2020. *Estudos e Pesquisas Informação Demográfica e Socioeconômica 43*. Rio de Janeiro: IBGE.

———. 2021. *Estudos e Pesquisas, Informação Demográfica e Socioeconômica 44*. Rio de Janeiro: IBGE.

Jardim, Maria Chaves and Márcio Rogério Silva. 2015. *Programa de aceleração do crescimento (PAC): Neodesenvolvimentismo?*. São Paulo: Cultura Acadêmica. (Coleção PROPG Digital – UNESP).<https://static.scielo.org/scielobooks/s5k33/pdf/jardim-9788579837432.pdf>, accessed 11-05-2022.

Krein, José Dari, Marcelo Manzano and Marilane Oliveira Teixeira. 2020. *Utopias do trabalho: desafios e perspectivas para o pós pandemia*. São Paulo: Friedrich Ebert Stiftung.

Krein, José Dari, Roberto Véras de Oliveira and Vitor Araújo Filgueiras (eds.). 2019. *Reforma trabalhista no Brasil: Promessas e realidade* (1st ed.). Campinas: Curt Nimuendajú.

Krein, José Dari, Anselmo Santos and Amilton Moretto. 2013. "Trabalho no Brasil: evolução recente e desafios". *Revista Paranaense de Desenvolvimento*, 34(124): 27–53.

Lavinas, Lena. 2010. "Pobreza: Métricas e evolução recente no Brasil e no Nordeste". *Cadernos do Desenvolvimento*, 5(7): 126–148.

Lima, Jacob Carlos. 2002. *As artimanhas da flexibilização: O trabalho terceirizado em cooperativas de produção*. São Paulo: Terceira Margem.

Máximo, Rérisson. 2020. "Efeitos territoriais de políticas educacionais: A recente expansão e interiorização do ensino federal em cidades não-metropolitanas no Ceará". *URBE – Revista Brasileira de Gestão Urbana*, 12: 1–17.

Melo, Maria Cristina Pereira de. 2013. "Comércio exterior da região Nordeste na esteira do 'Efeito China'". *Revista Econômica do Nordeste*, 44(2): 453–474.

Milla, Debora Cristina Alves da Cunha. 2020. *A narrativa do jornal O Globo sobre o ex-presidente Lula durante o processo da Lava-Jato*. Dissertação (Mestrado em Comunicação), Universidade Federal do Paraná.

Monteiro Neto, Aristides, Marco Aurélio Costa, Guilherme Mendes Resende, Constantino Cronemberger Mendes and Ernesto Pereira Galindo. 2017. "Desenvolvimento territorial no Brasil: Reflexões sobre políticas e instrumentos no período recente e propostas de aperfeiçoamento" in Aristides Monteiro Neto, César Nunes de Castro and Carlos Antonio Brandão (eds.): *Desenvolvimento regional no Brasil: políticas, estratégias e perspectivas* (pp. 37–50). Rio de Janeiro: IPEA.

Oliveira, Francisco de. 1972. "A economia brasileira: Crítica à razão dualista". *Novos Estudos CEBRAP*, 2: 3–82.

———. 1981. *Elegia para uma re(li)gião: Sudene, Nordeste, planejamento e conflito de classes*. Rio de Janeiro: Paz e Terra.

———. 2003. *O elo perdido: Classe e identidade de classe na Bahia*. São Paulo: Fundação Perseu Abramo.

Paiva, Maria das Graças de Menezes Venâncio. 2010. "Análise do programa de desenvolvimento do turismo do nordeste (Prodetur/NE) na perspectiva do planejamento estratégico". *Revista de Administração Pública*, 44(2): 197–213.

Paula, Luiz Fernando de and Rafael Moura. 2019. "Economic consequences of Operação Lava-Jato". *Valor Econômico*, 28 August. <http://www.luizfernandodepaula.com.br/ups/consequencias-economicas-da-operacao-lava-jato-valor-economico.pdf>

Pêgo, Bolívar and Carlos Àlvares da Silva Campos Neto. 2008. *O PAC e o setor elétrico: Desafios para o abastecimento do mercado brasileiro (2007–2010)*. Texto para Discussão 1329. Brasília: IPEA.

Peruchetti, Paulo and Laísa Richter. 2020. "Quem são os desalentados do Brasil?". *Blog do IBRE*. Rio de Janeiro: Fundação Getúlio Vargas. <https://blogdoibre.fgv.br/posts/quem-sao-os-desalentados-no-brasil>.

Pochmann, Marcio. 2008. *O emprego no desenvolvimento da nação*. São Paulo: Boitempo.

———. 2020. "Tendências estruturais do mundo do trabalho no Brasil". *Ciência & Saúde Coletiva*, 25(1): 89–99.

Saboia, João. 2001. *A dinâmica da descentralização industrial no Brasil*. Texto para Discussão 452. Rio de Janeiro: UFRJ-IE.

Silva, Andréa Ferreira da, Jair Andrade Araujo, Wellington Ribeiro Justo and Kilmer Coelho Campos. 2017. "Análise da pobreza multidimensional no Brasil no período de 2009 a 2015". *Revista Econômica do Nordeste*, 48(2): 9–24.

Silva, Ricardo Azevedo. 2005. "Crescimento econômico, desenvolvimento social e regional: O caso do Ceará no contexto da região Nordeste (1970–1998)". *Revista do Desenvolvimento Regional/REDES*, 10(2): 153–180.

Singer, André. 2013. "Brasil, junho de 2013, classes e ideologias cruzadas". *Novos Estudos CEBRAP*, 97: 23–40.

Trovão, Cassiano José Bezerra Marques, Juliana Bacelar de Araújo and Rafael Fernandes Montenegro. 2019. "Economia, trabalho e renda no Nordeste brasileiro do início do século XXI." *Revista de Desenvolvimento Econômico*, Ano XXI, 1(42): 134–160.

Valente Junior, Airton Saboya and João Marcos Rodrigues da Silva. 2019. "O setor de serviços do Nordeste no início do século XXI". *BNB Conjuntura Econômica*, Edição Especial 15 Anos: 163–175.

Véras de Oliveira, Roberto. 2011. *Sindicalismo e democracia no Brasil*: *Do novo sindicalismo*. São Paulo: Anneblume.

Vidal, Antônio Ricardo de Norões. 2019. "Investimentos federais na região Nordeste no período de 2010 a 2018". *Informe ETENE*, 4(3): 11p.

3 The labour regime

1 Introduction

The system of labour regulation in Brazil is broad and systematic in its scope, but partial in its coverage. It is broad, in that it covers not only employment relationships, conditions of employment, social protection, and other labour standards through the CLT (*Consolidação das Leis de Trabalho*[1]), along with the means for enforcement through labour inspection and the Labour Courts, but also the organization of workers and employers, their roles in the economy and the rules for collective bargaining. It is backed up by a wide-ranging system of training, largely managed by employers' organizations, which delivers skills and professional qualifications. However, it is partial, since a significant proportion of wage earners and vast numbers of non-wage workers are not included in the system, or only partly so, either because their situations are not considered in the legislative framework, or because the formal system of regulation is not implemented in all parts of the economy (Véras de Oliveira, 2018). In reality, there exists a substantial informal economy alongside the formal, regulated system. But contrary to a widespread assumption, the informal economy is not unregulated. Informal employment practices depend on social norms of behaviour and practice, and are influenced to some degree by the system of formal regulation. Parts of the informal economy are connected directly or indirectly with formal production systems. Even within the formal economy, there is a great deal of diversity in the ways in which labour is used and managed, leading to variation in the quality and productivity of employment. The labour regime, that is to say the structures and processes through which work is organized and governed, thus involves a wide variety of social and economic institutions, both formal and informal, which condition employment relationships in different parts of the production system, influence the development path and affect the nature and extent of inequality.

The formal regulation of work and employment in the Northeast follows the same rules as the rest of the Brazilian economy: there is a unitary national system, with little regional variation. In practice, however, the informal economy accounts for a much larger share of production and

DOI: 10.4324/9781003326670-3

employment in the Northeast than in other parts of Brazil, and many of the formal institutions – of representation, protection and enforcement – are weaker. The pattern of production in the Northeast is also different, with less industry and more agriculture, greater heterogeneity in production arrangements and a sharper dualism between large and small enterprises, all of which modifies the nature of employment relations. And the distinctive historical and social characteristics of the region also have an important influence. So while in principle the labour regime of the Northeast is merely the regional reflection of the national model, in practice it has its own character, which has consequences for the pattern of development of the region; and, as we saw in the last chapter, the development regime in the region in turn has consequences for the labour regime.

This chapter considers three key aspects of the labour regime:

- The overall framework of labour regulation and worker organization. We review how regulation has changed over time, the evolving role of state labour policy and trade union action, and the situation today;
- The nature of employment relationships, and the corresponding pattern of "labour status". We use survey data to examine differences in the character and quality of work in different types of economic activity;
- The relationship between the labour regime and inequality of income, including discrimination and differentiation by gender and race.

We also discuss the consequences for these labour market institutions and outcomes of the persistent political and economic crisis since 2015.

2 The regulation of the labour market: the State and the trade unions

The origins of the system of labour regulation in Brazil, and its distinctive character, lie in the measures adopted during the first Getulio Vargas government (1930–1945). This was a system of "regulated citizenship" (dos Santos, 1987), built around a hierarchy of occupations that were recognized and regulated, a signed labour card (*carteira assinada*) in which were specified the terms – the rights and duties of employers and workers – of wage labour contracts, and a corporatist system of unions representing workers and employers. A variety of institutions was put in place to manage this system – the Ministry of Labour, Labour Courts, Social Security institutions, labour legislation (the CLT), the minimum wage, and a formal training system (the "S" system – SENAI, SENAC, etc., training organizations that correspond to economic sectors).

This system of labour regulation was at the heart of a developmentalist project driven by a strong, centralizing and entrepreneurial State in the decades after the Second World War, capable of promoting accelerated industrialization. In particular, it provided the means to meet, but also to control the demands of the emerging industrial workforce (Cardoso, 1999, p.28). The trade union structure was the main instrument of this control. Unions were to be recognized, maintained and supervised by the State. Only one union was recognized for each economic sector and occupational category within each territory, funded by an obligatory tax on workers, collected by enterprises. Collective bargaining was highly regulated, and strict rules were established to circumscribe the right to strike. The minimum wage was a key mechanism for managing the distribution of the gains from industrial development, and wages above the minimum were, and still are, often described in terms of multiples of the minimum wage (as are social security benefits). For much of the post-war period, however, the minimum wage, while ostensibly a floor, was in practice a means to limit wage increases – it fell steadily in real terms from the mid-1950s to the early 1990s (Cacciamali et al., 2015).

Despite the enormous political, social and economic changes since 1945, much of this structure remains in place, notwithstanding repeated political efforts to change it. The carteira assinada remains a key dividing line in the labour market between protected and precarious workers, and the minimum wage remains a central instrument of national labour policy. The training institutions are still powerful actors. The trade union system has evolved and become more fragmented (both at the base – unions – and, more recently, at the top – union confederations), but its organization and role in collective bargaining still bear traces of these corporatist origins. Labour regulation remains heavily focussed on formal wage labour, a legacy of the original focus on the industrial proletariat, although industrial workers constitute only a fraction of the workforce today. This latter point is particularly true of the Northeast, where industry accounts for a smaller share of employment than in the rest of the country. In this region the formal labour institutions often appear to be ill-adapted to the labour markets in which they are supposed to be applied. To understand the labour regime today, it is necessary to set it in historical context.

After the trauma of the military regime (1964–1985, but much weakened after 1980), the 1980s was a period of institutional reconfiguration. The passage from the 1970s to the 1980s was marked by a wave of strikes, triggered by industrial conflicts in the ABC region of São Paulo State, which spread throughout the country, involving various categories of workers, such as metalworkers, bank workers, oil workers, civil servants, teachers, and sugarcane workers, among others. There emerged a union pole of political opposition to the government, critical of the corporatist union system, which later became known as "new unionism."

However, according to Rodrigues (1990), the "advantages" of the prevailing union system (such as the monopoly of representation, union unity, the union tax, etc.) were such that the new unions found it difficult to break with the earlier model. Despite a widespread rhetoric in favour of class-based unionism, in practice there was, over time, a certain accommodation to the corporatist structure. Nevertheless, important new political and social movements emerged from the reconstruction of the union system, including the Workers' Party (*Partido dos Trabalhadores* – PT) in 1980, the United Workers' Central (*Central Única dos Trabalhadores* – CUT) in 1983, and the Landless Workers Movement (*Movimento dos Trabalhadores Rurais Sem Terra* – MST) in 1984, among others.

With regard to the Northeast, authors such as Oliveira (1987) were sceptical about the possibilities of organizing and mobilizing workers in the new industries that had developed with support from Sudene (discussed in Chapter 2). In a study on industrialization in Bahia from the 1970s onwards, including an oil refinery, petrochemicals and other industries, Oliveira (1987) concluded that effective unionization was "a quasi-impossibility", because of segmentation and hierarchization among workers, a weak tradition of union organization and political repression. Nevertheless, in the 1980s the "new unionism" had an impact in the Northeast, with a growth of class consciousness among industrial workers, for instance among the growing numbers of metalworkers in Bahia and Pernambuco (Lima, 1996, p.175). There was also a resurgence of militantism among sugarcane workers. There were strikes by sugarcane workers in Pernambuco almost every year from 1979 until the 1990s, also involving other Northeastern sugarcane-producing states, such as Alagoas, Paraíba and Rio Grande do Norte. This cycle of strikes had important national repercussions during the democratic transition in the 1980s, by reinforcing a political project focussed on the social demands of workers, which translated into the creation and projection of the PT on the national scene. Trade union mobilization grew in the Northeast during this period, though less than in São Paulo, and it was mainly concentrated among white-collar workers (teachers, civil servants, bankers) and among rural workers, rather than in industry, which only accounted for a small share of employment (Castro, 1991).

The fall of the military regime and the rise of unions and popular movements in the 1980s created a political environment that was more conducive to the recognition of social, labour and political rights. These were most clearly expressed in the new Constitution that was promulgated in 1988: the State, on the one hand, expanded its functions as a provider of social services to the population (health, education, social security, social assistance, housing, basic sanitation, etc.); and, on the other hand, it lost the power of direct intervention over the organization and management of unions. At the same time ways were developed for organized civil society to participate in the development and oversight of public policies. New mechanisms of support to workers were created, such as the FAT (*Fundo de Amparo ao Trabalhador*, Worker Support Fund), a large fund based on social contributions collected by companies, which started to finance unemployment insurance and development projects. Above all, the notion of universal social rights called into question the historically constructed reference of "regulated citizenship" (Telles and Paoli, 1994).

But the promise of the 1988 Constitution met with strong resistance in the 1990s, when an agenda of economic restructuring, privatization and reform of the State was associated with attempts to flexibilize the labour market, which resulted in an increase in informal employment and growing precariousness of work (Pochmann, 2009). A series of government measures reduced or weakened the scope of labour regulation: an end to the automatic indexation of wages to inflation, weakening of labour inspection, greater flexibility of working time, creation of a fixed-term contract, an end to the principle of persistence of collective agreements, and modifications to the Labour Court, among others (Krein, 2007). The CUT, other union federations and some business organizations developed an alternative project for a "Democratic Labour Relations System," involving the promotion of trade union and worker rights, collective bargaining, and a state role in mediating the relations between capital and labour. But this project foundered in the face of neoliberal policies and divergences within the trade union movement. Trade unions were divided among several confederations, with differing political affiliations and strategy, though the CUT remained the largest confederation, including in the Northeast, despite the increasing share of the more liberal, "results-oriented" confederation, *Força Sindical.*

In the period from 1987 to 2001, there were two contrasting tendencies. First, the number of workers' trade unions grew substantially, from 5,648 to 11,354 in Brazil as a whole, and from 1,758 to 3,179 in the Northeast. But this increase in union density did not lead to a corresponding increase in the unionization rates of workers: the proportion of unionized workers hardly changed in the country as a whole in the 1990s, and only rose modestly in the Northeast, reaching some 17% of all workers in 2001, close to the average for Brazil.[2] In reality the geographical and sectoral expansion of unions seemed to mainly reflect a bureaucratic logic, as unions were created to fill territorial and occupational spaces. This was particularly the case in the Northeast, where almost half of all trade unions were rural in 2001, compared with only one third in Brazil as a whole. Among urban unions, those in the Northeast were much more likely to represent the public sector, and much less likely to represent manufacturing industry, than in the rest of the country (in particular, when compared to more industrialized regions). And there is evidence that the effectiveness of trade unions in the region was not commensurate with their formal presence. According to the IBGE *Pesquisa Sindical* (trade union survey), there were less workplace trade union delegates in the Northeast than in other parts of Brazil, less enterprise trade union committees and commissions, less tripartite bodies at the municipal level, less knowledge of and participation in mediation and conciliation, fewer strikes, and above all fewer agreements arising out of collective bargaining – in short, less institutional presence and correspondingly weaker actions and results.

The national situation changed, with respect to both state labour policy and the role of trade unions, after the installation of a government led by the Workers' Party (PT) in 2003. Earlier attempts to weaken labour regulation were reversed (at least partially), and labour policies and institutions were reinforced. This included enhanced employment protection, a variety of new social programmes, better connections between government and unions, and the creation of new mechanisms for social dialogue. The minimum wage was regularly readjusted, with real gains, collective bargaining was promoted, and measures were taken to expand formal employment. This policy approach particularly benefited the Northeast, where average wages are lower, so more workers benefited from the increase in the minimum wage. Furthermore, in the region there was more space for formalizing employment due to the high prevailing levels of informality.

The trade unions, in particular the CUT, but also other national confederations, supported and were involved in government initiatives in favour of social concertation, notably the creation of the Council for Social and Economic Development and the National Labour Forum (Araújo and Véras de Oliveira, 2014). Unions helped to reinforce labour inspection and the enforcement of labour legislation, and contributed to the work of the Labour Courts, helping to promote labour rights. On balance, this was a time of gains for unions and workers, with a majority of collective agreements resulting in real wage increases (Amorim, 2015). The main achievement of union action at the national level in this period concerned the minimum wage. United in a national campaign, the union confederations organized three marches to Brasilia, in 2004, 2005 and 2006, resulting in substantial increases in the minimum wage, and a law that guaranteed long-term adjustments in the minimum wage in excess of inflation.

The unionization rate increased both in the Northeast and in the rest of the country, but more so in the former. The overall union membership rate for the period 2002–2015 (the proportion of unionized workers in the employed population, calculated using PNAD data) for Brazil and the Northeast is given in Figure 3.1. Three periods can be identified: from 2002 to 2006, rising; from 2006 to 2013, falling; and from 2013 to 2015, rising sharply. In 2015 almost 13 million workers were affiliated to one of the national union bodies. This pattern is the same for the Northeast and for the country as a whole, but it can be seen that from a similar starting point in 2002, the unionization rate in the Northeast rose more or declined less than in the country as a whole, so the gap between the two increased. The share of women in union membership has been rising, from 37.5% in 2002 to 42.1% in 2015 in Brazil as a whole; and, in the Northeast, from 40% to 44.9%.

One of the reasons for the higher unionization rate in the Northeast is the greater weight in the region of union membership in the agricultural sector, where union coverage expanded (including a majority of self-employed workers[3]), and an increasing share of employment in the more unionized public sector. But a higher level of membership did not lead to more effective trade union action in the region.

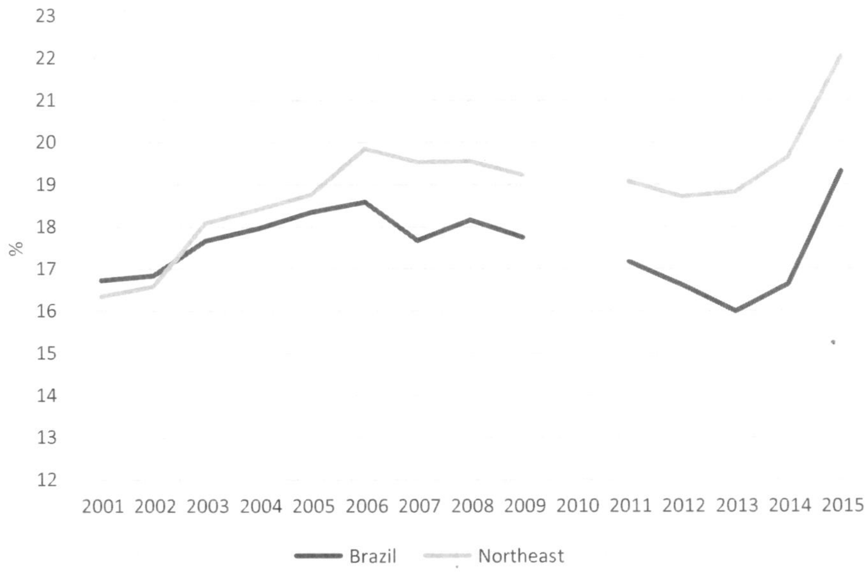

Figure 3.1 Unionization rate, Brazil and the Northeast, 2001–2015 (%).
Source: IBGE, *Pesquisa Nacional por Amostra de Domicílios* (PNAD) (2002–2015).
Note: The PNAD was not carried out in the census year 2010.

The synergy between government and trade union agendas in this period did not reduce strike activity in the country as a whole; on the contrary the number of strikes remained at a high level throughout the period, both during the economic boom from 2004 to 2008, and especially in the economically more difficult years after the global financial crisis. For instance, in 2011 and 2012 two waves of strikes broke out in public infrastructure construction projects across the country, especially the North and Northeast, around basic labour issues such as the payment of overtime, right to visit family members, improvements in the supply of food and drinking water, and relationships with supervisors. There was a particular concern with the precarious employment of construction workers, cleaning workers, security guards, and others. The political strengthening of the trade union movement thus created a space for greater militancy (Boito and Marcelino, 2010; DIEESE, 2015).

The situation then changed radically with the economic crisis from 2015 onwards, and with the change of government in 2016. The negative effects on the labour market of the economic crisis directly affected trade union strength in collective bargaining, but above all the new government came to power with an agenda to weaken trade unions and reduce legal protections in the labour market. There had long been a current of business and conservative political opinion that argued that the extensive system of labour market regulation undermined competitiveness and adversely affected employment creation. These voices were muffled during the period of relatively high economic growth under the first three PT-led governments, up to 2014, since during this period both output and formal employment grew substantially, which made it difficult to argue that labour market regulation was an obstacle to employment creation. But with the economic recession from 2015 onwards, the issue of labour market flexibility returned to the political agenda, and in a more extreme form than in the 1990s, despite its adverse consequences at that time.

The key policy changes were embedded in the 2017 Labour Reform. It was implemented with the promise of "modernization" of labour relations, job creation, the formalization of employment and the encouragement of "free negotiation" between employees and employers. But what actually occurred was the liberalization of outsourcing, the primacy of the negotiated over the legislated, the encouragement of individual negotiation to the detriment of the collective, the legalization of atypical and precarious contracts, the weakening of the Labour Courts, and the reduction of state intervention in the resolution of labour conflicts. These changes undermined trade union action; in particular, the labour reform eliminated a key component of the corporatist union system, the obligation for workers to pay the union tax, which greatly affected unions' financial capacity. The reform also restricted the space for collective bargaining, decentralizing negotiations and transferring responsibility for some tasks previously performed by unions to the sphere of individual bargaining between the worker and the employer (Véras de Oliveira et al., 2019, p.671). All of these changes were national in scope, but their effects in the Northeast were particularly marked. One consequence was to increase the discretionary power of companies to determine working relationships and conditions. This can be seen in some of the case studies discussed in the next chapter, for example, in call centres in Paraíba and the automobile industry in Goiana, Pernambuco.

So after the successes of the 2003–2015 period the Brazilian union movement found itself in some difficulty. In addition to the persistence of old problems (such as lack of workplace presence, low average levels of union membership, and organizational fragmentation, among others), the movement was no longer able to rely on government policies that gave priority to employment and income generation, nor on an economic environment that favoured collective bargaining, nor even on a continuation of the tendency, during the PT period, for businesses to refrain from attacking workers' rights.

The inevitable consequence of the weakening of union power was that the upward trend in unionization rates was reversed. Between 2012 and 2019 unionization rates fell, by 30% in Brazil as a whole, and by 23% in the Northeast (Table 3.1).[4] As in the earlier data the higher rate in the Northeast reflects a larger proportion of workers in public services and in agriculture, rather than unionization of industrial workers, which was low.

Table 3.1 Unionization rate, Brazil and Northeast, 2012–2019 (%)

	Brazil	*Northeast*
2012	16.1	16.7
2016	14.9	15.7
2017	14.4	15.0
2018	12.5	14.1
2019	11.2	12.8

Source: IBGE, *Pesquisa Nacional por Amostra de Domicílios Contínua* (PNADC) (2012–2019).

Despite these difficulties, collective bargaining continued, and delivered widespread, if small, real wage increases in 2018 (DIESSE, 2019, p.3). But pressures for labour market reform continued under the Bolsonaro government, and it remains to be seen whether unions can develop new actions in favour of employment, income and rights at work. In the Northeast, in particular, there is a widely recognized need to move away from formal, even symbolic representation of workers towards more effective actions in the workplace, and an adaptation of both legal instruments and trade union strategy to the heterogeneous structure of the Northeastern labour market.

So far we have only been considering formal regulation. But one of the main characteristics of the labour regime in Brazil is the importance of informality, both in wage work and self-employment. The level of informality is also a key factor in differentiating the Northeast from the rest of the country, as it is much higher in the former, as shown in Chapter 2.[5] This is important for several reasons. First, the rights of informal workers are far less well defended than formal ones, and formal institutions of representation – unions and other associations – inevitably give priority to their core of formal workers. Second, productivity and earnings are lower, on average, in informal work. Third, many vulnerable or discriminated groups, notably in relation to race and gender, are over-represented in informal work. Fourth, much informal work is effectively invisible, as the statistical and administrative system is not designed to capture it.

In our theoretical framework, informality is not an aberration or an accident, or even just the survival of non-capitalist forms of production, but a structural feature of the production and distribution system. In many economic activities formal enterprises employ informal wage workers (without carteira assinada), especially in temporary, secondary or outsourced work, because they are more easily fired and can be paid lower wages. Furthermore, many firms outsource to, or buy services from, informal self-employed workers and small firms, as a means of externalizing costs or as a way to circumvent labour legislation. Informal self-employment also acts as a buffer in the labour market by providing an alternative to unemployment. As the economic crisis that began in 2015 persisted, unemployment first rose and then reached a plateau before declining slowly (up to the first half of 2020);

meanwhile, the share of informal work also increased, and continued to increase slowly after unemployment had stabilized or started to fall, but with falling real incomes; we return to this below. Overall, informal work needs to be considered as an integral part of the production system and of the labour market, as Oliveira (1972) pointed out in the early 1970s in his critique of dualistic reasoning.

It is a mistake to think of the informal economy as unregulated. Informal work may not respect the formal structure of organization and regulation of the labour market, but it too is regulated, in its own terms, though social relations, informal organizations, community norms, power relations and traditional practice. The network of small garment producers in the Agreste region of Pernambuco, discussed in the next chapter, shows how informal relations among family firms can be stable and productive. In addition, as a large part of informal wage work falls, in theory, within the scope of labour, commercial and other laws, even if these are not fully applied, it is also regulated by the degree of willingness and of administrative ability to enforce such laws. In fact, the divide between formal and informal workers is not as sharp as the language would suggest. Formal workers are subject to informal practices; informal workers operate within a social sphere which reproduces some of the rules of the formal economy. For instance, while the minimum wage is often not respected by informal employers (nor by formal employers who hire informal workers), it remains a point of reference, and changes in the minimum wages have some influence on informal wages.

A considerable effort was made under the PT-led governments from 2003 to 2016 to formalize informal activities, and some progress was made, with respect to both wage work without carteira and self-employment. For example, with respect to the latter a special tax regime for micro- and small businesses was implemented and the legal status of "Individual Microentrepreneur" (MEI) was created, aiming to convert the "informal worker" into a legalized entrepreneur, with official registration and support from the small business service, Sebrae. But while the MEI has helped to formalize self-employment, it has also favoured the conversion, by companies, of employees into outsourced, notionally independent self-employed workers, facilitated by the labour reform of 2017 (Krein et al., 2019).

An important issue concerns the organization of informal workers. The instability and insecurity of precarious workers makes their organization difficult, but there have been some successes. The Landless Rural Workers Movement (MST) is probably the most prominent, with a long history of success in land occupations and in establishing forms of organization and the promotion of rights for rural workers. There have been many other experiences of organizing informal workers, with greater or lesser degrees of success, such as the Movement of Homeless Workers (MTST), and other associations and cooperatives in the Solidarity Economy, as well as trade union actions aimed at this group, such as the promotion of unions of self-employed workers (see, for example, Singer and Souza, 2000; Goulart, 2012; Kalil, 2012).

The difficulty faced by informal workers in claiming their status as workers is well illustrated by the long struggle of domestic workers, a majority of them women. The country's first association of domestic workers was created in 1936, but it took 77 years for their status as workers to be recognized. For many years the labour legislation (CLT) did not recognize domestic work as an "economic" activity and excluded domestic workers from regulation. Even the Constitution of 1988 reproduced the exclusion of domestic workers from the CLT. Only after years of mobilizations and pressure did domestic workers finally obtain recognition and equal rights with other workers through a constitutional amendment in 2013 (Roberts, 2018).

So the overall regulation of the labour market depends on a complex set of formal and informal institutions that have been built up over time, often contested politically, often difficult to change once they are in place. They concern both legal frameworks established by the State and socially embedded power relations and patterns of behaviour, which give rise to structural characteristics and differentiations in work, including but by no means confined to the formal-informal dichotomy. In the next section we explore some of these differentiations further.

3 Labour status

The labour regime is not only defined by the pattern of regulation of the labour market and the organization of workers. A central element of the labour regime is the "labour status", that is to say the nature of the employment relation for each worker, and her or his position within the production system and the labour process. The distribution of workers across different labour statuses reflects the diverse ways in which labour is incorporated into production systems, the segmentation of the labour market, and differences between workers in employment opportunities and benefits. More or less "formal" labour statuses can be distinguished, with greater or lesser degrees of protection or autonomy.

In this section we examine the characteristics of labour status in the Northeast, comparing the region with the rest of Brazil. Mapping the pattern of labour status provides the empirical foundation for the analysis of the labour regime, and helps to understand the ways employment and work are organized, and the consequences for production and distribution. We concentrate on work in the standard economic sense, i.e. activities that contribute to measurable output, undertaken on own account or for others. This is incomplete, since many activities, such as domestic work, care for others and voluntary contributions to the community, all disproportionately undertaken by women, require time and effort, and contribute to well-being, but are generally neglected in the analysis of employment. We concentrate on labour and employment in the more limited economic sense, because that is what existing data permit, but it is wise to bear this incompleteness in mind, especially when dealing with work in the informal economy.

Labour status then, in the sense we use the term, refers to the nature of the employment relationship. Important factors that contribute to labour status include:

- Autonomy: is the worker in a dependent relationship (undertaking work on someone else's instructions) or acting independently? The fundamental divide is between the self-employed and wage employees. However, there are also intermediate categories, because some self-employment is undertaken within a relationship of dependency, as in various types of outsourced work and work under contract.
- Continuity and regularity: How reliable is the work? Is it done regularly and for an extended period? Many jobs, both waged and on own account, are seasonal or of fixed duration.
- Protection and security: is the worker protected, by law or practice, against dismissal, against personal contingencies, against adverse working conditions? This includes both protections through labour legislation and participation in a social security system. In Brazil legal protection for wage workers is mainly assured through the signed labour card (*carteira de trabalho assinada*). In the case of the self-employed it may come through the registration of the enterprise, or through contributions to social security.
- Remuneration: is income adequate and secure? The main reference point in Brazil is the minimum wage, as noted above, though its adequacy depends on factors such as household status and dependency, and its real value has varied over time.
- Skill, qualification and occupation: are there opportunities to apply and develop skills and knowledge? More skilled jobs may have greater autonomy, or provide greater job satisfaction, in addition to generating higher incomes. "White-collar" jobs often have greater social status, and greater security, than "blue-collar".
- Representation and voice: is there collective organization to defend the interests of workers? In addition to membership of a trade union, or representation in negotiations by a trade union, there are other forms of organization and association, for instance, among the self-employed.

These factors could be used to classify work in many different ways. There is a long-standing practice in labour statistics to distinguish employers, wage workers, the self-employed and unpaid family workers. This limited breakdown, however, "obscures many differences between workers which reflect different labour processes or modes of insertion into labour markets" (Harriss et al., 1990, p.1). In the literature a variety of efforts have been made to expand this classification by identifying employment situations with differing characteristics, relevant for the workers themselves and for the production in which they are engaged (e.g. Standing, 1999). Brazilian official labour market statistics usually divide wage workers by whether or not they have a carteira assinada, and whether they are working in private or public sectors, or in domestic service. But this categorization still fails to capture some important differences between jobs and workers.

In order to analyse the labour regime in the Northeast in greater depth we have developed an expanded breakdown that includes a wider range of aspects of labour status. The aim has been not only to identify differences in the character and quality of work itself, but also categories of employment that contribute to labour market segmentation and play distinct roles in the production system.[6] We identify 16 categories of labour status, which are listed in Table 3.2. These categories have been identified on the basis of data available in the IBGE National Household Sample Survey, the PNADC, which provides indicators for many of the factors listed above. The labour statuses identified all constitute a significant percentage of employment in the Northeast. For other regional or national situations, the choice of labour statuses would no doubt be different. Details of the methods and indicators used to identify these categories are given in an annex to this chapter.

Table 3.2, then, gives the overall percentage distribution of the occupied workforce by labour status in the Northeast of Brazil in the third quarter of 2019, and the corresponding distribution in the rest of Brazil.[7]

Workers in the Northeast are fairly evenly distributed across these 16 categories, showing the considerably diversity in employment patterns. Self-employment and wage work without carteira[8] in agriculture account for 11.5% of employment, most of it self-employment in small farms. About a quarter of all employment is private sector wage work with carteira, with more white-collar than blue-collar workers. The largest category consists of lower white-collar workers such as administrative support staff, call centre operators, shop assistants in commercial centres and the like. There are relatively few unskilled workers with carteira – these workers are concentrated in jobs without carteira, which account for 13% of private sector employment (18% if we include agriculture, 23% if we include the public sector and almost 30% if we include domestic service, most of which is without carteira). Employment without carteira is much more common among small firms than large, but the use of informal wage labour is also a widespread practice in larger firms, accounting for 5% of all employment.

The public sector too is a substantial employer, 15% of employment, two thirds of it in regular, protected work. Overall, about 35% of employment is formal or protected wage work, and about 30% is informal or without the protection of the carteira assinada.

The remaining 35% is distributed across the self-employed/employer categories. Formal, registered employers and self-employed workers contributing to social security are few in number; only one sixth of self-employed workers contribute. Informal self-employment accounts for over 20% of all employment (almost 30% including agriculture). But there are large differences among the self-employed. We distinguish "productive" informal self-employment (income at least equivalent to the minimum wage) from

Table 3.2 Labour status, % distribution, Northeast and Rest of Brazil, third quarter 2019

Labour status	*Northeast*	*Rest of Brazil*
1 Self-employed/family work in agriculture	7.2	4.5
2 Wage work without carteira in agriculture	4.3	1.5
3 Private sector wage work with carteira, upper white-collar	5.2	9.5
4 Private sector wage work with carteira, lower white-collar/services/trade	9.8	13.8
5 Private sector wage work with carteira, blue-collar, skilled or semi-skilled	5.8	9.9
6 Private sector wage work with carteira, blue-collar, unskilled	3.8	5.2
7 Private sector wage work without carteira, small enterprise (up to five workers)	8.1	4.7
8 Private sector wage work without carteira, medium/large enterprise (over five workers)	5.2	5.0
9 Domestic service work	6.8	6.7
10 Public sector work without carteira	4.7	2.2
11 Public sector work with carteira/military/civil servant	10.1	9.6
12 Formal employer (with CNPJ* registration)	2.3	4.2
13 Formal non-agricultural self-employed work (contributing to social security)	4.2	7.1
14 Informal "productive" non-agricultural self-employed work or employer	8.3	9.9
15 Informal "marginal" non-agricultural self-employed work or employer	12.5	5.3
16 Non-agricultural family work	1.6	1.0
Total	100.0	100.0
Grouped categories		
Total agricultural self-employment and wage work without carteira	11.5	6.0
Total protected wage work (private and public)	34.7	48.0
Total wage work without carteira (non-agricultural)/ domestic service	24.8	18.6
Total formal non-agricultural non-wage work	6.5	11.4
Total informal non-agricultural non-wage work	22.5	16.2

Source: Computed from PNADC micro-data (IBGE), 2019, 3rd quarter. Totals may not add to 100 because of rounding.

Note: * CNPJ is the *Cadastro Nacional da Pessoa Jurídica*, the official register of enterprises and organizations.

"marginal" self-employment (less than the minimum wage); 12.5% of employment is in the latter category (more if we include some unpaid family workers), the largest single category.

A simple division into formal and informal work does not capture this diversity. But 58.7% of employment is in categories that are entirely or mainly informal in the sense that they are not registered or without carteira.

There are substantial differences between the Northeast and the rest of Brazil. Wage work with carteira accounts for a much smaller share of employment in the Northeast (25% against 38%), and that is also true for each of the individual categories of wage work with carteira (lines 3–6 in the table). Among formal workers, the share of white-collar and similar work with carteira (lines 3 and 4) is much higher in the rest of Brazil, where it accounts for almost a quarter of all employment, against 16% in the Northeast. There is much more wage work without carteira in the Northeast, especially in small firms and the public sector. The total share of self-employment and employers is similar in the two regions, but the share of the formal and "productive" informal categories is much lower in the Northeast, while the share of "marginal" self-employment and unpaid work is much higher, 14% against 6%.

The overall informal share in the rest of Brazil, in the sense calculated above, amounts to 40.8%, compared with the 58.7% in the Northeast computed above.[9] The high level of informality and backwardness of the Northeastern labour market comes out clearly from this comparison.

There are large differences in income across all these different categories of labour status, as can be seen in Table 3.3.

Three categories stand out: upper white-collar workers, regular public sector workers and formal employers, who received on average three to five times the minimum wage (R$998 in 2019) in the Northeast. At the bottom, the "marginal" self-employed had the lowest incomes, less than half the minimum wage. In the Northeast, incomes in self-employment in agriculture were not much higher. Formal and "productive" self-employed workers had much higher incomes, averaging twice the minimum wage, and five to six times higher than the "marginal" self-employed. This difference is partly due to the definition, because an income equivalent to the minimum wage was set as the dividing line between "productive" and "marginal" workers, but the gap is so large that it confirms the existence of two very different categories of self-employment.[10] Another noteworthy result is the relatively high incomes of public sector workers without carteira, higher on average than private sector wage workers with carteira.[11] Clearly this labour status is quite different from informal wage work in the private sector. Other notable results include the low incomes of lower white-collar workers (lower than skilled production workers) and the low incomes of workers without carteira in small enterprises and in agriculture. In the Northeast a majority of workers without carteira in small firms received less than the minimum wage. However, workers without carteira in larger enterprises received relatively high wages, similar to or greater than those of skilled workers with carteira. Clearly there are two very different situations here, with the lack of carteira having an adverse impact on income mainly in small firms.

Income in the Northeast averaged almost 40% lower than in the rest of Brazil, but there were large differences in this gap between labour statuses. Agricultural incomes in the Northeast were particularly low, 70% lower than the rest of Brazil in agricultural self-employment. There was also a

Table 3.3 Mean (normal) income by labour status, R$ per month, Northeast and Rest of Brazil, third quarter 2019

Labour status	*Northeast*	*Rest of Brazil*
1 Self-employed/family work in agriculture	422	1,389
2 Wage work without carteira in agriculture	499	997
3 Private sector wage work with carteira, upper white-collar	3,054	4,092
4 Private sector wage work with carteira, lower white-collar/services/trade	1,309	1,666
5 Private sector wage work with carteira, blue-collar, skilled or semi-skilled	1,407	1,900
6 Private sector wage work with carteira, blue-collar, unskilled	1,073	1,315
7 Private sector wage work without carteira, small enterprise (up to five workers)	720	1,206
8 Private sector wage work without carteira, medium/large enterprise (over five workers)	1,381	2,289
9 Domestic service work	589	989
10 Public sector work without carteira	1,651	2,077
11 Public sector work with carteira/military/civil servant	3,467	4,361
12 Formal employer (with CNPJ registration)	5,301	6,487
13 Formal non-agricultural self-employed work (contributing to social security)	2,006	3,007
14 Informal "productive" non-agricultural self-employed work or employer	1,865	2,277
15 Informal "marginal" non-agricultural self-employed work or employer	407	477
16 Non-agricultural family work	.	.
Total	1,515	2,432
Grouped categories		
Total agricultural self-employment and wage work without carteira	451	986
Total protected wage work (private and public)	2,190	2,608
Total wage work without carteira (non-agricultural)/ domestic service	1,000	1,374
Total formal non-agricultural non-wage work	3,182	4,140
Total informal non-agricultural non-wage work	919	1,367

Source: Computed from PNADC micro-data (IBGE), 2019, 3rd quarter.

large gap for wage work without carteira, 40% lower in the Northeast and even more in agriculture. For other categories the gap was between 15% and 25%. But although incomes were lower in the Northeast, the income ranking of different labour statuses was similar across the two regions.

One important aspect of labour status is how it varies across different subregions within states, since this is connected with the production system in each. This can be seen more clearly within individual states than for the region or the country as a whole. Figure 3.2 shows how the pattern varies

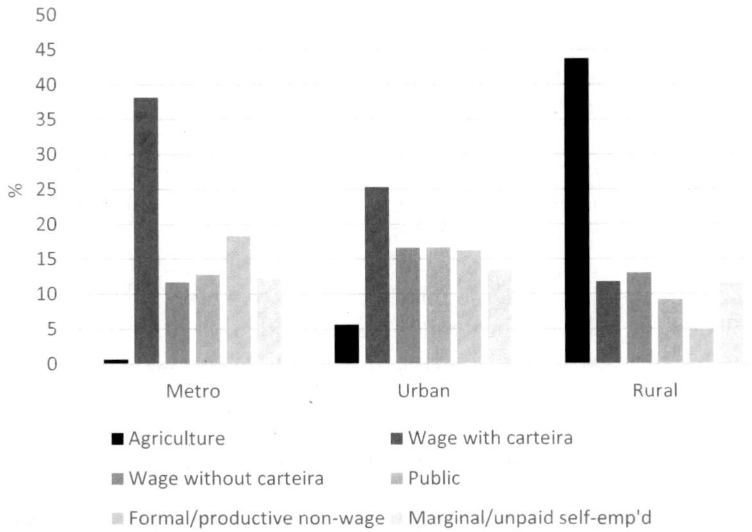

Figure 3.2 Consolidated labour status by subregion (metropolitan, other urban, rural), % distribution of workers, Pernambuco, 2019.
Source: Prepared on the basis of PNADC micro-data (IBGE), 2019, 3rd quarter.

between the metropolitan region, other urban areas and rural areas in one state of the Northeast, Pernambuco, grouping labour status in six categories.

Agricultural work, the first bar in each group, is of course concentrated in rural areas, but the other categories are more interesting. Private sector wage work with carteira, the second bar, accounts for the highest share of employment in the metropolitan region (Recife) – almost 40% – but distinctly less in other urban areas, and even less in rural areas. Wage work without carteira (the third bar) is distributed more evenly, with the largest share in other urban areas. The formal and productive self-employed status (second bar from the right) follows a pattern like that for wage work with carteira, but with a much lower share of employment, concentrated in metropolitan areas, less in other urban areas and much less in rural areas. Marginal self-employment (the right-hand bar) is distributed rather like wage work without carteira: most common in other urban areas but significant in both rural and metropolitan areas. Public employment also follows this pattern.

The metropolitan area, then, is dominated by formal wage work, and to a lesser extent by formal and productive self-employment and employers. In other urban areas the employment pattern is less formal than in metro areas and more evenly distributed between the different labour status categories. Clearly there is a great deal of diversity in economic activity in these smaller towns, and a correspondingly diverse labour market. In rural areas, apart from the dominance of agriculture, employment is distributed fairly evenly across labour statuses, but there is little formal non-agricultural employment. So informality has a very clear pattern across urban and rural settings, with the formal labour market concentrated in the largest cities.[12]

Up to this point we have been categorizing workers and jobs. In order to understand labour regimes the next step is to consider how different types of employment relationship are incorporated into production systems.

All production systems except simple self-employment use a variety of different types of labour. For example, it is common in enterprises for a core group of regular, protected workers to be complemented by a second group of temporary wage workers who are hired or fired as needs for labour vary. Or some activities may be outsourced to workers who are nominally self-employed but who are in reality in a dependent relationship. Complex production systems will involve firms of different types, each of them using a variety of types of labour.

Each production system generates its own pattern of labour status, and there are large differences across different industrial sectors, as we can see in Table 3.4, which gives the pattern in the Northeast.

Over half of agricultural work is self-employment. In reality there are two quite different agricultural sectors, one made up of small family holdings and the other consisting of large plantations and estates which employ wage labour. In the Northeast most agricultural wage work is without carteira, unlike the rest of Brazil where a majority of agricultural wage work is formal. Informality is pervasive in Northeastern agriculture.

Manufacturing industry uses a very wide range of forms of labour, reflecting the diversity of the sector. Over 40% of employment in the Northeast is wage work with carteira, dominated by skilled production workers, the only sector where this is the case, with a large minority of white-collar workers. There is also a great deal of wage work without carteira, in both small firms and large. Self-employment is less important, and it is concentrated in marginal self-employment, accounting for 20% of employment. The sector is therefore notably dualistic, with a substantial base of formal work in large firms, but a segment of low productivity self-employment as well.

Construction too is clearly segmented, but the employment structure is different from industry. Only half of employment is wage work, two thirds of it without carteira, mostly in small firms. The other half consists of self-employment, mainly informal and mostly marginal. The construction industry is very heterogeneous, with a great deal of outsourcing, subcontracting and temporary work, and this shows up clearly in the distribution of labour status. Many of the "productive" self-employed are probably workers providing special building skills – masons, electricians, plumbers etc. Some of this self-employment is disguised wage employment, but it is difficult to draw the line.

In the traditional private tertiary sectors – trade and commerce, transport, hotels and restaurants, personal services – there is a high share of self-employment, accounting for 50% or more of all employment, and except in transport most is marginal, low productivity self-employment. The highest

Labour status	*Agriculture, etc.*	*Industry*	*Construction*	*Trade*	*Transport*	*Hotels/ restaurants*	*Enterprise services*	*Public admin*	*Education and health*	*Other services*	*Total*
Self-employed/family worker in agriculture	55.5	0.0	0.0	0.0	0.0	0.0	0.0	0.0	0.0	0.0	7.2
Wage work without carteira in agriculture	33.7	0.0	0.0	0.0	0.0	0.0	0.0	0.0	0.0	0.0	4.3
Private sector wage work with carteira, upper white-collar	0.3	7.3	3.5	4.1	3.0	1.6	14.3	0.2	13.5	4.0	5.2
Private sector wage work with carteira, lower white-collar	0.7	6.9	1.9	19.3	6.9	13.2	30.7	0.4	8.0	6.5	9.8
Private sector wage work with carteira, blue-collar, skilled	4.1	25.1	10.5	4.9	12.5	1.1	5.3	0.1	0.3	2.1	5.8
Private sector wage work with carteira, blue-collar, unskilled	3.7	4.6	4.0	4.2	4.2	4.7	10.4	0.1	2.1	1.9	3.8
Private sector wage work without carteira, small enterprise	0.0	8.6	26.1	13.3	8.5	15.0	6.0	0.0	2.0	11.7	8.1
Private sector wage work without carteira, large enterprise	0.0	9.8	5.5	6.0	4.3	8.2	8.4	0.4	6.1	9.5	5.2
Public sector worker without carteira	0.0	0.5	0.1	0.1	0.7	0.0	0.5	31.8	19.6	0.7	4.7
Public sector worker with carteira/ military/civil servant	0.0	2.1	0.1	0.0	3.1	0.0	2.0	67.0	41.7	0.8	10.1
Formal employer (with CNPJ registration)	0.3	1.9	1.9	5.5	0.5	4.1	3.3	0.0	1.1	3.1	2.3
Formal non-agricultural self-employed (with social security)	0.0	4.5	3.5	7.5	9.9	5.9	5.7	0.0	1.6	10.1	4.2
Informal "productive" non-agric. self-employed or employer	1.1	7.1	19.0	11.9	25.3	12.0	9.3	0.0	1.6	16.9	8.3
Informal "marginal" non-agric. self-employed or employer	0.7	19.6	23.6	19.4	20.4	27.6	3.7	0.0	2.3	32.0	12.5
Non-agricultural family worker	0.0	2.1	0.4	4.0	0.7	6.5	0.4	0.0	0.1	0.9	1.6
Total	100.0	100.0	100.0	100.0	100.0	100.0	100.0	100.0	100.0	100.0	93.2*
% of all employment	12.9	9.3	7.3	20.5	4.6	6.3	8.0	6.1	13.2	5.0	93.2*

Source: Computed from PNADC micro-data (IBGE), 2019, 3rd quarter.
Note: * Domestic service excluded from the table (6.8% of employment), so right-hand column does not add to 100.

level of informality is found in personal services (including domestic service, not included in the table). Among wage workers in these sectors, there is again much less formal employment. Each sector has its own variation on this theme. Hotels and restaurants are notable for their high share of informal wage workers. Trade and commerce has a relatively high proportion of regular lower white-collar workers such as retail sales workers and clerks. In transport there is more formal and productive self-employment, and less informal wage labour. But the dominant pattern remains one of low levels of labour protection and high levels of informality.

The pattern is completely different in modern services – enterprise services, IT, education, health and public administration. These activities are dominated by protected wage work, in various forms; for instance, protected white-collar work accounts for 45% of employment in enterprise services. There is nevertheless a significant share of wage work without carteira, even in the public sector (mainly employed by municipal governments).

One important additional factor is the size of the enterprise. Large enterprises are dominated by formal employment relations and wage work with carteira; in small enterprises a substantial share of employment is informal, especially in the smallest firms. This is an important source of informality: in the Northeast only 20% of workers were employed in firms with more than 50 workers, mainly in manufacturing.

So there are very different labour arrangements in the different sectors of the economy. The bottom line of the table shows the share of each sector in total employment. The four sectors with the most formal employment – industry, enterprise services, public administration and education and health – account for 37% of the labour market in the Northeast. The more informal sectors – agriculture, construction, trade transport, hotels and restaurants, personal services and domestic service – account for 63%. When compared with the rest of Brazil, greater informality in the Northeast comes in part from this sectoral concentration – in the rest of Brazil 57% of employment is in these sectors where informality is greater. But this is not the main factor – the bulk of the difference in labour market structure comes from differences within each industrial sector, not from the sectoral pattern of production.

These differences between the Northeast and the rest of Brazil vary between sectors. In modern services, social services and the public sector, dominated by protected wage work, there is not much difference between the rest of Brazil and the Northeast. But in most other sectors, there is less wage work with carteira in the Northeast, and more informal and marginal self-employment. For instance, in manufacturing, where 44% of employment in the Northeast is with carteira, in the rest of Brazil the share is 64%. In other (personal) services, where over 60% of employment is self-employment in both the Northeast and the rest of Brazil, in the Northeast 32% is marginal (i.e. generating an income below the minimum wage), against only 16% in the rest of Brazil.

4 Inequality

The labour regime is highly unequal. Opportunities vary greatly across social categories, and there are large differences in wages and earnings between workers. How do these labour market patterns relate to the overall level of income inequality?

Inequality in household income in Brazil peaked at very high levels in the early 1990s, but declined over the next two decades, especially during the period 2002–2014. The IBGE *Pesquisa de Orçamentos Familiares* (POF – Household Budget Survey) gives a Gini coefficient of inequality of household income per capita of 0.591, 0.561 and 0.535 in 2002–2003, 2008–2009 and 2017–2018, respectively (Hoffman and Vaz, 2020). The PNAD gives a similar trend up to 2014 in the inequality of labour income. Other estimates using income tax data (Medeiros and Souza, 2016) suggest that the decline may have been exaggerated, because top income groups maintained their income share, but the bulk of the evidence suggests the income share of poorer groups rose and measures of overall inequality fell. However, the decline came to an end in 2014. Neri (2019), using data from the PNADC, shows that inequality measured by the Gini coefficient of labour income per capita reached a minimum in the fourth quarter of 2014, and then rose steadily until 2019. During this latter period, the bottom 50% of the income distribution lost 17% of their income, while the top 10% gained 2.5%, and the top 1% gained over 10%.[13]

During the period when overall income inequality was declining, inequality between the Northeast and the rest of the country was declining too, though it remained substantial. In the POF, in 2002 average family income per capita was 57% higher in Brazil as a whole than in the Northeast; in the 2008 survey it was 54%; in 2017 51%. Because of the dates when the POF was carried out it provides no information about what happened during the recession after 2014, but data from the PNADC suggests that reductions in regional inequality came to a halt: in 2014 the average labour income was 46% higher in Brazil as a whole than in the Northeast, and the gap remained unchanged in 2017 and 2019. Moreover, these figures do not include those who are in the labour force but have no labour income, essentially the unemployed, and unemployment rose faster in the Northeast after 2014. So overall there was a deterioration in the relative position of the Northeast during the recession, reversing the earlier trend.

What are the sources of this inequality? These numbers show the aggregate trends, but tell us little about causes. For that we have to explore the some of the underlying structural factors:

- First, there is extreme inequality in the distribution of wealth, and while accurate information on wealth is scarce, the overall shares of wages and of returns to capital (and land) in value added provide some indication of the consequences for income inequality.

- Second, other non-labour income sources, such as social transfers and pensions, have an impact on the overall distribution of household income.
- Third, as we have seen, there is deep inequality in the labour regime and the structure of labour use.
- And fourth, embedded discriminations and differentiations, notably by gender and race, also play a part.

4.1 Wage and capital shares

On the first of these factors, detailed information is lacking, but some estimates are available in the national and regional accounts of the income shares of capital and labour.[14] The national accounts show that the share of wages in national income was around 39% in the period 2000–2005, rising to 44%–45% in 2015–2017, but then falling at least up to 2019. The capital share was almost as large in 2002–2005, around 34%–35%, falling to 32% in 2015, before starting to rise again, slowly. The share of self-employed income declined from over 12% to under 9%, mostly in the period 2000–2010. There were two distinct processes at work in this period: first, a shift of income from profits to wages, which was partially reversed during the recession after 2015; and second, a longer-term replacement of self-employment by wage employment. Only the former has an unambiguous impact on inequality, but the observed shift was only of the order of 2% of national income, which is rather small. Still, this is consistent with the overall trend towards lower inequality during the period up to 2014, which also reflected a formalization of the labour market and rising minimum wages.

These national trends were replicated in the Northeast, at least after 2010, but changes were smaller than at the national level. Regional accounts, available from 2010 to 2019, show that the wage share was somewhat higher in the Northeast than in the rest of Brazil – presumably reflecting the greater labour-intensity of production in the region, rather than a more egalitarian distribution – rising from 45.5% in 2010 to 47.8% in 2015, and then declining to 46.7% in 2019, a similar trend to that for Brazil as a whole. The share of non-wage income in the Northeast showed a corresponding tendency to fall up to 2015, and then stabilize. The regional accounts do not separate out self-employed income from the capital share, but there was a sharp reduction in self-employment in the Northeast up to 2014, so the rise in the wage share in the region was probably mainly substituting for self-employed incomes.

4.2 Other non-labour income sources

With respect to the second factor, the contribution of non-labour sources of income to household income inequality, the POF 2017–2018 indicates that in Brazil as a whole 72% of income came from work; 19.5% from transfers; and 8.5% from capital, rent and other sources (IBGE, 2017–2018, Tabela 2.1.8). The last figure is much lower than the profit share in national accounts, but income of employers, which includes some capital income, is included with income from work in the POF. In addition, income from capital is generally underestimated in household surveys.

Income from capital is of course concentrated in the highest income groups, where it accounted for 15% of income (to which should be added income of employers, accounting for another 20%). It provided less than 2% of income in the lowest income groups.

Transfers accounted for almost 30% of income among lower-income groups, compared with less than 20% in higher-income groups. More than 10% of income in the bottom income group came from social programmes such as *Bolsa Família* and food programmes. So social transfers played a significant equalizing role. The same was not true of pensions, however. These accounted for the bulk of all transfers, and constituted almost as large a share of income among upper income groups as among the poorest. Public sector pensions were notably disequalizing (Hoffman and Vaz, 2020).

Those figures refer to Brazil as a whole, and there were some differences in the Northeast, where households had less income from work (68.3%), less income from capital (7%) and were much more dependent on transfers (24.6%). In the Northeast one third of income in the bottom income groups came from transfers in 2017–2018. The role of transfers has been increasing over time both in the Northeast and in Brazil as a whole, but especially in the former where their share in income in the lowest income groups had risen by 3–5 percentage points since the previous POF in 2008.

Although inequality of labour income within the Northeast was greater than in Brazil as a whole (see below), the opposite was true of inequality of household income per capita (Hoffman and Vaz, 2020). This suggests that higher social transfers to low-income households in the Northeast helped to offset the greater inequality of labour income.

4.3 The role of labour status

As we saw above, there are large differences in income between labour statuses. The inequality of labour income is lower in Brazil as a whole (including the Northeast) than within the Northeast, on both Gini and Theil measures (Table 3.5). This is contrary to expectations, because overall inequality in Brazil includes inequality between regions as well as within them. We can infer that there is significantly greater inequality in the Northeast region than elsewhere in the country.

To assess the implications for overall inequality, we decomposed a measure of inequality of labour income by labour status. The Theil index is convenient for this purpose because it breaks down easily into additive components. Results are given in Table 3.5.

The decomposition of the 2019 Theil index shows that a large share of inequality is explained by differences between labour status categories (last column of the table). The effect is stronger in the Northeast, where 42.6% of

Table 3.5 Indicators of inequality of labour income and their decomposition, Northeast and Brazil, 2019

	Gini	*Theil*	*Theil "within"**	*Theil "between"**	*Within (%)*	*Between (%)*
Northeast	0.524	0.593	0.341	0.253	57.4	42.6
Brazil	0.500	0.532	0.349	0.182	65.7	34.3

Source: Prepared on the basis of PNADC micro-data (IBGE), 2019, 3rd quarter.
Note: * Decomposition of the Theil index into two components: within the labour status groups, and between them. The Brazilian figure relates to the whole of Brazil, including the Northeast.

the Theil index is explained by income differences between labour statuses (last column), than in Brazil as a whole, where the figure is 34.3%. It is not surprising that the contribution of labour status to inequality is lower at the national level than within the Northeast, since as noted above the national figure also reflects interregional differences in income. What is more surprising is the high level of explanation within the Northeast. Incomes can vary for many reasons apart from labour status – differences in effort among individuals, health and family situations, local variations within the region, chance and random factors. In addition, these estimates are based on survey data, with a large margin of error. Even so, labour status accounts for almost half of the measure of inequality.

Moreover, this is an underestimate of the contribution of the labour market situation to inequality, because these figures only include those persons in the labour force reporting an income. Since there are many people in the labour force without income, notably the unemployed, the share of income inequality explained by the labour market situation is even higher. We can conclude that these differences in labour status, and the labour regime of which they are a part, play a critical role in overall inequality.

How should we interpret this? In the conventional economics literature, part of the inequality of labour income would be attributed to productivity differences, in turn resulting from differences in education levels and professional experience. But in the heterogeneous and segmented labour market that we observe in Brazil, education acts as a filter rather than a force determining productivity – a filter which permits incomes to remain high in upper white-collar jobs and the public sector, for instance. Inequality in access to education, which in turn has economic and social roots, maps directly onto inequality in access to employment. Many labour market segments are protected by barriers to entry, among which educational qualifications play an important role.

The diversity of incomes in self-employment shows that this part of the labour regime is highly segmented too. The high income of employers sets them apart, but we also identified two very different groups of (non-agricultural) self-employed – one group with higher incomes, some of them formal (registered or contributing to social security); and a large second group of marginal self-employed with low productivity and low incomes, unable to access wage labour markets and living at survival levels. In the Northeast, 12% of workers fall in this second category. There is also a substantial group of self-employed agricultural workers, also with very low incomes in the Northeast, even if many of them are able to produce for their own subsistence.

So there are diverse segments in the labour market with different conditions of access, productivity and income, and this maintains persistent income differentials between groups of workers. During the period up to 2014, some of these segmentations were becoming weaker. Access to formal wage work became easier, and the share of self-employment fell. There was clearly a widening of opportunities. Then from 2014 to 2019, when inequality rose in the Northeast and in Brazil as a whole, the share of inequality explained by labour status differences also increased, especially in the Northeast, so gaps between workers widened again. We examine these trends further below.

4.4 Social differentiation and discrimination

The fourth source of inequality, social differentiation and discrimination, is pervasive. Much analysis of this issue addresses labour market differentiation by gender and race. In 2014, the income of black workers averaged 40%–45% less than whites, and that of women 25%–30% less than men, giving rise to a persistent income hierarchy – white men at the top, followed by white women, followed by black men and then by black women. We consider this aspect of inequality in more detail in the next section.

5 Gender and race/colour

5.1 Theoretical approach

Inequalities in the production system and the labour regime interact with other sources of inequality. People do not all have the same employment opportunities. Many factors – gender, race/colour, ethnicity, migrant status, age, physical or mental disability, sexual orientation, social class, religion, etc. – influence access to employment and the nature of that employment. The persistence of these inequalities indicates that their reproduction is the result of powerful processes and that we need to pay attention to their effects and their dynamics.

Various economic theories try to explain unequal inclusion in the labour market, including theories of human capital, segmentation, and discrimination. But attempts to understand occupational inequalities often fail to consider the many barriers that are erected upstream, notably in educational qualifications or social origin. Human capital theory, for instance, addresses differences in returns to work in relation to skills and qualifications, but those inequalities are rooted in the social and economic conditions that lead to unequal access to education and training. Inequality tends to result from the accumulation and interaction of different factors, and it is not possible to understand them in isolation. In particular, they reflect not only economic forces but also relations among multiple identities, involving family, community, enterprise and State. Their analysis requires an approach that goes beyond the simple recognition of multiple sources of discrimination.

Among these factors, gender and race play a particularly important role in conditioning unequal labour market access in Brazil. The key concepts are intersectionality and consubstantiality, the former emerging from the Anglo-Saxon academic literature, the latter from French feminism. The term intersectionality was coined by Crenshaw (1989, 2002) in order to study the position of black women in American society. She defined intersectionality as "the way of capturing the consequences of the interaction between two or more forms of subordination: sexism, racism, patriarchy." Intersectionality focuses on the intersection between these categories of oppression and the analysis of how they are experienced in everyday life (Guimarães, 2016, p.44). The notion of consubstantiality was developed by Kergoat (1982) as a way to conceptualize the constitutive dynamics of social relations of power and domination. This approach contextualizes the social relations between women and men in the world of work. For Kergoat "the actors' positions are not fixed; they are in perpetual evolution and renegotiation" (Kergoat, 2010, p.98).

The concepts of intersectionality and consubstantiality converge on a consistent paradigm. Gender and race/colour intertwine with social class in the world of work and produce economic and social hierarchies (Hirata, 2014; Abreu et al., 2016). Discriminatory processes operate to restrict the opportunities of identifiable groups and are constantly renewed. Each social configuration produces its own forms of inequalities.

In this section we consider the influence of gender and race/colour. Four distinct segments of the workforce are considered: white men, black/brown men, white women and black/brown women. These groups are not homogenous as various personal attributes determine a worker's participation in the labour market apart from sex and race: education, age, family situation, geographic location, sector of activity, socioeconomic status, etc. In addition, certain public policies influence participation, such as those aimed at reconciling work and family life (e.g. day care centres) or those aimed at reducing poverty.

Race is of course a social construct,[15] and one which has a very specific character in Brazil because of the history of colonial conquest, slavery and migration into the country. The prevailing statistical convention is for race to be identified with skin colour, with the exception of native peoples. The *Instituto Brasileiro de Geografia e Estatística* (IBGE) classifies the Brazilian population in five categories: *branco* (white), *pardo* (brown), *preto* (black), *amarelo* (yellow), and indigenous. The category is obtained through self-identification in surveys and censuses (Osorio, 2003; Petruccelli and Saboia, 2013). The breakdown of the labour force in these terms, in the Northeast and the rest of Brazil, is given in Table 3.6.

Table 3.6 Distribution of the labour force by sex and race, Northeast and Brazil, 2019 (%)

Race/colour	*Northeast*		*Rest of Brazil*	
	Men	*Women*	*Men*	*Women*
White	12.6	11.1	26.6	23.1
Black	7.5	5.6	5.0	4.1
Yellow	0.2	0.2	0.4	0.4
Brown	35.6	26.8	22.4	17.7
Indígenous	0.2	0.2	0.2	0.1
Total	56.1	43.9	54.6	45.4

Source: IBGE, PNADC, 2019, 3rd quarter.

This system of race/colour classification has generated much criticism and debate. Some critics have pointed out that the official categories do not map well onto the categories Brazilians use to identify themselves in daily life, others that the brown category is ambiguous and may soften the appearance of racial divide. The now standard convention in academic research and affirmative action policies is to collapse brown and black groups into one category for the analysis of racial disparities in Brazil. This derives from two decades of sociological research after Carlos Hasenbalg (1985) and Nelson do Valle Silva (1985) documented strikingly similar socioeconomic profiles of black and brown populations compared to whites and argued that in terms of statistical analyses of race/colour inequality, a white vs. non-white classification scheme was most appropriate (Loveman et al., 2012; Silva, 2016). We follow this practice, and refer to "black" and "white" populations (i.e. we use "black" as a shorthand for "black" and "brown", bearing in mind that the boundaries between groups are blurred and ambiguous). We exclude from the analysis the "yellow" and indigenous populations, which constitute less than 1% of the labour force (see Table 3.6). We use the term "race" below; in Brazil it is frequent to refer to "*cor*" (colour) rather than race.

5.2 *The pattern of participation*

The point of departure is the overall make-up of the labour market. Table 3.6 shows that the distribution of the workforce by sex is similar in both the Northeast and the rest of Brazil: women constitute 44%–45% of the workforce and men 55%–56%, with slightly less women in the Northeast. But the incidence of race varies by region: the share of black workers is greater in the Northeast (i.e. adding the "black" and "brown" categories in Table 3.6), and the share of white workers correspondingly less.

The overall labour force participation rates are given in Figure 3.3. Participation rates of both sexes are lower in the Northeast than in the rest of the country, by 10–12 percentage points. In both regions the participation

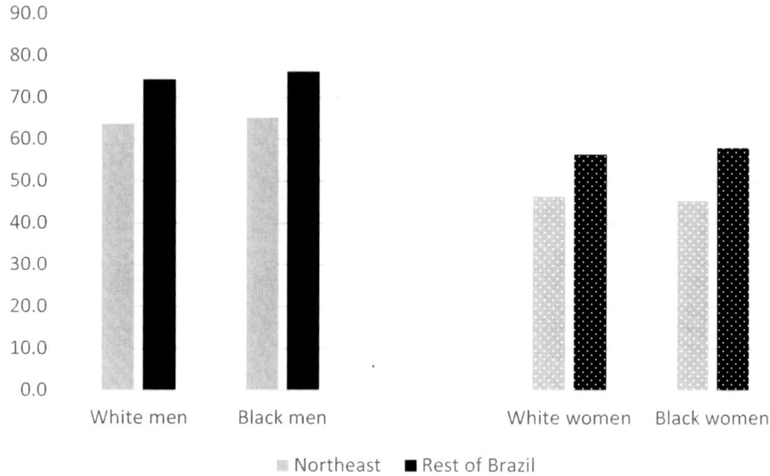

Figure 3.3 Labour force participation rate by sex and race, 14+ years of age, Northeast and Rest of Brazil, 2019 (%).
Source: IBGE, PNADC, 2019, 3rd quarter.

of women is lower than that of men, by 17–20 percentage points. The pattern by race is less consistent. Black men have a slightly higher labour force participation rate than white men in both the Northeast and the rest of Brazil, but the reverse is true among women, since white women have a higher participation rate than black women in both regions. But the differences are small, much smaller than the difference between genders.

Previous studies show that in recent decades the participation of women has tended to increase and that of men to decrease, and that the female labour force participation rate increases with years of schooling, as well as with increases in income (Scorzafave and Menezes-Filho, 2001; Bruschini and Lombardi, 2003; Barbosa, 2014). But the relationships are not simple. Women, both white and black, have higher education levels than men in both the Northeast and Brazil as a whole, but lower labour force participation. White workers, both men and women, have higher levels of education than black workers, but labour force participation is not greatly different. The role of education lies more in differentiating opportunities within the labour market.

5.3 Differences in labour status

Men and women tend to work in different sectors and occupations. In industry, construction, agriculture and transport the workforce is dominated by men, while women are over-represented in education, health and social services, and in domestic service. There are also differences in the sectoral distribution of white and black workers. For instance, black workers are more likely to be in agriculture and domestic service, and less in trade and in modern services, though the gaps are smaller than by gender. We look at this differentiation through the prism of labour status. The pattern by sex and race is given in Table 3.7, which disaggregates the overall structure reported in Table 3.2.

We can see how the interaction between gender and race creates patterns which vary from one labour status to another.

- In agriculture (categories 1 and 2) the dominance of male workers is clear, stronger for white than for black workers.
- Women are more likely than men to occupy white-collar jobs (categories 3 and 4), especially lower-level white-collar jobs; and white workers are

Table 3.7 Distribution of labour status by race and sex, Northeast, 2019 (%)

Labour Status	*Men*		*Women*		*Total*
	White	*Black*	*White*	*Black*	
1 Self-employed/family worker in agriculture	9.0	9.5	2.8	4.8	7.2
2 Wage worker without carteira in agriculture	4.3	6.8	0.5	0.7	4.3
3 Private sector wage worker with carteira, upper white-collar	6.9	4.1	8.2	5.1	5.2
4 Private sector wage worker with carteira, lower white-collar/services/trade	8.4	8.7	13.3	11.0	9.8
5 Private sector wage worker with carteira, blue-collar, skilled or semi-skilled	7.2	9.7	1.5	1.7	5.8
6 Private sector wage worker with carteira, blue-collar, unskilled	3.5	4.9	2.2	3.0	3.8
7 Private sector wage worker without carteira, small enterprise (up to five workers)	9.2	10.3	5.5	5.5	8.1
8 Private sector wage worker without carteira, medium/large enterprise (over five workers)	6.5	6.3	5.0	5.2	5.2
9 Domestic service worker	0.7	0.9	10.4	16.4	6.8
10 Public sector worker without carteira	3.3	3.1	7.1	6.7	4.7
11 Public sector worker with carteira/military/civil servant	9.9	7.2	15.8	12.4	10.1
12 Formal employer (with CNPJ registration)	3.8	1.5	2.6	0.9	2.3
13 Formal non-agricultural self-employed worker (contributing to social security)	5.0	4.2	4.8	3.8	4.2
14 Informal "productive" non-agricultural self-employed worker or employer	11.7	10.4	6.4	5.1	8.3
15 Informal "marginal" non-agricultural self-employed worker or employer	9.5	11.7	11.2	15.3	12.5
16 Non-agricultural family worker	1.1	1.0	2.7	2.4	1.6
Total	100	100	100	100	100

Source: Computed from PNADC micro-data (IBGE), 2019, 3rd quarter.

more likely to occupy these jobs than black workers, especially upper-level jobs. The combined gender/race hierarchy is particularly clear.

- Men are more likely than women to occupy other wage jobs with carteira (categories 5 and 6), especially skilled jobs. The share of black workers in these jobs is higher too.
- There are also relatively more men in wage jobs without carteira (categories 7 and 8), but the gap between men and women is less than for jobs with carteira, and there is little difference by race.
- Domestic service workers (category 9) show the sharpest pattern of all, concentrated among women, and especially black women.
- Public sector workers (categories 10 and 11) are highly feminized, but with a visible bias against black workers, both men and women, especially in regular jobs.
- Women are underrepresented among formal employers (category 12), and the same is even more true of black workers.
- Among self-employed workers, white men are disproportionately represented among the formal (13) and productive (14) categories, and black women underrepresented; whereas for the informal, marginal category (15) the situation is the reverse. The more marginal the self-employment (lower income), the more likely we are to find black and female workers. Unpaid family workers too (16) are disproportionately female.

So this table gives a fine-grained picture of differentiation in the Northeastern labour market. Women are more likely to be found in the precarious and low-income categories of domestic service and marginal self-employment, and this is especially true of black women; but women are also disproportionately found in white-collar and public sector jobs, and that is especially true for white women. Black workers show less differentiation compared with white than do women compared with men; but there is a tendency for them to be underrepresented in upper class jobs – white-collar occupations, employers, regular civil servants – and over-represented in blue-collar wage jobs, but also among the marginal self-employed. So differential access to the hierarchy of labour statuses is a significant mechanism contributing to labour market inequality.

Is this picture for the Northeast different from that for Brazil as a whole? There are relatively more black workers in the Northeast (Table 3.6), which makes a difference in the absolute numbers; and as we have seen there is more wage work with carteira, and less informal work, in the rest of Brazil (Table 3.2). After we allow for those differences, gender and racial patterns are broadly comparable between the Northeast and the rest of Brazil. The labour status categories where women, or black workers, are underrepresented in the Northeast are also those where they are underrepresented in the rest of the country. In other words, while black workers, in general, and black women, in particular, have more limited labour market options, there is no sign that this is particularly acute in the Northeast. The pattern of inequality and discrimination is present across the country.

5.4 *Income*

One further way of looking at this issue is in terms of income. In the Northeast in 2019, white men had an average monthly income of R$1,798; white women R$1,371; black men R$1,077; and black women R$920. Table 3.8 shows the ratio (percentage) of the average income of groups of workers compared with each other. The first and second rows give the income ratio, between gender and race groups, for Brazil and the Northeast. We can see that although the overall pattern of inequality is similar, the gender and racial gaps are somewhat less (the ratio is higher) in the Northeast than in the country as a whole.

This overall ratio can be decomposed into two factors: differences in income within each labour status group, and the distribution of workers across labour status groups. We might conceive of the first as wage discrimination, and the second as employment discrimination. The third row gives the average, for the Northeast, of the income ratio for each labour status group (wage discrimination). The difference between the second and third rows gives an approximate estimate of the contribution to income differences of the distribution of workers across different labour market categories (employment discrimination), that we saw in Table 3.7. We can see that for black men compared with white men, there is an average 20% wage gap within each category (Northeast-2), but 40% overall (Northeast-1). So an additional 20% comes from employment discrimination. For white women compared with white men, again there is a little over 20% difference within each labour status group (Northeast-2), but nothing is added from disparities in opportunities. The disadvantage of white women, it seems, comes essentially from lower incomes within each job. For black women the situation is different. The last column, black women in relation to white women, like for black men compared with white men, shows a substantial contribution from both wage and employment discrimination. The third column, black women in relation to white men, combines these different elements, and shows the largest contribution coming from wage discrimination, but a significant contribution also coming from employment discrimination.

Table 3.8 Relative average income of different groups of workers by sex and race, Northeast and Brazil, 2019

	Black men as % of white men	*White women as % of white men*	*Black women as % of white men*	*Black women as % of white women*
Brazil	54.6	74.7	43.5	58.2
Northeast-1	59.8	76.3	51.2	67.1
Northeast-2	80.2	77.5	63.4	81.6

Source: Computed from PNADC micro-data (IBGE), 2019, 3rd quarter.
Notes: Northeast-1 refers to the overall income ratio. Northeast-2 refers to the average of income ratios in each labour status category.

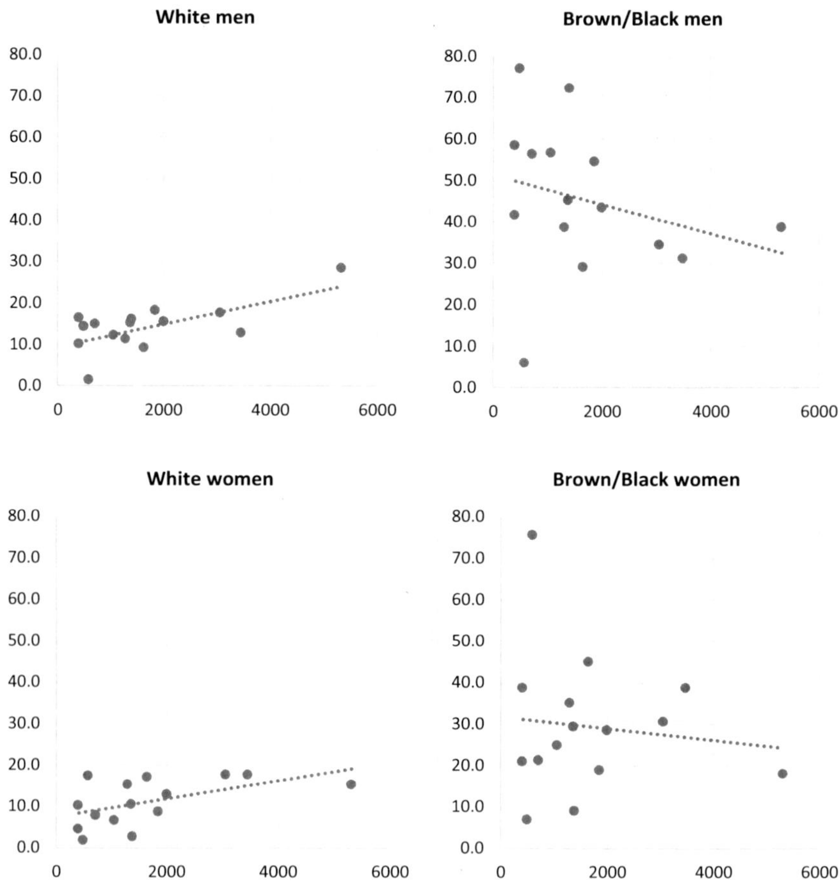

Figure 3.4 Percentage of workers in each labour status by level of earnings for each gender/race category, Northeast, 2019.

Source: Prepared on the basis of PNADC micro-data (IBGE), 2019, 3rd quarter.

Finally, Figure 3.4 provides another way of examining these difference. It consists of four sub-graphs, each of which refers to one category of workers: white men, black men, white women and black women. The vertical axis of each sub-graph is the percentage of workers who belong to this race/sex category, for each of the 16 categories of labour status, and these labour status categories are classified by average income along the horizontal axis. It can be seen in the top left-hand graph that there is a positive relationship between the percentage of employed white men and the income of the labour status in question. The top right-hand graph refers to the relationship for black male workers, showing a tendency for the proportion of black men to be highest in the low-income labour statuses. The only exception, in the lower left corner, concerns domestic service, where there are few male workers.

The two lower graphs show the same relationship for female workers. The pattern is similar to that of men, particularly for white workers.

These graphs clearly show the net impact on income of gender and racial differences in employment opportunities. The higher the income of a particular labour status, the higher the proportion of white workers, both male and female; while the reverse is true for black workers.

Overall we see that occupational segmentation by gender and race has a strong influence on earnings and other indicators of job quality. The disparity in employment opportunities between black and white workers is greater than the gender gap, but the gender gap in incomes is at least as important as the racial gap. The data presented in this section show that neither the region nor the workforce is homogeneous and that it is necessary to look at different social categories to understand the processes. The processes of production and reproduction of racial and gender inequalities are distinct, but they overlap, generating an interactive and cumulative effect. Integrating the joint influence of gender and race in the analysis of employment helps to better understand the functioning of the labour market as a whole.

6 Change and crisis in the labour market

Data on labour status discussed so far relate to the year 2019. But as we saw in Chapter 2, the Brazilian economy has gone through several different phases in recent decades. During the period from the turn of the century up to 2014, there were clear improvements in the Northeast labour market, with falling unemployment and increased formalization, and the gaps between the Northeast and the rest of Brazil were reduced. But the political, social and economic crisis after 2014 dramatically changed the trajectory of the Brazilian labour market, and many of these gains were lost. The economic recession led to layoffs and to unemployment, and also caused many discouraged workers to abandon the labour market. In this section we concentrate on how the labour regime and the labour market outcomes were affected by this period of crisis.

The impact of the crisis on unemployment and underemployment, and its regional pattern, were discussed in Chapter 2. As we saw, unemployment in the Northeast was higher than in the rest of Brazil, but followed a broadly similar trend. Figure 3.5 shows that this trend also has a distinct gender and racial profile. Women had a higher unemployment rate than men, for both white and black workers, and black workers had a higher unemployment rate than whites. All groups suffered a sharp increase in unemployment from 2014 to 2017, by 4–7 percentage points, followed by a stabilization or

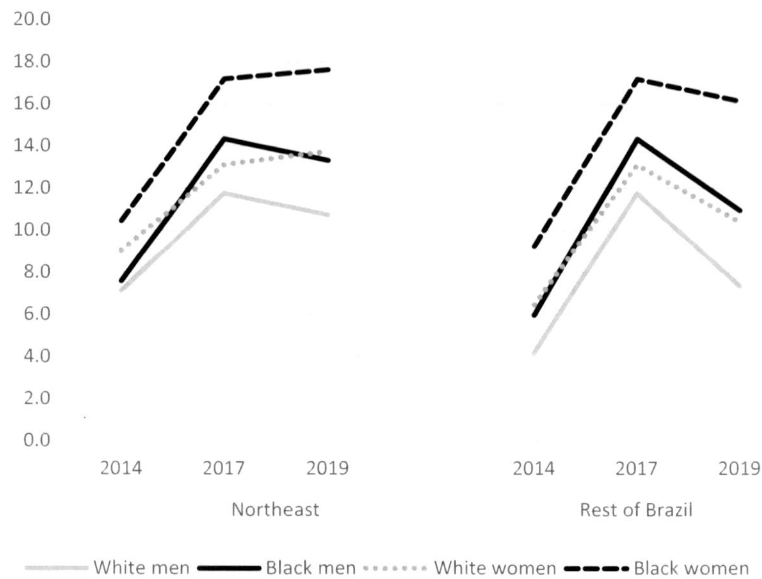

Figure 3.5 Unemployment rate by sex and race, Northeast and Rest of Brazil, 2014, 2017 and 2019 (%).

Source: IBGE, PNADC, third quarters of 2014, 2017, 2019.

a fall. After 2017 the gaps between groups tended to widen. The unemployment rate of men recovered faster than that of women, but more slowly in the Northeast than in the rest of Brazil; indeed, in the Northeast the unemployment rate of both white and black women continued to increase between 2017 and 2019.

The impact of the crisis was not confined to the overall level of employment and unemployment. It also affected the nature and quality of employment, and the pattern of employment in particular production arrangements.

Figure 3.6 shows changes in labour status between 2014 and 2019 for the Northeast and the rest of Brazil, consolidated into five categories: agricultural work, private sector wage work with carteira, wage work without carteira, public sector employment and non-wage work. Agriculture continued to decline, especially in the Northeast, with a further loss of about a quarter of the share in employment in 2014. So the crisis did not generate any significant return to agricultural work, on the contrary.

Wage employment with carteira also fell, with a loss of 3–5 percentage points in the employment share. This was only partially compensated by a shift to employment without carteira, which rose by only 1 or 2 percentage points. There was a small gain in public sector employment in the Northeast (not in the rest of Brazil) but most of the adjustment came through an increase in (non-agricultural) self-employment, which rose by 4–7 percentage points.

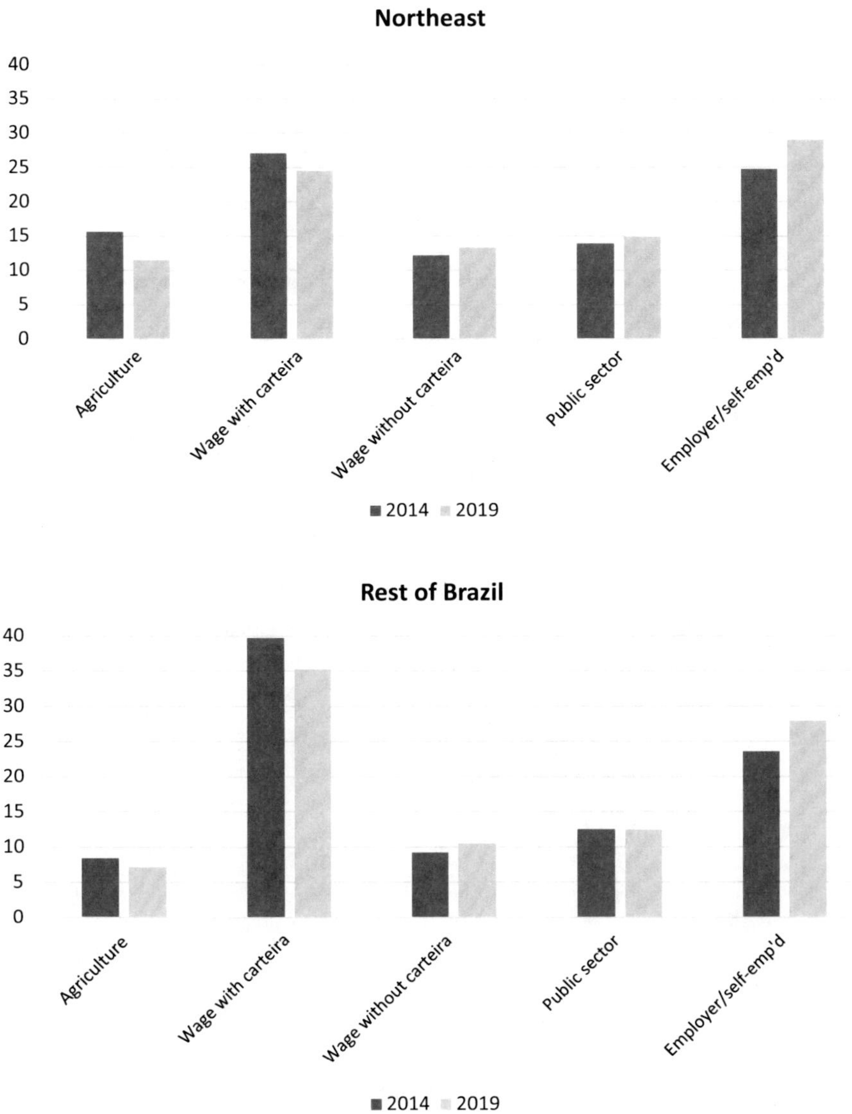

Figure 3.6 Distribution of workers in consolidated labour status categories, Northeast and Rest of Brazil, 2014 and 2019 (%).

Source: Prepared on the basis of PNADC micro-data (IBGE), 2014, 2019, 3rd quarters.

If we look in more detail at labour status, using the more disaggregated categories discussed above, several further patterns emerge, as Figure 3.7 shows. 2017 is included in the figure as well as 2014 and 2019 because there were some differences between the earlier and later parts of the recession.

First, there was a very steep decline in self-employment in agriculture in the Northeast, and a rise in wage work without carteira, suggesting a loss of

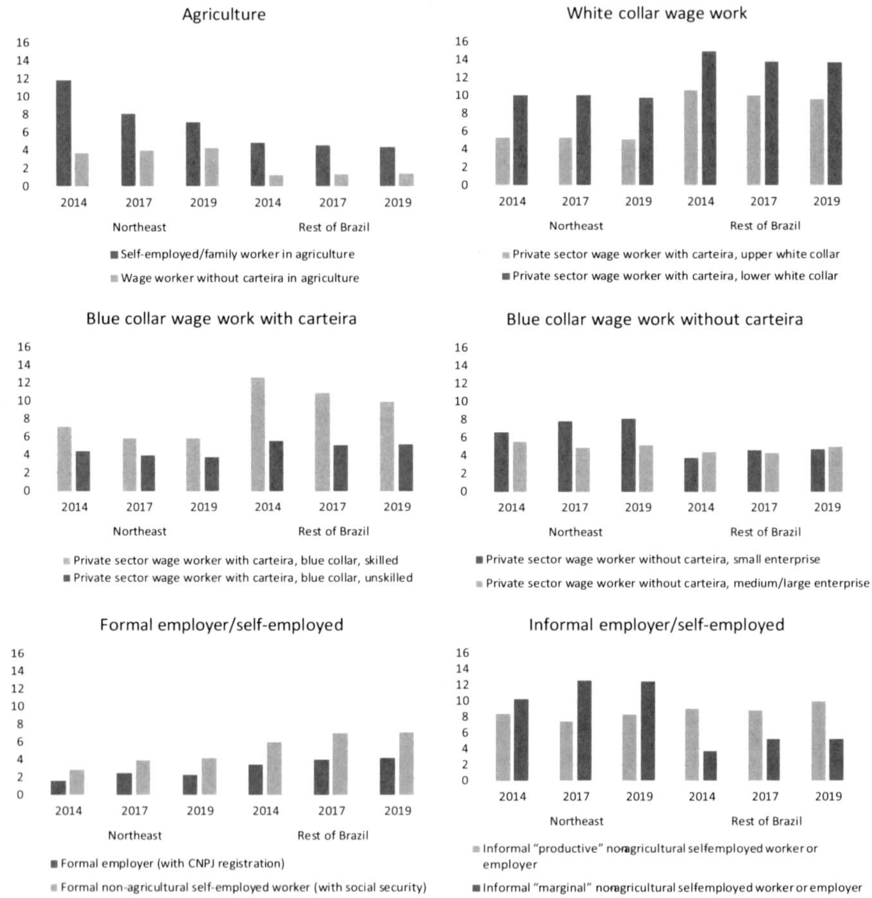

Figure 3.7 Trends in selected categories of labour status, Northeast and Rest of Brazil, 2014, 2017 and 2019 (% of all workers).

Source: Prepared on the basis of PNADC micro-data (IBGE), 2014, 2017, 2019, 3rd quarters.

livelihood among small farmers, which may also have contributed to labour force dropout. So there is no sign here of a return to subsistence farming as a survival strategy during the recession. This pattern was not nearly as important in other parts of Brazil, but in any case agriculture provides a much higher share of employment in the Northeast.

Among workers with carteira, all categories showed a decline during the period, much larger for blue-collar workers, especially skilled, than for white-collar workers. The share of public sector workers, shown in Figure 3.6, increased slightly in the Northeast and declined slightly elsewhere in Brazil, in both cases with a tendency for the share of workers without carteira to increase.

Private sector wage workers without carteira showed different trends in small and large enterprises, and between regions. The numbers in small enterprises rose, while the numbers in large enterprises fell at first before starting to rise again after 2017. This trend was stronger in the Northeast than elsewhere. There is a plausible explanation for this pattern in larger firms: when the recession hit, larger firms first fired workers without carteira, because that was the easiest adjustment. But as the recession continued and the employment situation stabilized, there was a more structural shift towards hiring workers without carteira rather than with carteira.

The four categories of self-employment (including employers) generally increased their share of employment. Among formal categories (employers and formal self-employed) there was a jump between 2014 and 2017, but then the situation tended to stabilize, in both the Northeast and the rest of Brazil. It seems that in the first phase of the recession, some of those who lost wage jobs were able to move into formal self-employment or to create independent enterprises. There was a similar increase in marginal self-employment, suggesting that this also provided a refuge for those losing wage jobs, but at a very low level of income. In contrast, in the higher-income ("productive") informal activities, there was first a fall in the share of employment, and then some recovery after 2017. These patterns of change were similar in the Northeast and the rest of Brazil, but the share of marginal self-employment in the Northeast was more than double that in the rest of Brazil.

So alongside the increase in unemployment and labour force dropout discussed above, there was significant absorption of workers in self-employment, both formal and informal, which played the role of a shock absorber between 2014 and 2017, absorbing around 5% of employment in different categories, somewhat more in the Northeast, and with a higher share of marginal self-employment, though the broad pattern was similar in the rest of Brazil. But after 2017 growth in self-employment slowed, suggesting that the limits of absorption had been reached.

The deterioration in the quality of employment affected all segments of the labour force. To compensate for the loss of waged jobs, male white workers were more able to move into formal self-employment, while black and female workers were more likely to resort to informal jobs. On the whole men were more affected than women in the early part of the crisis, with a larger shift into marginal self-employment, but recovered faster after 2017.

These patterns varied between different industrial sectors, reflecting the different production systems and labour regimes. The five-year time period we are discussing here is too short for there to be large changes in sectoral production structure, even during the recession, but some changes did occur. We have already noted the case of agriculture, where the long-term decline continued.[16] There were also declines in the share of industry and construction, while the share of many trade and service activities increased, with a particularly large increase for education and health services, though public administration did not share in the increase and the share of business services fell. The net impact on the labour market was ambiguous. There is more formal wage employment in manufacturing and business services, so their decline implied a loss of formal jobs, but this was partly offset by the increase in the social sector. On the other hand, the fall in the shares of agriculture and of construction, both with a great deal of informal employment, would imply a loss of informal jobs. Increases in the share of trade, personal services and transport might have the opposite effect. But overall, the shifts in the sectoral pattern of production were fairly small. As in the period before 2014, the more important labour market changes were happening within sectors.

One of the largest changes was in the construction sector, which was hit particularly hard by the recession. In this sector, wage work was dominated by two categories, skilled workers with carteira, and workers without carteira in small enterprises. The former group accounted for 16%–18% of construction workers in 2014 without much difference between Brazil and the Northeast, while the latter group was more important in the Northeast, where a quarter of workers were in this category, against 10% in the rest of Brazil.

Between 2014 and 2019 the share of workers with carteira declined quite sharply (Figure 3.8), both skilled and unskilled. In the Northeast the main adjustment occurred through a substitution of informal workers (without carteira) for formal workers (upper figure), without much change in the total share of wage work. The total share of self-employment did not change much, but there was a clear shift towards marginal, low-income self-employment. In the rest of Brazil, while wage work with carteira declined, there was less increase in wage work without carteira, and the main adjustment occurred through an increase in self-employment (lower figure), especially marginal self-employment. So there were two different processes at work during the recession, one involving the informalization of wage labour relations, the other a shift to low-income self-employment. Taking all forms of self-employment together, they accounted for almost half of employment in construction in the Northeast in 2019, and almost 60% in the rest of Brazil.

In other sectors the changes were diverse, but with a general tendency towards informalization. In manufacturing industry there was a downward trend in the proportion of formal wage workers, especially lower white-collar workers and unskilled workers. This was mostly compensated by a rise in self-employment, both formal and informal. In the Northeast the bulk of self-employed workers were in marginal self-employment, and the numbers increased during the recession.

Trade and commerce, which accounted for almost 20% of total employment, also showed some informalization. As in the case of construction, this probably reflects a process of subcontracting and outsourcing, as qualified wage workers were converted into self-employed. A similar process occurred

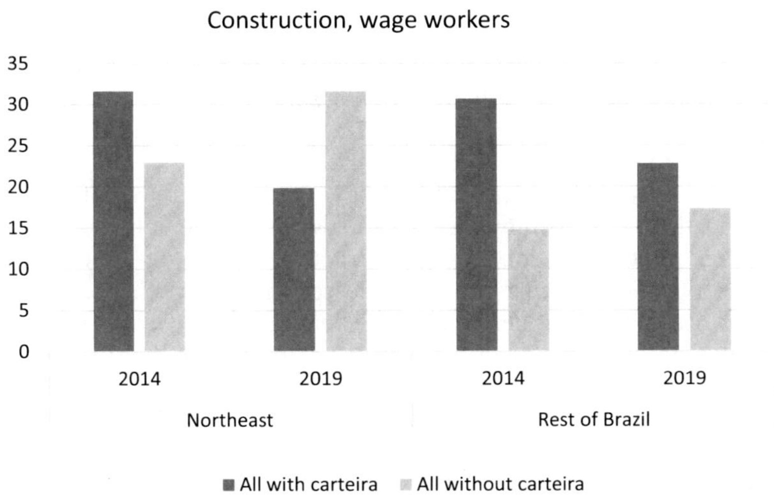

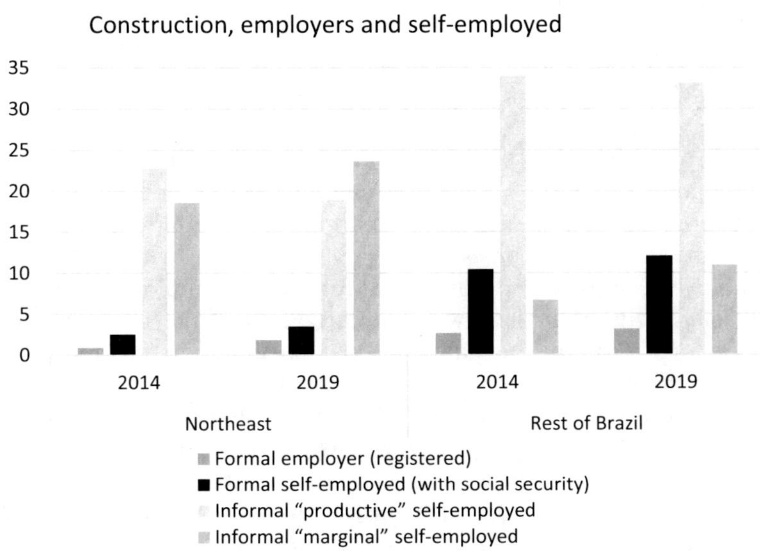

Figure 3.8 Changes in the labour status pattern in construction, Northeast and Rest of Brazil, 2014 and 2019 (% of workers).

Source: Prepared on the basis of PNADC micro-data (IBGE), 2019, 3rd quarter.

in hotels, restaurants and other personal services, with the difference that in these sectors there was a growth in marginal self-employment as well.

The transport sector showed a clear process of what might be called deproletarianization, for there was a decline in wage work between 2014 and 2019, both with and without carteira, and a substantial shift to self-employment. Clearly there was a change in the organization of the transport sectors towards small scale operations, although the degree to which these are truly autonomous is not clear. For instance, taxis may be run by self-employed people, but they may also form part of a system such as Uber, where their employment relation has some of the characteristics of wage labour. This is the subject of one of the case studies discussed in the next chapter.

Among other sectors, there was some tendency for regular public sector employment to fall and work without carteira to rise, but changes were small. In modern services, there was a clear shift away from formal wage work to self-employment of different types, but not to wage work without carteira.

Summing up, we can see striking differences in the pattern of adjustment among the sectors. There was a widespread tendency for the share of wage work with carteira to fall, but it was not uniform – stronger for blue-collar workers in some sectors, stronger for white-collar workers in others, generally stronger for skilled than unskilled. In some sectors – construction, trade and hotels and restaurants – work with carteira was partly substituted by wage work without carteira in small firms; but that was not the case in manufacturing, transport or other services, where the adjustment took place mainly through increases in self-employment, both formal and informal. But on balance there was a fall in the share of wage work in total employment. There was a rise in informal, marginal self-employment across the board, and a smaller but consistent rise in the share of formal self-employed and employers. However, productive informal self-employment tended to decline, suggesting that there was a polarization of the self-employed between the formal, on the one hand, and the marginal, on the other.

What do these labour status changes imply for changes in income for the different groups in the labour market? Table 3.9 shows average real income changes by labour status in the Northeast. Overall, real incomes hardly changed, but there were considerable differences between labour status categories. The main losers were in agriculture and in the different forms of self-employment, with real income declines of the order of 10% – more among the formal self-employed. The factors responsible for the decline in income are different in agriculture and in non-agricultural self-employment, since the share of employment fell in the former and rose in the latter. Falling incomes in non-agricultural self-employment no doubt reflect the crowding of workers into this category in the face of declining opportunities elsewhere.

Among wage workers, those working in the public sector did best, with significant income gains, but incomes fell for most private sector wage workers with carteira, except the upper white-collar groups. The picture for

Table 3.9 Real income changes* by labour status, Northeast, 2014–2019 (%)

1 Self-employed/family worker in agriculture	−10.7
2 Wage worker without carteira in agriculture	−9.4
3 Private sector wage worker with carteira, upper white-collar	4.5
4 Private sector wage worker with carteira, lower white-collar/services/trade	−1.4
5 Private sector wage worker with carteira, blue-collar, skilled or semi-skilled	−5.2
6 Private sector wage worker with carteira, blue-collar, unskilled	−1.9
7 Private sector wage worker without carteira, small enterprise (up to five workers)	−8.7
8 Private sector wage worker without carteira, medium/large enterprise (over five workers)	18.5
9 Domestic service worker	−2.9
10 Public sector worker without carteira	11.5
11 Public sector worker with carteira/military/civil servant	7.7
12 Formal employer (with CNPJ registration)	−11.7
13 Formal non-agricultural self-employed worker (contributing to social security)	−25.3
14 Informal "productive" non-agricultural self-employed worker or employer	−9.3
15 Informal "marginal" non-agricultural self-employed worker or employer	−8.3
Total	−0.1

Source: Computed from PNADC micro-data (IBGE), 2014, 2019, 3rd quarters.
Note: * Money values deflated by the IBGE consumer price index.

workers without carteira was mixed, with those in small firms doing badly, in large firms relatively well – as noted above, the latter group has relatively high incomes, but this was a category where employment fell.

A breakdown by race and gender gives a mixed picture. White men and black women did badly, with falling real incomes, while the incomes of white women and black men rose, but these changes offset each other for each gender and racial group. The main effect on income inequality did not come from the relative gains of different groups, but rather from the relationship of income with labour status, within the sex-race groups. In particular, inequality rose among white men (the change in income for each labour status category was positively related with income in 2014) but fell within all other groups, especially for women.

7 Conclusion: the overall picture

This chapter examines the labour regime in the Northeast from several angles: the pattern of regulation, how it has evolved over time, the situation of different groups of workers, the patterns of inequality, the consequences of economic change and the contrast between the Northeast and the rest of Brazil. First, we mapped out the formal institutions of the labour market, including the CLT and its application, the organizations of workers and employers, the process of dialogue among them, and the roles different labour institutions play in regulating conditions of work and representing the interests of different parties. Then we examined employment relationships in more detail, identifying different labour statuses, assessing their relative importance in the labour market and the production system, and examining the patterns of inequality to which they give rise. We looked in more detail at two key factors of inequality within the labour regime, gender and race, and how they connect with labour market structures and segmentations. And we then considered in more detail how different groups in the labour market have been affected by the persistent economic, social and political crisis in the country since 2015, and how patterns of labour use have been affected in different sectors of the economy.

The picture that emerges is one of a labour regime that is fragmented and unequal, although articulated between its distinct parts. A substantial fraction of the labour market functions under a formal structure of regulation, often with trade union presence and collective bargaining, a minimum wage, guarantees of a range of labour rights and a system of social protection providing coverage against a range of contingencies. This part of the labour market is dominated by wage work in large manufacturing firms and the public sector, but it extends to a range of "modern" economic activities, from information technology services to commercial centres, from health care to financial activities, even reaching a fraction of employment in agribusiness. Within this part of the labour market employment relations respect a set of legal standards through the carteira assinada, or through registration and participation in the social security system for the self-employed. In theory this structure of regulation applies to the country as a whole. What distinguishes the Northeast from the rest of Brazil is less the nature of employment relations in this formal segment, and more its relative size, for in the Northeast this is a minority of the labour market, while in the rest of Brazil it accounts for well over half.

This can be seen clearly from the analysis of labour status. Protected wage work accounts for a little over one third of employment in the Northeast, and unprotected wage work a little less. The remaining one third of employment consists of extremely diverse types of self-employment, a small fraction formal, but mostly informal, much of it marginal work delivering very low incomes.

This labour system is both segmented and integrated. Segmented because there is a large gap in incomes and security between different parts of the labour market. But it is integrated because different forms of labour are involved within a single production system. Because of outsourcing, unprotected and low-income workers contribute to formal production chains – the example of construction is discussed above. In addition, much of the consumption of workers in formal employment consists of low-priced basic consumer goods and personal services produced under informal conditions. We explore these patterns further in Chapter 4.

This diverse set of labour statuses delivers highly unequal incomes. Within the Northeast, income differences between labour statuses account for well over 40% of all inequality of labour income. Income in the highest labour status group is more than 12 times the lowest, and the large numbers of workers in marginal self-employment and in agriculture receive on average less than half the minimum wage.

This labour system interacts with other sources of inequality. We consider, in particular, gender and race, factors which intersect. A part of gender and race inequality comes from unequal access to different statuses in the labour market, and a part from lower incomes for black or female workers within each labour status. Our analysis suggests that both factors are important.

Obviously, the system of formal regulation is a strong factor in combatting these sources of inequality, but much of the inequality comes from factors outside the formal system, or from differences between formal and informal work.

These patterns are persistent. The overall share of unprotected wage work in the Northeast was much the same in 2019 as in the mid-1990s. There was some progress in formalization in the Brazilian labour market as a whole between 2002 and 2014 (Chapter 2), and some signs of improvement in the situation of women, but the analysis of the crisis years after 2014 shows that much of the gain has been lost, as unemployment rose, formal jobs were lost, there was significant dropout from the labour force in the Northeast, and self-employment, notably marginal, low-income self-employment, rose. The gap between the Northeastern labour market and the rest of the country, including with respect to the extent of formal employment and income differences, has shown little long-term sign of decline.

These patterns within the labour market interact with the broader question of access to employment. Unemployment rates, higher in the Northeast than the rest of the country, rose sharply during the crisis, reaching 12% for white men and almost 18% for black women. But it is also striking that labour force participation was lower in the Northeast than in the rest of the country, and it fell further during the economic crisis, especially for those aged less than 35. Adverse conditions in the labour market, with a low and declining share of "good" jobs, clearly leave many younger people on the margins, with little hope of stable employment and a decent income. And this exclusion from the labour market, and an associated decline in labour force commitment, is surely a major factor in social dysfunction and criminality. The official figures we have been using, even from household surveys, mainly relate to legal activities and incomes, but those who are unable to access adequate legal incomes find other means to survive on which reliable data are lacking.

What can we say about the overall labour regime on the basis of this analysis?

- First, there is considerable heterogeneity of labour relations. Not only do patterns differ between sectors, but so do trends. There seems to be an increasing fragmentation of production systems, leading to greater diversity of labour statuses in the same sector, and probably greater inequality overall.

- Second, the different forms of labour relations are nevertheless articulated, either through the strategies of private and public employers (such as outsourcing and hiring both formal and informal workers), or through the survival strategies of families (whose members may be distributed between formal and informal occupations, as well as between wage- and self-employment, with the purpose of increasing income security by diversifying income sources[17]). Furthermore, the formal regulatory system and the social institutions that regulate the informal economy also interact. Hence the importance of the notion of labour regime for this study, which attempts to take all of these elements into account.
- Third, the process of informalization in the 1990s, which was reversed in the 2000s, re-emerged during the crisis since 2014. In some cases formal jobs were replaced by outsourcing to self-employment (in construction, for instance); in others, workers who lost their jobs were forced into low productivity work if they could not survive while unemployed; in yet others, formal wage work was simply replaced by informal wage work, notably in smaller enterprises.
- Fourth, comparing the Northeast with the rest of Brazil, the economic disadvantage of the Northeast comes out clearly, with far fewer white-collar workers, fewer skilled workers, more wage workers without carteira in small enterprises, and many more self-employed, concentrated in low-income self-employment, or in agriculture. The self-employed elsewhere in Brazil are much more likely to have some social security and higher incomes. Overall labour incomes are almost 40% lower in the Northeast.
- Fifth, the average income difference between the Northeast and the rest of Brazil is less for higher-income labour status groups (20%–25%) than it is for lower-income groups (50%–60%); and a larger share of workers is concentrated in lower-income groups in the Northeast.
- Sixth, the interaction between the labour regime and the dynamics of regional development does not generate inclusive labour markets. Capital accumulation tends to be concentrated in large scale production, with only modest employment creation, and this leads to the creation of islands of protected employment in a sea of informal work. Processes of subcontracting and outsourcing tend to reinforce unequal labour market structures. The economy as a whole is characterized by substantial inequality between large capital-intensive firms, on the one hand, and small enterprises and self-employment, on the other, much of the latter informal and low-income.
- Seventh, these inequalities are compounded by the difficulties of labour market access for young people, which show up in high levels of unemployment and labour market dropout.

If we return to the classic notion of "regulated citizenship", then the reality of the Northeastern labour market is that this regulated citizenship only reaches a minority of workers. There is a clear difference with most other parts of Brazil. The production system in Northeast Brazil is more heterogeneous, and this gives rise to a corresponding heterogeneity within the labour regime, with a wide variety of employment relations, structural segmentations and differences between social groups in situations and opportunities. A substantial fraction of the population lives on the margins, whether or not linked to the core of the productive system. The pattern and dynamics of inequality, both within the Northeast and between the Northeast and the rest of Brazil, to a large extent derive from these social and economic structures and institutions.

Annex to Chapter 3

An extended breakdown of labour status

The breakdown of labour status discussed in this chapter uses information from the national household survey, the PNADC, to characterize employment relations. The PNADC is used by IBGE to create a standard classification of *posição na ocupação* (occupational status), shown in Table 3A.1, which gives the overall percentage distribution of the workforce in the Northeast of Brazil and the rest of Brazil in the third quarter of 2019.

This provides useful information about the overall pattern of employment relationships. We can already see large differences between the Northeast and the rest of Brazil in the share of formal (with carteira assinada) and informal (without) wage work. But what it tells us is limited. Eighty per cent of workers fall in just four categories. And there are large differences in the quality and nature of employment within each of categories in the table. In order to properly understand the labour regime we need more detail.

In the body of the chapter a number of factors are identified that are relevant for the classification of labour status: autonomy, reliability, protection and security, remuneration and skill, and representation. The extent to which these can be captured with existing data varies. With respect to autonomy, the standard categories (employer, self-employed, unpaid family worker and wage employee) are available in the PNADC, but it is more difficult to identify ambiguous situations of disguised wage work. On continuity and regularity, it is possible to identify temporary work in the PNADC, which also provides information on the time spent in the present job, but this is of limited value as an indicator. With respect to protection and security of wage workers, information on possession of the labour card (carteira), which provides legal protection of basic rights, is available. For the self-employed and employers the PNADC provides indicators such as the registration of the enterprise and whether or not contributions are made to social security. The PNADC also provides information on labour income. With

Table 3A.1 Labour (occupational) status (PNADC categories), % distribution, Northeast and Rest of Brazil, third quarter 2019

Labour status in principal occupation	*Northeast*	*Rest of Brazil*
Wage worker in the private sector with signed labour card	24.6	38.4
Wage worker in the private sector without signed labour card	17.7	11.1
Domestic service worker with signed labour card	1.2	2.0
Domestic service worker without signed labour card	5.6	4.6
Public sector worker – military and established civil servants	9.1	8.1
Other public sector worker with signed labour card	1.0	1.5
Other public sector worker without signed labour card	4.7	2.2
Employer	3.5	5.0
Self-employed	29.6	25.0
Unpaid family worker	3.1	2.0
Total	100.0	100.0

Source: IBGE, PNADC, 2019, 3rd quarter.

respect to skills and qualifications, the main indicator is provided by the occupation, although data are also available on educational qualifications. Finally, trade union representation is not well captured.

So there are gaps. Nevertheless, a considerable amount of information is available on at least some of the dimensions of labour status, and other factors with an indirect effect on labour status such as the size of firm and the sector of activity can also be taken into account. There are too many situations for all to be distinguished, but with PNADC data it is possible to take some account of occupation, sector, type of firm, income and indicators of formality to establish a finer disaggregation. This classification is based on principal occupation. In principle it would be possible to take secondary occupations into account, but that has not been attempted here.

First, agriculture is quite different from other sectors. It is dominated by self-employment and unpaid family work (56% in the Northeast in 2019). Most wage labour in agriculture is without carteira, often seasonal or in small farms. We therefore separate out these two categories. There is also some wage work with carteira in agriculture, and some employers, but these are smaller categories, largely confined to commercial production on large plantations, and closer in nature to arrangements in other sectors.

Second, it is possible to identify different categories among workers with carteira. One important distinction is in terms of occupation, which can also provide a proxy for class and skill. Workers in upper-level white-collar occupations (directors, managers, professional and technical workers) differ in important respects from others. They tend to be better paid and more stable, often with better working conditions. And there is a difference of class identity.

A second white-collar group consists of administrative and secretarial support and similar jobs with carteira. This group does not have high income levels (close to the average for all workers), but there is again a difference of class identity compared with both production workers and upper white-collar workers. We include with this group many workers in trade and services, such as call centre operators and shop assistants in larger shops and commercial centres.

Among production ("blue-collar") workers, the skill level is an important distinguishing factor, associated with both income and job stability. The best dividing line, in terms of income, seems to be between skilled and semi-skilled workers, on the one hand, and unskilled workers, on the other.

This gives us four groups of private sector wage workers with carteira:

- Upper white-collar workers (directors, managers, professionals and technical staff)
- Lower white-collar workers (administrative and secretarial, sales workers and similar)
- Skilled and semi-skilled production workers
- Unskilled production workers

Third, non-agricultural workers without carteira are widely spread across production sectors (especially construction, trade, hotels and restaurants and personal services). The main factor differentiating workers in this group seems to be less a question of occupation or sector and more one of enterprise size. We identify two distinct categories here: workers without carteira in small enterprises, where there is likely to be a personal relationship between employer and worker – over 60% of non-agricultural wage workers without carteira in the Northeast were in small firms with five or less workers in 2019; and workers without carteira in larger enterprises, which may reflect temporary use of specialized workers, but may also include an exploitative use of casual labour (in construction, for instance, or as occasional workers in industry).

Fourth, domestic workers are clearly a distinct category. We group together domestic workers with and without carteira, since the numbers in the former category are small, especially in the Northeast.

Fifth, three different situations in the public sector were identified in Table 3A.1: regular civil servants (and the military), and other public sector workers with and without carteira. The military and civil servants clearly constitute a distinct category of regular, protected workers. There is also a group of public sector workers with carteira, but this accounted for less than 1% of all workers, so we group them with other regular civil servants. On the other hand, public sector workers without carteira accounted for almost 5% of workers in the Northeast. This is a distinctive group that includes workers contracted on a temporary, political or otherwise non-standard basis in the public sector.

Sixth, employers accounted for over 4% of workers in Brazil as a whole, and 80% of them earned more than twice the minimum wage. The majority of employers are formal, in the sense that their enterprises are registered (in the *Cadastro Nacional da Pessoa Jurídica* – CNPJ). However, there is also a low-income, informal group among employers who are closer in character to the self-employed. We therefore distinguish employers with and without CNPJ registration, and group the latter with the informal self-employed.

Seventh, own account workers are a large and complex group, accounting for close to 30% of all workers in the Northeast. We have already separated out self-employed agricultural households. As in the case of employers, we distinguish formal and informal categories. Very few self-employed workers were registered with the CNPJ, but somewhat more (15%) contributed to social security, so we use that as an indicator of formality and separate out this group.

Among those who do not contribute to social security, there is a wide range of situations, and it is important to distinguish the marginal self-employed from productive small family enterprises. One way to do this would be on the basis of capital ownership, but on this the PNADC provides no information. Instead we use income as a proxy indicator of productivity. 50% of the non-agricultural self-employed in the Northeast earned less than one minimum wage in 2019, and we use this as a dividing line, distinguishing "productive" self-employment (at least the minimum wage) from "marginal" self-employment (less than the minimum wage). Informal employers are also included in these groups on the basis of the same criterion.

A final group consists of unpaid family workers outside agriculture.

This gives a total of 16 labour statuses.

1. Self-employed/family worker in agriculture
2. Wage worker without carteira in agriculture
3. Private sector wage worker with carteira, upper white-collar
4. Private sector wage worker with carteira, lower white-collar/services/trade
5. Private sector wage worker with carteira, blue-collar, skilled or semi-skilled
6. Private sector wage worker with carteira, blue-collar, unskilled
7. Private sector wage worker without carteira, small enterprise (up to five workers)
8. Private sector wage worker without carteira, medium/large enterprise (over five workers)
9. Domestic service worker
10. Public sector worker without carteira
11. Public sector worker with carteira/military/civil servant
12. Formal employer (with CNPJ registration)
13. Formal non-agricultural self-employed worker (contributing to social security)
14. Informal "productive" non-agricultural self-employed worker or employer
15. Informal "marginal" non-agricultural self-employed worker or employer
16. Non-agricultural family worker

Table 3.2 in the text gives the overall distribution of workers across these statuses in the Northeast and in Brazil as a whole in 2019, and Table 3.4 gives the distribution of workers by labour status in each industrial sector in the Northeast.

What important aspects of labour status are missing from our extended breakdown? One is the issue of continuity and security of employment, for which better indicators would be needed. Another is the issue of disguised wage employment among the self-employed, for instance, in the gig economy and in outsourced work from larger firms. We only have indirect information on skills and the content of work, and on working conditions. And we have no information about unionization. So there is scope for improvement. But this breakdown already gives us a good starting point to understand how different forms of employment relationship fit into the production system.

Notes

1 The CLT refers to the consolidation of labour laws first approved in 1943, and its extensions and revisions since that date, incorporating the norms and standards that regulate individual and collective labour relations.

2 Data from IBGE, *Pesquisa Sindical* for 1987–1992 and the PNAD (IBGE, *Pesquisa Nacional por Amostra de Domicílios*) for subsequent years. Different data sources give different estimates; the *Pesquisa Sindical* shows a higher unionization rate than the PNAD. But they agree that the overall trend was for a relative stability in unionization rates. The numbers do not include organizations of employers and of self-employed workers, which in 2001 accounted for 29% of all unions in Brazil as a whole, and 22% in the Northeast.

3 55% of workers in the sector were self-employed in 2019. See Table 3.4.

4 Data from the PNADC (IBGE). The methodology of the PNADC gives lower estimates than the PNAD (Figure 3.1) but the difference between the Northeast and the rest of Brazil is maintained.

5 Higher than in the Southeast, the South and the Centre-West. The North has more in common with the Northeast in this respect.

6 See the discussion of labour market segmentation in Chapter 1. The considerable literature on this subject includes Wilkinson (1979) and Deakin (2013), and in Latin America Tokman (1989, 2004).

7 This reference period was initially chosen because these were the most recent data available at the time this analysis was carried out. Later information subsequently became available, but from 2020 onward the pattern was distorted by the impact of the pandemic, so 2019 provides a better reference point.

8 Henceforth we refer to wage work with or without labour card as "with carteira" (or formal) or "without carteira" (or informal).

9 In Chapter 2, taking the fourth quarter as a reference, we found an informality rate of 48.2% for Brazil and 60.2% for the Northeast. The difference between the two calculations (which use the same database) is mainly due to two reasons. First, in Chapter 2 we used the fourth quarter as a reference, and here the third (seasonally, between the third and fourth quarters, the proportion of informal work grows due to temporary hires at the end of the year). Second, and more importantly, in the estimate in Chapter 2 we considered all self-employment as informal work. In this more detailed breakdown we are able to separate formal and informal self-employment. On the other hand, here we treated all domestic service workers as belonging to the informal category.

10 We do not put inverted commas around "marginal" and "productive" in the rest of this text, but it should be considered that these are labels rather than a precise reflection of the content of the labour status concerned.

11 This average is probably increased by the presence, among these workers, of "commissioned positions", persons who are appointed by newly elected governments, employed under informal contracts but benefiting from relatively high wages. At the other extreme are workers hired mainly by municipalities for local functions (for example, community health agents), who receive very low wages.

12 The pattern is similar in Paraíba. We have not examined other states.

13 There are several different ways to estimate these indicators of inequality. Hoffmann and Vaz (2020) present indicators based on inequality in total household income per capita. Neri's estimates are of labour income per capita, i.e. also referring to households. Our estimates (below) are of inequality of labour income, among individuals receiving some labour income, and therefore refer to inequality between workers. These different measures give different estimates, of Gini coefficients for example, though trends and differences among regions are likely to be similar.

14 IBGE, System of National and Regional Accounts: https://www.ibge.gov.br/estatisticas/economicas/contas-nacionais/9052-sistema-de-contas-nacionais-brasil.html?=&t=o-que-e. Accessed on 23-02-2022. The categories in the national accounts refer to *remuneração dos empregados* (wages); *excedente operacional bruto* (considered equivalent to capital share); and *rendimento misto bruto* (self-employed share). There are conceptual issues in the definition of these categories, but they provide a first approximation to the overall trends.

15 So is gender, but available data do not permit one to go further than the traditional male-female breakdown.

16 As we saw in the previous chapter, although agribusiness has been expanding to the detriment of traditional agriculture, especially family-based agriculture, this expansion is occurring with relatively little absorption of labour.

17 See, for example, Motta and Scott (1983).

References

Abreu, Alice Rangel de Paiva, Helena Hirata and Maria Rosa Lombardi (eds.). 2016. *Gênero e trabalho no Brasil e na França*. São Paulo: Boitempo.

Amorim, Wilson Aparecido Costa de. 2015. *Negociações coletivas no Brasil: 50 anos de aprendizado*. São Paulo: Atlas.

Araújo, Angela and Roberto Véras de Oliveira. 2014. "O sindicalismo na era Lula: Entre paradoxos e novas perspectivas" in Roberto Véras De Oliveira, Maria Aparecida Bridi and Marcos Ferraz (eds.): *O sindicalismo na era Lula: Paradoxos, perspectivas e olhares* (pp. 29–59). Belo Horizonte: Fino Traço Editora.

Barbosa, Ana Luiza Neves de Holanda. 2014. "Participação feminina no mercado de trabalho brasileiro". *Boletim Mercado de Trabalho – Conjuntura e Análise*, 57: 31–41. Brasilia: IPEA.

Boito Jr, Armando, and Paula Marcelino. 2010. "O sindicalismo deixou a crise para trás? Um novo ciclo de greves na decada de 2000". *Caderno CRH*, 23(59): 323–338.

Bruschini, Cristina and Maria Rosa Lombardi. 2003. "Mulheres e homens no mercado de trabalho brasileiro: Um retrato dos anos 1990" in Margaret Maruani and Helena Hirata (eds.): *As novas fronteiras da desigualdade: Homens e mulheres no mercado de trabalho*. São Paulo: SENAC.

Cacciamali, Maria-Cristina, Taniya Chakrabarty, Gerry Rodgers and Fabio Tatei. 2015. *Minimum wage policy in Brazil and India and its impact on labour market inequality*. Working Paper 02/2015. New Delhi: Institute for Human Development.

Cardoso, Adalberto. 1999. *Sindicatos, trabalhadores e a coqueluche neoliberal: A era Vargas acabou?* Rio de Janeiro: Fundação Getulio Vargas.

Castro, Nadya. 1991. "Sindicalismo metalúrgico: Mesmas cenas em outros cenários?". *Cadernos CRH*, Salvador, 14(14): 73–96.

Crenshaw, Kimberle. 1989. "Demarginalizing the intersection of race and sex: A black feminist critique of antidiscrimination doctrine, feminist theory and antiracist politics". *University of Chicago Legal Forum*, 1989(1): 139–167.

———. 2002. "Documento para o encontro de especialistas em aspectos da discriminação racial relativos ao gênero". *Estudos feministas*, 10(1): 171–188.

Deakin, Simon. 2013. *Addressing labour market segmentation: The role of labour law*. Working Paper 446. Cambridge: Centre for Business Research, University of Cambridge.

DIEESE (*Departamento Intersindical de Estatística e Estudos Socioeconômicos*). 2015. *Balanço das greves em 2013*. Estudos e Pesquisas, 79. São Paulo: DIEESE.

———. 2019. *Balanço das negociações dos reajustes salariais de 2018*. Estudos e Pesquisas, 90. São Paulo: DIEESE.

Dos Santos, Wanderley Guilherme. 1987. *Cidadania e justiça: A política social na ordem brasileira*. 2nd edition. Rio de Janeiro: Campus.

Goulart, Débora Cristina. 2012. "Movimento dos Trabalhadores Sem-Teto e subproletarização: Elementos para um debate sobre a classe trabalhadora no Brasil". *Lutas Sociais*, 29: 160–171.

Guimarães, Antonio Sérgio Alfredo. 2016. "Sociologia e natureza: classes, raças e sexos" in Alice Rangel de Paiva Abreu, Helena Hirata and Maria Rosa Lombardi (eds.): *Gênero e trabalho no Brasil e na França* (pp. 27–36). São Paulo: Boitempo.

Harriss, John, K.P. Kannan and Gerry Rodgers. 1990. *Urban labour market structure and job access in India: A study of Coimbatore*. Research Series 92. Geneva: International Institute for Labour Studies.

Hasenbalg, Carlos. 1985. "Race and socioeconomic inequalities in Brazil" in Pierre-Michel Fontaine (ed.): *Race, class, and power in Brazil* (pp. 25–41). Los Angeles: Center for Afro-American Studies, University of California.

Hirata, Helena. 2014. "Gênero, classe e raça: Interseccionalidade e consubstancialidade das relações sociais". *Tempo Social*, 26(1): 61–73.

Hoffmann, Rodolfo and Daniela Verzola Vaz. 2020. *Mensurando a desigualdade no Brasil: Evidências a partir da renda e dos gastos das famílias*. Texto para Discussão No. 63. Rio de Janeiro: IEPE/Casa das Garças, June.

IBGE (Instituto Brasileiro de Geografia e Estatística). Various dates. *PNAD (Pesquisa Nacional por Amostra de Domicílios)*. Rio de Janeiro: IBGE.

———. Various dates. *PNADC (Pesquisa Nacional por Amostra de Domicílios Contínua)*. Rio de Janeiro: IBGE.

———. Various dates. *Pesquisa Sindical*. Rio de Janeiro: IBGE.

———. 2002–2003; 2008–2009; 2017–2018. *Pesquisa de Orçamentos Familiares*. Rio de Janeiro: IBGE.

Kalil, Renan Bernardi. 2012. *A organização e a atuação coletivas dos trabalhadores informais: Sindicatos, cooperativas e associações*. Dissertação (Mestrado em Direito), University of São Paulo (USP).

Kergoat, Danièle. 1982. *Les ouvrières*. Paris: Le Sycomore.

———. 2010. "Dinâmica e consubstancialidade das relações sociais". *Novos Estudos CEBRAP*, 86: 93–103. <http://www.scielo.br/pdf/nec/n86/n86a05.pdf>, accessed 1-06-2019.

Krein, Dari. 2007. *Tendências recentes nas relações de emprego no Brasil – 1990/2005*. Thesis (Doutorado em Economía), Universidade Estadual de Campinas (UNICAMP). Campinas-SP.

Krein, José Dari, Roberto Véras de Oliveira and Vitor Filgueiras (eds.). 2019. *Reforma trabalhista no Brasil: Promessas e realidade*. Campinas: Curt Nimuendajú.

Lima, Jacob. 1996. *Trabalho, mercado e formação de classe: Estudo sobre operários fabris em Pernambuco*. João Pessoa: Editora Universitária.

Loveman, Mara, Jeronimo O. Muniz and Stanley R. Bailey. 2012. "Brazil in black and white? Race categories, the census, and the study of inequality". *Ethnic and Racial Studies*, 35(8): 1466–1483.

Medeiros, Marcelo and Pedro H. G. F. Souza. 2016. *A estabilidade da desigualdade no Brasil entre 2006 e 2012: Resultados adicionais*. Texto para discussão 2017. Brasilia: IPEA.

Motta, Roberto and Parry Scott. 1983. *Sobrevivência e fontes de renda: Estratégias das famílias de baixa renda no Recife*. Série População e Emprego. Recife: Sudene/Editora Massangana.

Neri, Marcelo. 2019. *A escalada da desigualdade. Qual foi o impacto da crise sobre a distribuição de renda e a pobreza?*. Rio de Janeiro, FGV Social. <https://cps.fgv.br/desigualdade>, accessed 14-05-2022.

Oliveira, Francisco de. 1972. *Crítica à razão dualista: O ornitorrinco*. São Paulo: Boitempo.

———. 1987. *O elo perdido: Classe e identidade de classe na Bahia*. São Paulo: Fundação Perseu Abramo.

Osorio, Rafael Guerreiro. 2003. *O sistema classificatório de cor ou raça do IBGE*. Texto para discussão 996. Brasilia: IPEA.

Petruccelli, José Luis and Ana Lucia Saboia (eds.). 2013. *Características étnico-raciais da população – Classificações e identidades*. Estudos e Análises – Informação demográfica e socioeconómica, 2. Rio de Janeiro: IBGE.

Pochmann, Marcio. 2009. "What Brazil learned from labour flexibilization in the 1990s". *International Labour Review*, 148(1): 269–282.

Roberts, Madeleine Octavia. 2018. "De 'um pé na cozinha' a 'um pé na porta': A PEC das domésticas no Brasil, suas oportunidades e seus desafios". *Revista Mundos do Trabalho*, 10(20): 31–59.

Rodrigues, Leôncio Martins. 1990. "As tendências políticas na formação das centrais sindicais" in Armando Boito Jr. (ed.): *O sindicalismo brasileiro nos anos 80* (pp. 11–42). Rio de Janeiro: Paz e Terra.

Scorzafave, Luiz Guiherme and Naércio Aquino Menezes-Filho. 2001. "Participação feminina no mercado de trabalho brasileiro: Evolução e determinantes". *Pesquisa e Planejamento Econômico*, 31(3): 441–478. Brasilia: IPEA.

Silva, Nelson do Valle. 1985. "Updating the cost of not being white in Brazil" in Pierre-Michel Fontaine (ed.): *Race, class, and power in Brazil* (pp. 42–55). Los Angeles: Center for Afro-American Studies, University of California.

Silva, Graziella Moraes. 2016. "After racial democracy: Contemporary puzzles in race relations in Brazil, Latin America and beyond from a boundaries perspective". *Current Sociology*, 64(5): 794–812.

Singer, Paul and André Ricardo Souza. 2000. *A economia solidária no Brasil: A autogestão como resposta ao desemprego*. São Paulo: Contexto.

Standing, Guy. 1999. *Global labour flexibility: Seeking distributive justice*. Basingstoke: Macmillan.

Telles, Vera da Silva and Maria Célia Paoli. 1994. "Social rights: Conflicts and negotiations in contemporary Brazil" in Sonia Alvarez, Evelyn Dagnino and Arturo Escobar (eds.): *Cultures of politics/politics of cultures: Revisioning Latin American social movements* (pp. 64–92). Boulder, CO: Westview Press.

Tokman, Victor E. 1989. "Economic development and labor market segmentation in the Latin American periphery". *Journal of Interamerican Studies and World Affairs*, 31(1–2): 23–48.

———. 2004. *Una voz en el camino: Empleo y equidad en América Latina: 40 Años de búsqueda*. Santiago de Chile: Fondo de Cultura Económica.

Véras de Oliveira, Roberto. 2018. "Brazilian labour reform in historical perspective". *Global Labour Journal*, 9(3): 319–338.

Véras de Oliveira, Roberto, Andréia Galvão and Anderson Campos. 2019. "Reforma trabalhista: Impactos imediatos sobre os sindicatos e primeiras reações". *Cadernos do CEAS*, 248: 668–689.

Wilkinson, Frank (ed.). 1981. *The dynamics of labour market segmentation*. London: Academic Press.

4 Diversity in production systems and labour relations

1 Introduction

This chapter summarizes the results of individual studies of production systems. They complement the general picture of development and labour regimes presented in the previous chapters of the book, by providing evidence on how local and sectoral factors influence and are reflected in production and employment patterns. What happens in the region is partly the aggregation of these different production processes, but the broader development regime, in turn, conditions and influences the level and quality of local employment. Local labour relations and institutions are therefore interconnected with the general process of capital accumulation in Brazil and play an important role in determining patterns of growth and distributing the benefits of development.

These case studies, carried out by researchers from the Federal University of Campina Grande – UFCG and the Federal University of Paraíba – UFPB within a research project on the reproduction of inequalities in Northeast Brazil (*A Reprodução das Desigualdades no Nordeste do Brasil: Regimes de Trabalho e Desenvolvimento*), aimed to analyse the constitution and reconfiguration of productive sectors located in the Northeast, mainly in the states of Paraíba and Pernambuco. The underlying hypothesis that guided these studies was that the patterns of labour relations historically constituted in the Northeast are reproduced and remodelled in segmented and precarious ways. The levels of segmentation and precariousness depend on the way productive units are inserted into the economic, organizational and institutional fabric of the region, namely in terms of their public or private character, the level of capital mobilization, their capital-intensive or labour-intensive profile, the agents involved and the effective respect for social and labour rights.

The following economic sectors are included: sugar and ethanol production in Pernambuco and Paraíba; fruit growing in Petrolina (Pernambuco) and Juazeiro (Bahia); mining in the Seridó of Paraíba; the garment pole in the Agreste region of Pernambuco; the footwear sector in Campina Grande; shipyards in the Suape Industrial and Port Complex (Pernambuco); the civil

DOI: 10.4324/9781003326670-4

construction sector in Paraíba; information technology in Pernambuco; call centres in João Pessoa and Campina Grande (Paraíba); Uber passenger transport service in Rio Grande do Norte; and the automotive pole of Goiana (Pernambuco).[1]

While not a comprehensive or even a representative selection of productive situations and sectors, the case studies presented here do cover a wide range of institutional and organizational forms – both formal and informal – and most sectors of the economy. The main gaps concern parts of the trade and services sectors. As such, these case studies illustrate many of the situations, production relationships, and employment patterns found in the Northeast.

Though the book deals with the Northeast as a whole, the empirical material presented here is mainly anchored in two states: Pernambuco and Paraíba. Neither the region nor individual states are homogeneous regarding the level of industrialization, the degree of formality of the labour market, the average wage patterns, etc. While Pernambuco has been historically situated above the average indicators for the region, Paraíba has been below. The differences between them can illustrate the diversity of situations in the region. Other parts of the Northeast, notably Bahia, Ceará and Maranhão, also have distinct characteristics. However, while each state in the Northeast has its own profile, culture, history and economic structure they display common elements that imply that the differences between the states of the region are (from the point of view of the subject of this book) less significant than the difference between the region as a whole and the rest of Brazil. Therefore, we believe that these studies of a part of the Northeast help to understand the economic and social trajectory of the region as a whole.

The sectoral studies aimed to articulate empirical enquiries with analytical-conceptual frameworks. A first level drew on the empirical findings of each case study to dialogue critically with other studies carried out, at the local, national and international levels, on the same theme, seeking to trace the state of the art in each case and the identification of the most appropriate approach.

A second level, of a more general nature, referred to the broader debate about production systems and labour relations and, above all, about the transformations that the world economy has been going through. In general, the concern was to identify the connections, the similarities and the differences between the local, national and international contexts, highlighting the peripheral position of Brazil in global capitalism and, internally, the peripheral situation of the Northeast in the national context. Some thematic areas were given particular attention, such as the role of Taylorist or Fordist production processes, restructuring of production, flexibilization of labour relations and labour reforms, past and present forms of informality, outsourcing and entrepreneurship.

These studies combine qualitative and quantitative approaches, aiming to capture both objective and subjective aspects of the situations studied. In order to give greater coherence to the studies a common analytical matrix was constructed. The structure of this matrix was an adaptation of the five institutional domains that the French School of Regulation proposes as playing a central role in the regulation of production and distribution (Chapter 1). The matrix was built around the following axes: macroeconomic context and relationships; competition regime and production system; labour market structures and institutions; role of the State (and other actors); and the form of national and international integration. In addition, two transversal themes were integrated into the reflections: inequality between social groups (gender, colour, age, etc.), and the impact of the 2017 Labour Reform.

2 The sugarcane agroindustry in the Northeast[2]

Historically, sugarcane cultivation has been an iconic activity, representative of the Brazilian Northeast. Its history throws light on the socioeconomic formation of the region, where it moulded a specific agrarian system. Sugarcane cultivation was introduced by the Portuguese colonizers in the first half of the sixteenth century. Over the following centuries the sugar economy flourished, albeit with ups and downs, and, nowadays, Brazil is the first producer of sugar in the world and the second producer of ethanol.[3] Until the middle of the twentieth century the Northeast dominated sugar production in Brazil. But the growth of demand for ethanol, the concentration of production and the increased participation of foreign capital[4] led to substantial changes in the production process. Northeastern plantations and sugar factories were unable to compete, and production mainly migrated to the Southeast region of Brazil, which had more modern industrial zones, greater access to financial capital and a more dynamic consumer market (Andrade, 2001).[5]

The world oil crisis in the 1970s motivated the creation of the National Alcohol Programme by the federal government, which allocated large volumes of resources to the sector. By encouraging the production of ethanol, in addition to offering an alternative to fossil fuel, Proálcool aimed to revitalize the sugar and ethanol industry in Brazil (Andrade, 2001).

However, in the course of the 1980s, the national alcohol sector experienced a new crisis, due to changes in the international situation (of the oil market), to public indebtedness (both at the federal and state levels) and to the inability of producers to meet the growing demand for fuel in the country (Ramos, 2016).

In the 1990s, the difficulties facing the northeastern sugar producers worsened. The area under sugarcane decreased by 21% in the region and it fell by a further 23% between 2000 and 2018, while it increased 106% in Brazil as a whole (see Figure 4.1). The share of the Northeast in national sugarcane production decreased from 18% to 6.5%. Several factors contributed to this decline: the reduction in the participation of the State, the deregulation of prices,[6] the relocation of economic groups to other parts of the country and the occurrence of environmental problems (droughts and soil erosion). In

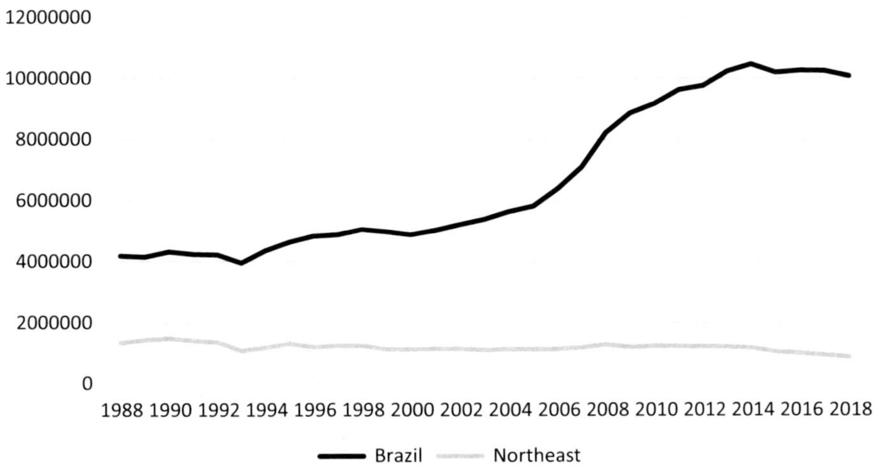

Figure 4.1 Trend in area under sugarcane in Brazil and the Northeast, 1988–2018 (in hectares).

Source: Danato and Dantas (2022), Graph 1.

the Northeast sugarcane productivity is currently well below the national average. In 2018, the regional average yield was 56,043 kilogrammes per hectare while it was 74,369 for Brazil as a whole (IBGE, 2020).

2.1 Changes in the labour market

With the decadence of the regional sugar economy, employment decreased. The number of sugar mills in operation decreased, and, according to the Ministry of Agriculture (Sapcana), the number of production units in Pernambuco dropped from 32 to 14 between the 1996/1997 and 2018/2019 harvests. Hence it was estimated that, in Pernambuco, the level of employment fell from 240,000 workers in 1979 to 130,000 at the end of the 1990s.

At the same time, the structure of employment changed: the number of permanent sugarcane workers decreased, and the number of temporary workers and seasonal migrants increased. However, the Northeast made some significant advances in the formalization of labour, though it remained below the national average. According to PNAD data, between 1992 and 2006 the percentage of sugarcane workers in formal employment increased from 56% to 74% among permanent workers and from 23% to 56% among temporary workers. For Brazil as a whole the corresponding increases were from 76% to 87% among permanent workers and from 37% to 68% among temporary workers. In 2006, the Northeast had provided 27.5% of the formal jobs in the cultivation of sugarcane generated in the country, in 2019 the percentage had dropped to 23% (RAIS data).

On the plantations, the bulk of the work is done manually by cane cutters. Men constitute more than 90% of the workforce of the sector. In 2006, the percentage of women in formal employment in the sugarcane harvest was just 4.4%, a percentage that rose to 6.7% in 2011 but dropped to 3.7% in 2019.

In the Northeast, the majority of sugarcane workers earned between 1 and 1.5 minimum wages. Between 2003 and 2019, there was a slight improvement in Pernambuco as the proportion of earners in the lowest range (0.51–1.00 minimum wage) decreased from 22% to 14% and the proportion of earners in the 1.01–1.50 range increased from 55% to 64%. The distribution of higher earnings did not change (17% in the 1.51–2.00 range and 4% in the 2.01–3.00 range) (RAIS). Wage inequalities between men and women are particularly large in higher earning brackets. 19% of men were earning between 1.51 and 2 minimum wages against 5% among women. Less than 0.5% of women and around 4% of men were found in the 2.01–3.00 minimum wages range.

2.2 Evolution of labour relations

The labour system that was set up after the abolition of slavery in 1888 had guaranteed a stable and compliant labour force to the sugar planters. *Moradores* were resident workers who received a house and a subsistence plot on condition that they would work on the plantation, receiving a low wage or no pay at all, and they were not allowed to work for any other employer. They were maintained in a regime of dependence on and subordination to the owners. In the second half of the twentieth century, the state-sponsored centralization and modernization of agricultural production brought about changes in production techniques and work relations. The increasing concentration of land ownership led to the expulsion of workers living on the plantations, and the struggle for land intensified[7] (Medeiros, 1989). Rural workers became wage workers whose pay rates were determined by the employers, while their employment situation and well-being continued to be precarious.

The extension to rural workers of labour rights took place belatedly because the agrarian elites opposed the enactment and enforcement of the 1943 Consolidation of Labour Laws (CLT) for rural workers. It was only in 1963 that rural workers' rights were recognized (*Estatuto do Trabalhador Rural*). The same year, the first collective agreement was signed in Pernambuco under pressure from a workers' general strike. It included, in particular, a so-called "Task Table" (*Tabela de Tarefas*), which fixed daily work schedules, salary adjustment and the recognition of union representation in the plantations (Abreu e Lima, 2012). It was a point of rupture between two epochs. Though this process was negatively impacted by the 1964 military coup, a new collective bargaining agreement was signed in 1979. It included, in particular, some clauses referring to the formalization of the employment contract of *clandestinos* (informal workers often recruited on a daily or weekly basis via labour intermediaries (Sigaud, 1980, 1986)).

Between 1979 and 1989, wage negotiations were difficult (accompanied by strikes that occurred almost every year) and were predominantly settled by the Labour Court; only three collective agreements emerged from stakeholders' bargaining (Fetape, 2018). In the 1990s collective agreements brought some advances regarding the following topics: (i) women's health and work; (ii) safety in transport; (iii) first aid in case of work accidents; (iv) workplace improvements; (v) prohibition of punishment of workers involved in struggles for better working conditions. In the 2000s, wage campaigns for sugarcane plantations in Pernambuco resulted in negotiated agreements without strikes (except for a strike by one category of workers in 2005). From 2004 until 2013, the sugarcane workers achieved real gains with yearly wage readjustments constantly greater than 2% above inflation, with a peak gain of 14% in 2006 (data from DIESSE). In 2008, a national tripartite dialogue between the federal government, employers and workers resulted in the signature of the national commitment for "improvement" of working conditions in sugarcane production (*Compromisso Nacional para Aperfeiçoar as Condições de Trabalho na Cana-de-Açúcar*). Some advances were made in clauses referring to women's work and measures to protect health and safety at work. But the 2014–2016 crisis and the 2017 labour reform have put a brake on improving working conditions in the sector.

2.3 Summing up

Formalization has not yet brought real improvements in employment and wage security within the plantation economy of Northeast Brazil but has reconfigured the historical pattern of precariousness. For Queiroz and Vanderstraeten (2018, p.141) "What has been formalized is a precarious, permanently temporary situation or a 'job for life' characterized by insecurities and instabilities within the formal labour market." These findings suggest that current forms of precariousness are the result of both past control structures and new labour market regulations. With the decline of the sector in the Northeast, its capacity to generate employment has fallen steadily.

3 The irrigated fruit-growing pole of Petrolina and Juazeiro[8]

The irrigated fruit-growing area of Petrolina-Juazeiro, located in the lower middle San Francisco River valley, is a lifeline for the semiarid region of the Northeast. The production of mangoes and grapes accounts for more than 90% of table grape exports of Brazil and for about 80% of its mango exports (2019 data from SECEX, the Brazilian Foreign Trade Secretariat). The Brazilian State played a leading role in consolidating a development strategy based on high commercial value crops that attracted national and international capital. In the Petrolina-Juazeiro micro-region, the area under mango and grapes expanded from 2,029 hectares in 1990 to 14,847 hectares in 2000 and reached 34,066 hectares in 2018 (IBGE-PAM, 2020).

The fruit-growing cluster is the result of a long tradition of state intervention in the region, which gained momentum in the 1960s, with the creation of the São Francisco Valley Superintendency (SUVALE) and, in the following decade, of the São Francisco Valley Development Company (CODEVASF).[9] The foundations of the project were laid with the creation of more than a dozen irrigated zones, most of which were transferred to agricultural companies.

Large and medium-sized farms contributed to the shift to fruit production for export. Their capital mainly came from international and national industrial or commercial business. The global retail revolution had induced a transformation of world agricultural markets, and buyer-specified requirements in terms of fruit quality and conditions of production have raised entry barriers to small producers (Selwyn, 2010, 2013).

3.1 The labour market in the Petrolina-Juazeiro fruit-growing pole

Organized around the export dynamics of fruit production, the local labour market displays specific characteristics and (like the cultivation of sugarcane) seasonality is its main feature. On the one hand, producers need to recruit and retain skilled workers and on the other hand, they try to minimize labour costs. Short-term contracts and informality are widespread, but formal employment has also increased. Between the 2000 and 2010 censuses the percentage of informal workers in the agriculture and aquaculture sectors dropped from 67% to 44% in Petrolina and from 58% to 47% in Juazeiro. And informality was lower in grape cultivation (27% in Petrolina, and 15% in Juazeiro).

Fruit growing is a highly seasonal activity. Peak hiring is from August to September for activities related to harvesting and the preparation for export. Lay-offs occur predominantly in November and December, when the international export window of Brazilian mangoes and grapes ends. Informal work tends to expand at the end of the harvest period when workers are recruited for fruit packing, truck loading, clearing and weeding.

Temporary hiring has become functional for the labour arrangements of fruit growing. Harvest contracts[10] guarantee companies the availability of labour they need while enabling them to lower their production costs by not paying social contributions. Beyond restricted access to labour rights, harvest contracts represent a situation of instability for workers, contributing to situations of exploitation and harassment. Since 2010, trade unions and employers' representatives negotiate the rules that govern the use of such contracts. The 2016 agreement specified that the duration of a harvest contract could not be less than 30 days and could extend up to five months. Over the period 2008–2019, in grape cultivation, contracts shorter than three months have tended to decrease. Their reduction is explained by (i) the implementation of new forms of work management that include mechanisms to intensify work, and (ii) the introduction of new technologies, in particular, introducing grape varieties that demand less manual work during the growing stage of the grape.

The consolidation of the São Francisco Valley as a development enclave has attracted workers from the Northeast and other regions of Brazil. The Petrolina-Juazeiro pole became one of the few areas in the Northeast (outside metropolitan areas) where net migration is positive (Cavalcanti, 1997; Damiani, 2003; Pereira, 2012). Two migration streams are linked to work: a permanent migratory stream and seasonal and pendular migratory movements. In their majority, seasonal migrants are young adult male workers with a low level of education. They migrate alone and return to their place of origin during the off-season. In the Petrolina-Juazeiro area, daily commuters from urban centres to rural fields are also numerous.

Since the 1990s the number of female workers in the fruit export sector has grown significantly. Selwyn (2010) argued that farm managers responded to rising demands from fruit retailers by altering the gender division of labour. Most women are engaged in the fruit-growing labour market with harvest contracts, for part-time work, and often in informal jobs, performing activities that, even if they require a qualification, are poorly paid. Although equal pay is expressly guaranteed by collective agreements, the remuneration pattern is different for men and women.

Many of the wage workers in mango and grape production are engaged in other activities during the off-season. Some workers own rural properties or belong to subsistence farm families who at the end of the fruit harvest return to work their land. Some women workers may combine agricultural wage work and urban activities, such as domestic work, during the off-season.

3.2 Working conditions

Fruit export farming requires considerable manpower. Pre-harvest manual tasks, predominantly performed by women, represent about 40% of total production costs (Leite, 2013). To minimize their costs farming companies impose a stringent control over the pace and intensity of production. Some companies have set daily production targets under the control of field inspectors (Selwyn, 2007; Leite, 2013; Silva G., 2016). Such a system puts pressure on the workers who fear, if considered underperforming, not to have their contracts extended or renewed. Large companies have also instituted "hours bank" systems which enable them to increase the length of the working day during the peak season without having to pay overtime. The intensification of work translates not only into quantitative targets, but also into qualitative improvement of the production process since the maintenance of quality standards is fundamental in the international commercialization of fruit (Selwyn, 2009).

The vast majority of formal workers (89% in 2019) earned between one and two minimum wages. The minimum wage in irrigated fruit farming is determined by a collective bargaining agreement between workers' unions and employers' associations; historically it has been slightly above the national minimum wage.[11] In 2020, it was established at R$1,088 per month, R$43 above the national minimum wage.

3.3 Collective action

In the past, the rural workers' unions in the São Francisco region had been associated with family farming (Selwyn, 2007). Since the 1980s and the expansion of irrigated fruit growing, those unions reoriented their policies and actions to also address rural wage earners' concerns, including those of women workers. From 1994 onwards, employers' and workers' representatives of the fruit industry have met annually to negotiate economic and social guidelines related to labour issues (remuneration, health and accident risks, breaks, etc.) which allowed for some improvement in working conditions (Souto Jr., 2013). But the difficulties encountered in negotiating the 2019 and 2020 collective agreements have shown that the process of deregulation of labour relations implemented since the 2017 national labour reform has given a new contour to labour relations in irrigated fruit farming in this region.[12]

3.4 Summing up

Although most of the region's fruit production is commercialized on the domestic market, the work relations prevailing in irrigated agriculture are conditioned by the possibility of accessing the international market. The dominance of fixed-term hiring contracts, the intensification of work, the rigid quality control and inspection, and the flexible working hours are dynamics linked to a productive logic required by international competition. In irrigated fruit growing, the precariousness of work appears to be a way of guaranteeing the patterns of capitalist accumulation in the face of high production and export costs. However, unionism is active in the sector, and has brought about improvements in the employment contracts and conditions of work, although not in a way that produces more fundamental changes.

4 Mining non-metallic minerals in the Seridó Paraibano[13]

From the 1950s to the 1960s, mining was integrated into the Sudene's development plans, and public incentives and loans began to attract companies to the mineral deposits of the Northeast. It is estimated that around 7% of FINOR's investments (a financing mechanism used by Sudene) were allocated to the mineral sector in the region between 1974 and 2000 (Brazil, 2001). In the 2000s, the demand for non-metallic minerals increased, in particular, in the construction industry,[14] but also from a variety of manufacturing industries as some minerals enter in the manufacture of steel, fertilizers, cement, pharmaceuticals, shoes, etc.

Large capitalist companies from outside the Northeast own the mining rights to exploit the most profitable mineral deposits but subcontract their rights to smaller local enterprises. In the Northeast, mining activities are undertaken by small enterprises that extract between 10,000 and 100,000 ton a year of minerals. They are small enterprises with limited financial capital that operate at a low technological level (Vasconcelos, 2006).

4.1 Mining is a segmented and pyramidal production process

Local enterprises buy ore from prospectors (*garimpeiros*) and process it to improve its quality and sell it with higher added value. In Paraíba the number of non-metallic mineral enterprises has steadily increased. There were 27 establishments in 1988, 56 in 1998, 88 in 2008 and 100 in 2018. About 60% of those enterprises had less than 20 formal employees in 1988, and the proportion had increased to about 80% in 2018 (data from RAIS). Most entrepreneurs invest in excavator machines for opening prospecting sites, but ore extraction is carried out by informal workers in association with formal workers specialized in operating machinery, detonating explosives, transport and other types of services that support the extraction process.

So, a mix of informal and formal actors intervene at different stages of the production process. In 2010, it was estimated that about 65% of the category "non-metallic mining workers" were informal in the Northeast and 45% in Brazil as a whole. Informality was higher in Paraíba (73%) (IBGE, 2010 Census). In the Northeast about half of formal workers are skilled workers while informal workers are mostly engaged manually in the extraction phase (Nóbrega, 2019).

Garimpeiros are informal own account workers. They are remunerated either per day of work or by quantity of ore extracted (e.g. by lorry load) and they do not have access to social security. Work is intense and dangerous; they work either underground or in open-air mining and extract the ore manually. Most live in urban areas and travel to and from work in the trucks that carry the ore, or on their own motorcycles.

Between 2005 and 2012, with the help of the state government seven cooperatives of *garimpeiros* were created. At the time of their creation, they had a total of 344 members. However, by 2017 the membership had dropped by 25%. Cooperatives hold very few mining rights, which explains the decrease of members.

Middlemen are the link between *garimpeiros* and local processing enterprises (Vasconcelos, 2006). They mobilize the manual workforce, negotiate authorization to enter the land, etc. Some middlemen are formal employees of mineral processing enterprises, others are independent middlemen who have obtained an exploitation licence over an area. They exercise control over the workers. Some of these middlemen are exclusive suppliers for a particular enterprise and others look for opportunities to sell the ore at the best price.

Local enterprises have different arrangements. Some local enterprises have a mining licence and authorize *garimpeiros* to extract in the area covered by their licence on condition of buying all their production. Some enterprises do not have any licence but negotiate directly with *garimpeiros* from cooperatives to buy their production at the lowest price. Another group of enterprises, with or without mining licence, buys ore from middlemen without being involved in the organization of the miners and extraction work.

As for skilled formal workers, there are three types of specialization or skill: a first group is concerned with geological surveys and extraction planning; a second group is concerned with the extraction phase itself; and the third is concerned with the improvement of the ore. In the Northeast, the proportion of skilled occupations in total non-metallic mining formal jobs has fluctuated around 50% between 1997 and 2018, but in Paraíba it has steadily decreased, from a very high level when almost all formal employment was skilled in 1997 down to one third in 2018. The common entrepreneurial discourse is that it is not economically viable to invest in heavy machinery and hire personnel for the extraction stage. It is more profitable to buy raw material from *garimpeiros* or middlemen and focus on the processing stage to sell minerals with higher added value.[15]

4.2 Summing up

Mining rights are fundamental in structuring the relations of production and labour use in the sector. The segmentation of the production process generates a system of dependence that allows control of both the workforce and the work process. Formal and informal labour statuses are found in different stages of the production process and precariousness and informality predominate at the extraction stage. The degree of informality is higher in the Northeast than in Brazil as a whole. The importance of mining in Paraíba is less related to the volume of extracted ore, and the size of the enterprises concerned, and more to the ability of local mineral processing enterprises to participate in regional, national and international production chains.

5 The garment pole of the Agreste region of Pernambuco[16]

This production pole is a network of micro, small and medium enterprises engaged in the production of garments and their sale at popular prices, located in a cluster of municipalities in the Agreste region of Pernambuco.[17] The activity originated in 1940–1950 as a system of informal artisanal production sold in local fairs.[18] Since the 1980s it has modernized and expanded on an industrial scale while still maintaining and reproducing earlier production features. The constant imbrication between the new and the traditional, and the formal and the informal, characterizes the complexity of this clothing cluster. Manufacturing and commercial units are articulated within an intricate network of interdependence and hierarchical exchanges.

5.1 Manufacturing

It was estimated that over 225 million pieces of garments were manufactured in 2019, representing a turnover of approximately 6 billion Reais and employing around 250,000 persons (ADEPE, 2019).

Within this production system, which is both hierarchical and horizontal, cooperation and competition coexist between home-based productive units, permeated by bonds of trust and proximity, but also by the logic of mercantile exchanges, mobilizing and exchanging positions, sometimes for suppliers, sometimes for customers.

The structure of manufacturing

Facções

These are informal workshops to which *fabricos* and *fábricas* subcontract specific tasks of the production process. Home-based units, they need little initial capital (sewing machines) and working capital (to cover only maintenance costs such as payment of labour, electricity, water, etc.).

Fabricos

Fabricos may carry out all stages or just part of the production of garments, initially on a semi-industrial scale. There is intensive use of the workforce and low integration of advanced technology. The owners are responsible for the purchase of raw materials and for marketing their product. They assume the risks and control over the gains of the business. They may operate informally or formally, through direct contracts or subcontracting to *facções*.

Fábricas

In the 1980s factories with legal registration (*Cadastro Nacional da Pessoa Jurídica* – CNPJ) started to emerge. They hire workers with formal contracts and use modern technology, but they also outsource/subcontract work to informal units (*facções*) and hire informal workers when they need to temporarily increase their labour force.

***Processing laundries* (for the manufacture of denim pieces)**

These add value to manufactured items through washing, bleaching, softening, dyeing, and the application of manual effects on different types of wear. They are service providers to *fabricos* and *fábricas*.

According to the 2010 Census, 70% of the workers engaged in the clothing sector of the Pernambuco Pole were informal, and 80% of those informal workers were engaged in manufacturing. There has been a tendency towards formalization among both enterprises and workers. Between 1994 and 2018, the number of formal manufacturing units jumped from 73 to 1,406[19] and the number of formal workers employed in textiles/garments jumped from 1,103 to 13,166. The breakdown of formal enterprises by size shows that the vast majority are micro-enterprises and that there are no large industrial plants: micro-enterprises (up to 19 workers) represented 87.6% of the manufacturing units, small enterprises (from 20 to 99 workers) 11.9% and medium size enterprises (from 100 to 499 workers) 0.5%.

Labour status. Self-employment is found in both *facções* and *fabricos*. Workers without a formal contract are distributed over all production units, whether formal or informal. Wage workers with a formal contract are more frequently found in *fábricas* and laundries. However, in the region, a formal contract does not prevent the employer from circumventing the labour legislation. Another point to emphasize is the use of fixed-term and temporary contracts to meet peak demands for labour (Pereira, 2018). The less protected segments of the workforce are found in *facções*.

Facções recruit workers through informal kinship and proximity networks. *Fabricos*, *fábricas* and processing laundries recruit their workforce by means of notices posted on the doors of the units, announcements in the local radio stations and social networks. There is a large presence of female workers, mainly seamstresses and sewing assistants. In most cases, the way to enter the local job market has been through subcontracting. There is no educational requirement for seamstresses, but a tacit "know-how" is required which is usually acquired within the family environment. Some cases of formal training have been reported in *fábricas*. SENAI, IFPE, ETE also provide training through vocational schools. Specialized knowledge is required to fill a few technical, supervisory and strategic positions in small and medium-sized enterprises and in the processing laundries.

Working time. The standard working week is 44 hours for salaried workers with or without a formal contract. But overtime is frequent in the months preceding the June and Christmas festivities, and the longest working days are found mainly in the *facções*, reaching 12 hours a day (Zanatta, 2016; Pereira, 2018; Freire, 2019).

Remuneration. In legally constituted units, the wage is based on the collective agreement for each category of workers. In 2018, more than 80% of the workers employed in the textile/garment segments of *fábricas* were paid between 1.0 and 1.5 minimum wages (source: RAIS). These remunerations apply to seamstresses in *fábricas*, as well as to washers, ironers and dyers in the processing laundries. In addition, seamstresses receive bonuses for productivity, and ironers and dyers receive a bonus for unhealthy working conditions. In *facções* and *fabricos*, work is paid on a piece-rate base. Remuneration is unstable and variable, with a wider range in cutting and sewing and smaller in the finishing phase of a garment. Many workers "prefer" to work without a formal contract to earn higher pay. For tasks subcontracted to *facções*, workers are paid weekly or fortnightly as contractors are paid at the time of order or delivery.

Safety and health. Unfavourable environmental conditions (poor light, excess noise and heat, inadequate organization of the workstations), monotonous and repetitive tasks, and physical and mental stress are frequently reported, especially in *facções*. In processing laundries, workers are also exposed to toxic chemicals. In the best structured *fábricas* and laundries, personal protective equipment is provided, and their use is controlled by supervisors. Conflicts regarding the work environment are frequent and the workforce turnover high (Freire, 2019).

5.2 Commercialization of garments

The manufacture of garments and their commercialization are closely linked and several types of commercial outlets function side by side. In an attempt to modernize the commercialization of garments three large commercial centres were built in the area of the Pernambuco Garment Pole, in the main producing cities, with both public and private investment, in order to replace the popular clothing fairs in the region. Informal traders from the traditional fairs had to adapt to a new institutional framework, new rules and new management procedures. But this led to contradictory processes: the more attempts were made to institutionalize, formalize and regulate work, the more informality resisted, metamorphosed itself and even generated more precarious working conditions (Braga, 2014, 2019).

5.3 Summing up

The labour market of the Pernambuco Garment Pole continues to be dominated by informality though formalization has made some progress. Manufacturing and commercial enterprises, mostly micro and small scale, are increasingly integrated into regional and national circuits. Kinship relationships dominate business regardless of the size or the legal status of enterprises. In the first decade of the twenty-first century, the garment sector acquired some modern features more closely linked to capitalist dynamics, which created some differentiation within production and also trade. But the ongoing "modernization" process is deeply permeated by traditional elements, which results in the configuration of a formal/informal hybrid and symbiotic model.

6 Footwear production in Campina Grande, Paraíba[20]

In 2018, Brazil produced 944 million pairs of shoes, of which more than half (53%) were manufactured in the Northeast of the country (Abicalçados,

2019).[21] Historically, the Brazilian footwear industry had been more concentrated in the South and Southeast regions, but after the 1990s, it expanded to the Northeast when companies adopted a strategy of relocation to benefit from lower taxes and lower wages (Navarro and Prazeres, 2010). This case study presents the features of the footwear industry in the micro-region of Campina Grande, in the state of Paraíba, where an old artisanal tradition of shoemaking linked to the local leather industry had flourished in the past.[22]

6.1 The structure of production

In 2006, in the Campina Grande micro-region there were 58 formally registered shoemaking enterprises; their number reached 87 in 2012 but came down to 50 in 2019 due to the economic recession (data from RAIS). In 2018, three quarters of the units were micro-enterprises employing less than 20 workers, 18% were small enterprises employing between 20 and 99 workers, and the remaining units consisted of one medium size enterprise and two large companies: Alpargatas SA with around 8,000 employees, and Tess with approximately 1,400 employees (Abicalçados, 2019).

According to the 2010 Census, 85% of workers in the shoemaking sector of the state of Paraíba were in formal employment, 10% were informal workers, 4% were self-employed, and 0.6% were employers. The distribution of labour statuses depends on the type and size of the production units. In the Campina Grande region, dominated by the large Alpargatas firm, 90% of the workers were formal. In contrast, in the region of Patos where micro and small production units dominate, one third of the workers were formal and two-thirds informal.

6.2 Large-scale production at Alpargatas SA

The São Paulo-based company *Alpargatas SA* is a corporation with national capital and the characteristics of a multinational (Ferreira, 2018). The Campina Grande factory has become the main manufacturing unit of the company's famous *havaiana* sandals (but R&D and management are concentrated in São Paulo). It functions 24 hours a day in three shifts from Monday to Saturday. Sunday is a non-working day. The company outsources some services in the fields of training, factory safety, cleaning, restaurant, shipping, machine repairs, etc.

The production process includes the transformation of raw material (rubber, kaolin/carbonate, pigment and chemical additives), the moulding of the soles, and the finishing and packaging of sandals. It requires workers with physical strength, technical abilities, concentration and skills. In 2019, the workforce was overwhelmingly made up of young men, women representing only 6.3% of all workers (their highest share was 13.8% in 2011). On the shopfloor women worked in the finishing stage of the production process. In the administrative sections of the enterprise, women were more present in activities that required greater qualifications. The management expressed its intention to recruit more women in the production line in the future.

Some production stages are organized on a Taylorist/Fordist model but for other stages workers perform multiple functions and are organized in teams. Production targets are established for each type of product in terms of both volume and time. In 2019, during a visit to the factory, it was observed that around 624,000 sandals were produced in a day.[23]

Work is intense, tasks are repetitive and the work environment not easy: noise level of machines is very high, men are exposed to high temperatures, steam and toxic chemicals, there is a strong smell of melted rubber and paint. Although workers have a 10-minute break in each shift to perform physical exercises at their workstation, and every hour the tasks are rotated within a team, physical, mental and auditory wear and tear is widespread. Every month, there is a staff turnover of 100–150 employees. At recruitment, workers are given some training to check their skills and the type of tasks they are best suited to. If the evaluation is not satisfactory, they are not hired.

The wages of shopfloor workers varied between 1,000 and 2,000 reais (between one and two minimum wages).[24] Workers praised the social benefits that the company offered to their employees: a health plan and also leisure activities that included workers' family members. Regarding union organization, it was reported that workers who had been involved in strikes or demonstrations had been dismissed.

6.3 The Bodocongó Footwear Pole

Located in Campina Grande, the Bodocongó Footwear Pole is a cluster of micro and small enterprises created in 2007 with the support of the state government, the Brazilian service of assistance to micro and small enterprises (Sebrae) and the Leather and Footwear Technology Centre. The state government provided the land and the factory buildings.[25]

The profile of workers was mixed. Some had acquired their knowledge of the trade in their childhood within their family and others had acquired a professional training through SENAI courses. For most, footwear manufacturing had been their first job. Some had left and tried their hand at other informal activities but returned to shoemaking later. A few had worked in large companies in the footwear sector, such as Alpargatas SA and Tess, for a while.

The enterprises used low technology, often old machines, and in some units the production was artisanal, and the shoes handcrafted. Workers took on multiple functions. It was common to work overtime, depending on demand. To supplement their income some workers carried out some work at night, at home, and involved family members. To reduce costs, some enterprises outsourced, formally or informally, some stages of the production process. However, there were cases of better qualified workers from outside being contracted temporarily to perform a specific task within an enterprise.

Working conditions varied widely among the enterprises of the Bodocongó Pole. Logistics planning regarding the storage of materials, the stockage of products and the distribution of space on the shopfloor was deficient. In general, health and safety protection was poor and the risk of accident not negligible. Some workers were wearing protective equipment, but many were not.

Among the workers who were interviewed for the study, 55% were earning between one and two minimum wages per month, 32% were receiving the minimum wage and the remaining 13% earned more than two minimum wages.

6.4 Summing up

The footwear sector of Campina Grande showed the coexistence of two production systems: a large-scale production model (Alpargatas), with professional managers and the decision-making located in São Paulo, and a local, small-scale production model with family management. Large factories demanded a 'new' type of worker, more qualified, with ability to work in teams, and disconnected from trade unions and collective action. The intensification of the work tempo to meet production targets and a difficult physical working environment characterized both models. The most adverse situations in terms of labour conditions were found in the micro and small companies.

The two systems operate in different markets. Alpargatas sells to national and international markets, and the micro and small companies of the Bodocongó Pole sell to local and regional markets.

7 Shipbuilding in Suape Industrial Port Complex[26]

Over the last century Brazilian shipbuilding went through ups and downs, and suffered an almost total dismantling in the 1990s. But the discovery of oil reserves in the territorial waters of the country, associated with the developmental policies of the Lula and Dilma governments, opened up the possibility of offshore exploration and the revitalization of the industry. The construction of ships requires specific infrastructure in seaports and logistics for transporting raw materials. The Suape Industrial Port Complex, in Pernambuco, created in 1978, was chosen as one of the locations for this revitalization process and became the largest public port of the Northeast region. This case study focusses on shipbuilding in Suape.

Two shipyards were located in Suape: The *Estaleiro Atlantico Sul*, inaugurated in 2008 (with a portfolio of 22 oil tankers), and the *Vard Promar* shipyard, which started operations in 2013 (with a portfolio of eight gas carriers). Both shipyards were private companies linked to national and international conglomerates.[27] They did not develop their own shipbuilding technology, but focussed on assembly. Their sole client was Transpetro, a fuel transportation subsidiary of Petrobras, the state-owned Brazilian company for the exploration, extraction, refining, transport and sale of oil.

7.1 Employment in the Suape shipyards

A shipyard recruits its workforce on the basis of its order book and creates employment for large contingents of workers. The Suape shipbuilding hub recruited several thousand workers locally and also employed some migrant workers from other Brazilian states, especially in leadership and management positions, and some skilled workers with experience in the Japanese shipbuilding industry (*dekasegi*) (Pereira, 2019).

The *Estaleiro Atlantico Sul* (EAS) started to recruit in 2008 and its workforce reached a peak in 2013. Local workers were mostly unskilled and semi-skilled men. EAS was the only shipyard that hired some women in the production line. Initially, in 2008, women represented 18% of the workforce, but their proportion went down to 9% in 2013 and to 7% in 2018 (Figure 4.2).

Most workers had completed high school (the proportion increased from 69% to 82% between 2008 and 2018). However, for the shipyard managers qualifications were not just a question of schooling; they emphasized that the lack of technical skill and experience of the local workforce have been obstacles to high productivity. In the region, technical and vocational training started to be offered only after industries arrived in the Suape Complex (Pereira, 2019).

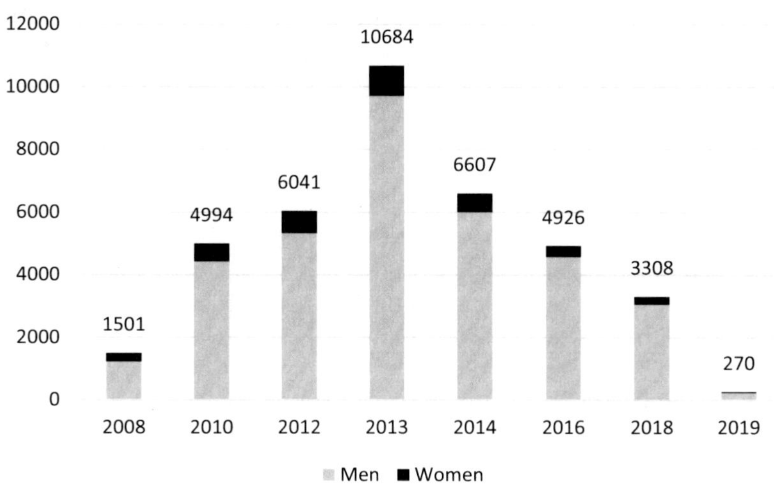

Figure 4.2 Formal employment in Suape shipyards.
Source: Based on Pereira et al. (2022), Graph 2.

In hiring new staff, recommendations from *in-situ* workers were frequently privileged over professional recruitment methods. Field interviews suggested that 60% of workers had been recruited on a close relative's recommendation and that 40% of the women interviewed had been instrumental in the recruitment of a relative or friend (Cardozo, 2020). For Moraes (2015), hiring family or friends of staff members was not a disinterested measure. A debt of gratitude and loyalty defined the workers' bonds with the company and led to greater tolerance of exploitation.

Over the years, the proportion of younger workers has fallen and that of older age groups increased (Cardozo, 2020). This evolution could be considered normal in enterprises where employment relations are stable. But both Pereira (2019) and Rodrigues (2020) discarded this hypothesis given the high turnover in the national and local labour markets. The evolution of the workers' age profile and the level of women's employment in the Suape naval hub between 2008 and 2018 reveals that, in a context of decline and crisis after 2014, women and young people were the most affected by lay-offs.

Wage levels were higher than those practised in the local labour market. In 2013, 22% of workers earned between two and three minimum wages; 15% earned between three and four minimum wages; 13% earned between four and five minimum wages; and 15% received between five and seven minimum wages. Among welders, the occupation that employed most workers, 38% received between two and three minimum wages.

Other material benefits and symbols linked to a formal contract contributed to the standard of living of shipyard workers (meal allowance, health plan, transport, etc.). So these workers had an ambivalent assessment of their position. On the one hand, they had some awareness of the exploitative conditions in their jobs. On the other hand, they had the satisfaction of wearing the shipyard uniform, were identified as a shipyard employee in the streets and had easy credit in local shops, which demonstrated the status of the shipbuilding industry employees within their community and circle of acquaintances (Pereira, 2019; Cardozo, 2020).

7.2 Industrial conflicts

A first strike was organized in 2008. Much of the day-to-day work was carried out in confined spaces and at great heights, factors that the labour legislation itself considered of high risk to the health and life of workers. Workers complained of the lack of personal protective equipment; the non-payment of bonuses for unhealthy work; shift of function (e.g. displacing welders towards cleaning tasks); the quality of the food; the state of the transport buses; harassment on the part of managers; and relationship with supervisors. There was also the complaint that the value of wages paid by EAS was below the salary floor of the metallurgical category in Pernambuco.[28] The strike ended after three days. Forty-eight workers were fired for actively participating in the movement and for forming a representation commission

(Rodrigues, 2020). A new strike was organized in 2011. The claims were very similar to those of 2008. At the end of the strike, salaries were increased by 10% and the management promised to resolve other issues (Queiroz, 2014; Rodrigues, 2020). But the conflict revealed mismatches between strikers' actions and the statements of union leaders. The legitimacy of Sindmetal-PE to represent Suape shipyard workers was questioned and led to the election of a group of dissident trade-unionists in 2014 (Rodrigues, 2020).

7.3 Decline of the Suape shipyards

In the case of EAS, two specific factors precipitated the decline. A first factor was the "Car Wash Operation" (*Operação Lava Jato*) initiated in 2014 to investigate corruption cases involving Petrobras managers, politicians and businessmen (Avritzer, 2019) (see Chapter 2). The impact of this operation was felt by the Suape shipyards due to the cancellation of Transpetro orders. A second factor was the neo-liberal turn in state policy after 2016. The National Petroleum Agency lowered the level of local content requirement in inputs to shipbuilding. Unable to compete with Asian prices and without orders, EAS made its last delivery of a vessel in June 2019. Without any orders, the company went into legal redress proceedings. Workers were massively laid off but a small group of workers was kept, only for work on ship repair. Some laid-off workers could find alternative employment in other enterprises of the Suape Complex, others became unemployed or took up informal work.

7.4 Summing up

The arrival of shipyards in Suape widened formal employment opportunities in a region where, in the past, a major part of the labour market was characterized by low skills, informality and precariousness. They offered new access to formal employment, work stability and the security of a regular income, to some segments of the population (Silva, 2017; Pereira, 2019). But shipbuilding is dependent on orders. The 2015 economic crisis and the political instability adversely impacted shipyards which had been deeply dependent on public protection and incentive measures. When those disappeared shipbuilding in Pernambuco became economically unsustainable.

8 The construction sector in Brazil and the Northeast[29]

The Growth Acceleration Programme (*Programa de Aceleração do Crescimento* – PAC), launched in 2007, established itself as the main programme to develop the construction sector through the expansion of social, urban, logistical and energy infrastructures (see Chapter 2). In the Northeast region it promoted, in particular, the construction of the Transnordestina Railway, the Transposition of the São Francisco River, the improvement of the main highway through the region, the BR 101, the construction/repair of several stadiums for the 2014 World Cup, the construction of a refinery and a petrochemical plant in Suape, and other works. In the wake of the PAC, the public programme *Minha Casa Minha Vida* ("My house, my life"), launched in 2009 to promote house ownership among low-income households, also led to an expansion of construction activities.

Over the period from 2007 to 2016, the construction sector was responsible for about 7% to 8% of total employment in the country.[30] The peak of employment in the sector was reached in 2013 with 2,773,953 workers for Brazil as a whole and 642,530 for the Northeast (IBGE, *Pesquisa Anual da Industria da Construction, 2007–2018*).

In 2017, in the Northeast, the construction of houses and buildings accounted for 53% of the construction sector's formal employment (41% in Brazil as a whole), infrastructure works 25% (29% in Brazil), and specialized services 22% (31% in Brazil) (Source: RAIS, 2017).

8.1 Structure of the enterprises in the construction sector

The number of enterprises in the construction sector more than doubled over the period 2007–2017, from 52,870 to 126,316 units,[31] due to the increase in investment but also the expansion of subcontracting to micro-enterprises. Over the period, 60% of the enterprises fell in the category employing up to four workers in both Brazil and the Northeast. In the Northeast, 3.2% of companies were employing more than 100 workers in 2007. The proportion increased to 3.8% in 2012 but dropped to 1.9% in 2017, no doubt affected by the economic crisis but also by the action of the *Lava Jato* investigation, which directly affected big construction companies such as Odebrecht.[32]

8.2 Employment conditions in the construction sector

The sector, which predominantly employs men, is characterized by extensive informality, temporary contracts, outsourcing, and high turnover (Cockell and Perticarrari, 2010; Costa, 2011). The nature of the construction process reinforces the mobility of the workforce. When work on a site is finished workers are dismissed and have to look for a new contract. Contracts "up to 6 months" are the most frequent category of formal employment; their incidence fell in the 2010s but started to rise again in 2017.

In the Northeast, about 50% of formal construction workers were in the age group 25–39 years and this proportion remained constant throughout the 2007–2017 period. The most noticeable change in the age structure was among younger workers (up to the age of 24 years) who represented 15% of formal workers in 2007; their participation increased to 18% in 2011 but dropped to 11% in 2017. The construction sector used to be a gateway for young workers looking for their first formal job, but the sector has shown signs of absorbing fewer young people and fewer people without experience.

Table 4.1 Distribution of formal construction workers over earning categories (minimum wages): Minimum-maximum shares over 2007–2017

	Up to 1 MW	*From 1 to 2 MW*	*From 2 to 4 MW*	*Over 4 MW*
Brazil	2.9%–3.5%	50.9%–55.9%	29.8%–34.5%	9.1%–12.2%
Northeast	4.7%–6.1%	63.1%–67.7%	18.6%–23.3%	6.3%–8.6%

Source: RAIS, 2007–2017.

The situation seemed worse in the Northeast. In 2010, 8.6% of formal construction workers were in their first job in the Northeast and 6% in Brazil, but by 2017 the incidence had dropped to 2.5% for both.

The construction industry covers several functions and skill levels. Table 4.1 presents the distribution of formal construction workers over ranges of earnings for the period 2007–2017 in both Brazil and the Northeast. It shows clearly that the incidence of lower earnings was significantly higher in the Northeast than in Brazil as a whole, and by the same token the reverse was true for higher earnings. The majority of formal construction workers received between one and two minimum wages. The proportion of workers in this category was about 13 percentage points higher in the Northeast than in Brazil.

Has the purchasing power of earnings been maintained over the years? Rombaldi (2014) noted that the wage agreements signed in 2011 and 2013 between trade unions and construction companies involved in the preparation of the 2014 football World Cup provided for increases 6.3% and 3.9% above inflation. But real wages fell during the recession from 2015 onwards.

Civil construction is among the sectors with the highest risk of work accidents, in particular, among outsourced enterprises (Rombaldi, 2014; Coutinho, 2015). According to the national association of occupational medicine (ANAMT, 2020) civil construction is the sector in Brazil with the highest incidence of permanent disability, the second for deaths (second only to land transport) and the fifth for sick leaves lasting more than 15 days.

8.3 Summing up

The sector is highly fragmented, outsourcing widespread and informality high. For the majority of construction workers employment is characterized by precariousness, job instability, low wages, and a high level of accidents at work. Invariably, the indicators for the Northeast are worse than national-level indicators. Public policies during the neodevelopmentalist period from 2002 to 2014 fostered the expansion of the construction sector and the development of private companies, and labour market indicators in the sector improved. But from 2014 onwards, the sector was severely affected by the *Operação Lava Jato* and by the effects of the economic crisis, which greatly affected employment levels and working conditions in the sector, even more in the Northeast than in the rest of Brazil.

9 Information technology workers in Pernambuco[33]

In Brazil, the spread of information technology (IT) gained momentum in the 1990s. Since then, the IT sector has grown at a fast rate, and the degree of formalization of the sector and the incidence of wage work are higher than in the economy as a whole (Porcaro, 2013). This case study focusses on formal employees in establishments devoted to the development of software and related consulting activities, provision of services, and processing of data in Pernambuco.[34] Initially, data processing was undertaken by public enterprises, but the arrival of private companies completely changed the profile of the sector's workers. In 2000, the creation of *Porto Digital de Recife*, a technology park organized as a public-private partnership, was the main milestone in consolidating an Information and Communication Technology (ICT) sector in Pernambuco. Over time, the technological park moved towards a greater and more diversified presence of private and international capital (Macêdo, 2017).

9.1 The structure of ICT enterprises

The ICT sector covers diverse activities. In 2019, IT represented 29% of ICT formal employment, telecommunications represented 21%, audiovisual production 2% and call centres 48%. Employment in telecommunications and audiovisual production services was concentrated in smaller firms; IT employment was spread over a wider range of micro, small and medium size enterprises; and 75% of formal employment in call centres was in enterprises with a thousand or more employees.

Between 2007 and 2019, IT employment grew more in larger firms; the proportion of employment in enterprises with 100 or more employees jumped from 38% to 51%. Considering that there were hardly any new hires in public enterprises (which also did not change in number), this growth signals a change in the average size of private enterprises, and greater concentration. In addition, the geographic concentration of IT jobs in the Metropolitan Region of Recife was reinforced.

9.2 Characteristics of IT employment

Between 2007 and 2019, IT employment grew 115% in the Northeast, above the Brazilian average of 104%.[35] In 2007, the Northeast accounted for 7.9% of IT formal employment in Brazil; in 2019 its share had increased to 8.3%. Within the Northeast, growth of IT formal employment varied across states. In 2007, the three states with highest level of IT employment were Bahia, Pernambuco and Ceará. This was still the case in 2019, but IT employment had grown by 49% in Bahia, by 122% in Pernambuco and by 186% in Ceará. Rio Grande do Norte was the only northeastern state with a negative balance over the period (–8%) (source: RAIS).

Formal employees in IT are better educated than formal employees in the economy as a whole. Almost 70% of IT employees had been through higher education (whether complete or incomplete), compared with 27% in the economy as a whole. The presence of graduates is relatively higher in public enterprises than in private firms. In the IT sector diplomas and training certification play an important role. The main reason expressed for joining the IT sector was professional vocation and a liking for informatics/technology (62%); the second most important reason was a job opportunity (29%).

Employment in IT is predominantly male (Castro, 2013) and Pernambuco is no exception; in 2019 men accounted for 69% of IT formal employment. The legal nature of enterprises and the size of establishments affect the gender profile of the workforce. The presence of women is relatively higher in public enterprises than in private firms; and relatively higher in bigger companies.[36]

IT workers are relatively young. In 2019, 72% of IT formal workers were below the age of 39 in Pernambuco against 57% in the Northeast economy as a whole and 58% in Brazil. The workforce is younger in private enterprises than in public enterprises.

Remuneration in the IT sector is higher than average. In 2019, 68% of all formal workers in the Northeast earned no more than two minimum wages[37] (56% in Brazil), but only 28% of IT formal workers in Pernambuco were in this low earning category. In contrast, at the upper end of earnings, 41% of IT formal workers were earning above four minimum wages, compared with 13% in the Northeast as a whole (16% in Brazil). It is also worth mentioning that almost 20% of IT workers in Pernambuco were receiving more than seven minimum wages. Women were disproportionately found in the lowest earnings group. With regard to colour/race, there was a higher representation of white workers, compared with black and brown, in the highest income groups and in smaller firms.

The legal status and the size of enterprises also combine to determine important segmentations in the wage patterns of IT workers in the Metropolitan Region of Recife. Individual income was higher in public enterprises than in private enterprises. The smaller firms tend to pay the lowest wages and the larger, the highest.

The vast majority of IT employees (93%) had full-time permanent contracts. Almost 80% of IT workers worked on average 40 hours a week, 7% worked more (up to 44 hours), 8% worked around 30 hours, and 5% had a shorter working week. With respect to occupational health the two complaints most frequently highlighted were repetitive strain injuries (25%) and stress (20%). Stress appeared to be more frequent in micro and in bigger enterprises (400 or more employees).

9.3 Trade union affiliation

In 2017, a survey, coordinated by Roberto Véras in collaboration with SINDPD/PE,[38] was carried out among IT workers in the Metropolitan Region of Recife. It showed that 18% of the interviewees were members of the union that represented that occupational category (12% in private enterprises and 54% in public enterprises). There was a startling contrast between the longer-established data processing sector, dominated by state-owned enterprises, where workers were older and unions were thriving, and private companies primarily focussed on software development, which now predominate in the sector, where workers were younger and unionization levels low.

9.4 Summing up

The IT sector has a profile which is quite different from that of the economy as a whole. Since the 1990s, it has displayed a higher pace of growth, a higher proportion of white-collar salaried workers and a higher degree of formalization. IT workers are prominently younger, more educated, better paid and more male. This sector generates a socio-professional group that stands out, with university education, professional qualifications, need for permanent training, and for whom the centrality of technical knowledge defines their identity.

The share of private enterprises has increased over time. The growing presence of private companies and the spread of new companies, small, medium and large, has changed the profile of IT workers. Several factors determine earnings segmentation among IT workers: professional qualification, sex, race/colour, private versus public status of enterprises, and the size of the enterprises.

10 Call centres in Paraíba[39]

In Brazil, call centre companies started to develop in the 1990s amidst the privatization of the telecommunications sector. Large companies were set up, mostly concentrated in large cities, in the state of São Paulo. In the 2000s, a process of spatial decentralization took place and activities were outsourced to mid-sized cities and other parts of the country. The state of Paraíba was a pioneer in this process, which eventually extended to the whole Northeast region.[40] This case study draws its evidence from the cities of Campina Grande and João Pessoa. Various factors favoured the territorial dispersion of call centres: high production costs in metropolises, tax incentives and less competition from other employers in peripheral areas. In the Northeast, the availability of an educated workforce without a strong union tradition was an important additional attraction (Almeida, 2014).

10.1 Structure of enterprises and employment

The Brazilian call centre sector has been consolidated as an oligopoly, with the two largest companies employing 47% of the country's telemarketers (Bono and Leite, 2016), and more than 70% of workers employed in five large companies. But while there was spatial dispersion of operating units, control remained centralized in São Paulo. From 2003 to 2011 the number of telemarketers grew extremely fast in the Northeast but only 7% of the companies had their headquarters in the region. Until 2017, the Northeast had 246 call centres out of 1938 for Brazil as a whole, including 35 centres with more than 1,000 employees (out of 139 in Brazil). After 2015, the expansion went into reverse due to the economic crisis, the labour reform and investment in artificial intelligence technologies.

In 2005, there were around 675,000 telemarketers in Brazil (Oliveira, 2005) and in 2012, *Sintelmark*[41] suggested that their number had increased to 1.4 million workers (home workers and on-premise agents). The share of the Northeast in call centre formal employment increased from 12% in 2007 to 30% in 2017 (RAIS, 2007–2019). In Paraíba, almost all call centre employment consisted of permanent contracts, beside a few apprentice contracts. This configuration changed in 2019 with the emergence of fixed-term contracts[42] which represented 30% of the total call centre employment in Campina Grande in that year and 51% in João Pessoa.

In call centres the workforce is predominantly young and feminine (70% of all employees). In regions with a low supply of formal jobs call centres attract young people in search of their first formal job, hence the concentration of call centre workers in the 18–24 age group. In 2013, about 53% of call centre employees were from this age group in Paraíba.

In 2017, the three most frequent occupations were "Telemarketing operator" (almost 90% of the workforce), "Telemarketing supervisor" (2%–3%), and "Teleservice monitor" (1%–2%). The minimum educational requirement for a telemarketing operator used to be "complete high school" but the incidence of workers with higher education has been increasing over time, which points to an overqualified workforce. In Paraíba, the proportion of workers in call centres with complete or incomplete higher education (25% in Campina Grande and 32% in João Pessoa, in 2019) was much higher than the average for the Northeast and Brazil (around 17% in 2017).

Most call centre employees worked between 30 to 39 hours a week. The incidence of part-time work was very small, though work in the range of 21–30 hours a week had been growing recently. In 2019, in João Pessoa, less than 40% of workers had been in the job for more than two years, but in Campina Grande, where call centres have been in operation for longer, the proportion was higher (65%) and growing.

The majority of call centre workers were remunerated between 1.01 and 1.5 minimum wages. In 2017, 80% of workers in Paraíba were in this earning bracket, 72% in the Northeast and 63% in Brazil as a whole. Earnings were lower in Paraíba than the average for the Northeast, and lower in the Northeast than in Brazil as a whole. Since 2015, remuneration in call centres has fallen somewhat in relation to the national minimum wage.

Call centre work blends cutting-edge technology with Taylorist and post-Fordist forms of organization, involving low pay, and intense, highly controlled, physically and emotionally strenuous work, fraught with instances of harassment and ill health. But although work was intense and strictly regulated, workers in Paraíba considered their work environment generally good. The sector provided opportunities for young people to enter the labour market and the use of communications technology offered opportunities for the workers' personal development.

10.2 Trade union action and resistance

Trade unions found it difficult to penetrate call centres. Most workers were not unionized, among other reasons for fear of reprisals from management, notably of losing their job. However, in Paraíban call centres, varied forms of resistance emerged, both individual and collective, with and without trade union intermediation, although they have yielded few gains for workers in the face of the companies' unwillingness to accept their demands.

10.3 Summing up

The characteristics of the call centre workforce are broadly aligned with employers' expectations when shifting call centre operations to the Northeast: a young, mostly female workforce with relatively high levels of education, receiving low wages, in a very flexible work environment that facilitates employers' control. Call centres resort to management mechanisms that replicate Fordist methods used to manage labour in some industrial lines of production. So technological innovation does not necessarily change the work regime. However, call centres bring new elements by expanding formal employment opportunities for young people and women, and they do it in the Northeast, where the deficit of jobs is greater. But the call centre sector is now advancing into a new phase marked by growing investments in robotization, artificial intelligence and the proliferation of self-service applications, leaving open the question of its future expansion and its spatial dynamics.

11 Uber drivers in Rio Grande do Norte[43]

This case study discusses the terms and conditions of work of Uber drivers in the northeastern state of Rio Grande do Norte. The Uber company[44] operates a digital platform where nominally self-employed drivers and customers seeking transport connect. Passenger transport through a mobile phone app was introduced in Brazil in 2014. Currently, Uber is present in more than 500 cities in the country and has 1 million drivers/delivery partners who provide services to at least 22 million users (Uber, 2020). Uber started operating in Rio Grande do Norte in August 2016. In 2019, it was estimated that there were a little under 11,000 Uber drivers in the state and that, each day, at least 6,000 drivers obtained some work through the Uber app (Tribuna do Norte, 2019).

11.1 Uber's business model

The Uber platform is a *lean platform* which operates on a business model of minimal asset ownership (Srnicek, 2016). The drivers use their own vehicles and assume all the risks arising from the transport service. Uber determines the price a customer pays. It applies a dynamic pricing model that adjusts rates according to not only the time and distance of the ride but also to the traffic and level of the rider-to-driver demand. So, Uber defines the "rules of the game". Algorithms are programmed to encourage drivers to remain connected as long as possible to the platform. This "gamification" consists of offering a "bonus" or "score" to drivers who maintain the longest running time (Abílio, 2020). Uber makes money by charging a commission to the drivers.

This case study draws on two in-depth interviews with Uber drivers.[45]

11.2 Fernando

Fernando was 51 years old and had been an Uber driver for three years. He was a widower with three children. He had some technical qualifications in advertising and had been a publicist for 25 years. In his last job, in São Paulo, he held an executive position in a law firm that went bankrupt. Becoming an Uber driver had been a drastic change of trajectory that coincided with the deep economic recession that hit Brazil and the arrival of Uber in the labour market of Rio Grande do Norte. In face of the difficulties of reinsertion in the labour market, he had decided to register on the Uber platform. It was his only source of income.

Fernando was making a monthly net income of between 3,000 and 3,500 reais a month (3–3.5 minimum wages at that time). His biggest costs were insurances (almost 5,000 reais a year for the car and 1,600 reais for a vehicle protection association, as assaults were quite frequent). Fernando had designed a work strategy that brought him a satisfactory level of income. He worked 10–14 hours a day, four days a week (Thursday to Sunday) – that is between 50 and 60 hours a week. He worked at periods that yield higher earnings, that is to say nights and weekends. His work allowed him some autonomy – he could choose when to work and how long for. This had enabled him to register for a law training course.

Fernando perceived his current work as a "business", not as a job. His professional trajectory made him stand out among his peers. He was a leader of the local cooperative of Uber drivers[46] and had contributed to the preparation of a municipal law to regulate the app-based private transport service. He managed to convert the experience accumulated in his past professional activities into a strategy to increase income as well as to distinguish himself from his peers.

11.3 Flávio

Flávio was 40 years old, twice divorced and father of a teenager. At the age of 15 he enrolled in a college of civil engineering but dropped out. Recently he resumed studying and was taking some technical courses. Before becoming an Uber driver, he had been employed in a succession of low-level formal jobs. His last job was administrative assistant in Queiroz Galvão, a construction company. He was laid off due to the economic crisis. For about six months he rented a taxi from a colleague and worked as taxi driver. He was working 12–16 hours a day and was earning on average 150 reais a day. When Uber started to operate in Rio Grande do Norte, he bought a car with his accumulated savings and began to work as an Uber driver. It was his only source of income.

Flávio worked between 10 and 12 hours a day from Monday to Saturday. He set himself a daily goal of 100–150 reais net (excluding fuel expenses) and was making between 2,000 and 2,500 reais a month (2–2.5 minimum wages). At the beginning, he could reach that goal working a stretch of eight hours, but earnings had been decreasing as the number of registered drivers increased.

Regarding his Uber activity, Flávio had several complaints: the insecurity at work, the price of car insurance and the level of fuel taxes. Nevertheless, he had declined to return to formal employment when the Queiroz Galvão enterprise invited him to return. On the one hand, the job would have interfered with his new studies, and, on the other, it would have yielded less earnings than his Uber activity. He appreciated that an Uber driver remained his own boss despite more accountability and responsibility. Flávio calculated how much time and days he had to work to achieve the income needed to meet his "basic needs".

11.4 Summing up

Uber has fixed new rules for the functioning of the passenger transport market. The self-employed Uber drivers assume all the risks of the service performed. The work flexibility, the lack of social protection and the long working hours are treated as challenges to be overcome individually and Uber drivers adopt different survival and adaptation strategies. As long he/she has a car, an Uber driver can earn above the average wage prevalent in the state. The relative autonomy and flexibility in the driver's work schedule seems attractive to many drivers as it enables them to pursue some studies or other activities. But their autonomy remains constrained by the platform's operating logic.

In Brazil, Uber was introduced in a context of deep economic crisis. It offered an alternative to unemployment, but there are two major caveats. The first caveat, inherent to the dynamic pricing system, is that as more drivers join the platform, the level of remuneration tends to decrease. The second refers to the fact that the costs of the activity are supported exclusively by the drivers. Any inflationary pressure on the price of fuel (as at the time of writing with the Russian-Ukrainian war), on the cost of insurance and car maintenance has a negative impact on the drivers' earnings.

Finally, the individualization of work strategies weakens the possibility of collective action to improve working conditions.[47]

12 The Automotive Pole of Goiana, Pernambuco[48]

The automotive pole of Goiana, in Pernambuco, comprises a Jeep factory and 16 first-line suppliers. The decision of Fiat-Chrysler Automobiles (FCA) to build a new industrial plant was the result of a clear market strategy. The aim was to meet the growing demand from Latin American and African middle-class consumers for luxury cars of the Sport Utility Vehicle (SUV) type. FCA made an initial investment of 7 billion reais of which two-thirds consisted of subsidized loans from the Brazilian federal government. The land was donated by the government of Pernambuco, and, in addition, the company benefitted from fiscal incentives. The factory was built over two and a half years, and production started in 2015.

The emergence of the automotive pole altered the structure of the local economy, adding a modern industrial pole to traditional agriculture and fishing activities.[49] The transformation of the economic structure had a profound impact on the local labour market. By 2019, the automotive pole was responsible for 74% of industrial employment in Goiana municipality and 60% of all formal jobs.

FCA's website reports that in October 2019 the pole had 9,050 employees (3,300 at Jeep; 4,900 at suppliers; and 850 indirect). 78% came from the state of Pernambuco itself, 4% from other parts of the Northeast, and the rest from other regions. The plant has a production capacity of 250,000 vehicles per annum. A total of 700 robots have been installed at the Jeep plant (650 for welding, 40 for painting and 10 for assembly). FCA says the facility has been engineered for "maximum flexibility" to be able to produce three models of vehicle simultaneously.

Men dominate the automotive workforce (around 85%). Women outnumber men only in the occupation of seat seamstresses. The age group with the largest share of workers is between 30 and 39 years old (on average 36% over the 2013–2019 period), followed by the groups 18–24 years and 25–29 years, with 27% and 26%, respectively. In 2015, the vast majority of workers (75%) had completed secondary education but, after 2016, there was an upward shift in educational qualifications. In 2019, 55% of the employees had been through higher education and 30% had completed secondary education (Rodrigues, 2020). However, the increase in education was not accompanied by a change in the average earnings.

Earnings in the Jeep factory are concentrated between one and two minimum wages among formal workers. Wages paid in Goiana are lower than those paid in the Betim factory of FCA (Minas Gerais) where the majority of workers earn above three minimum wages (see Figure 4.3). The figure also reflects differences in skill levels between the Goiana and Betim workforces, and a higher share of managerial and decision-making posts in the latter.

It must be pointed out that although significantly lower than the wages paid by the FCA group in Betim, the wages paid in the automotive pole of Goiana are slightly better than those paid in other parts of the municipality's formal labour market.

The automotive pole has absorbed a significant number of local workers but the conversion from agriculture or fishing into factory workers has not always been easy (Oliveira, 2017). Training a qualified labour force has been a concern. A partnership between FCA and eight educational institutions in Pernambuco and Paraíba, signed in 2014, has been the springboard for the emergence of the Automotive Knowledge Hub. SENAI has participated actively in the training of professionals for employment in the Jeep factory and its suppliers.

FCA has been successful in generating local formal employment and most workers show great pride in being part of FCA. This is one reason why the

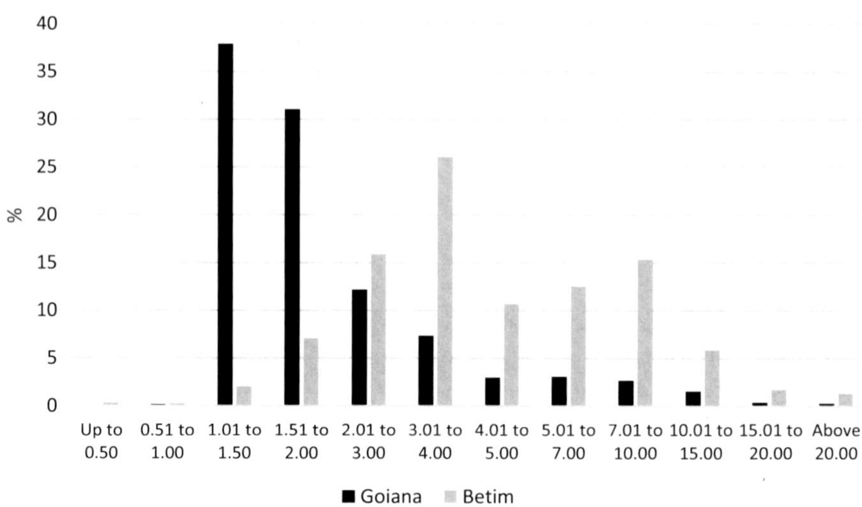

Figure 4.3 Distribution of wages in FCA automotive factories in Goiana and Betim, 2018 (in multiples of the minimum wage).

Source: Based on RAIS data presented in Rodrigues (2020), Table 8.

Metalworkers' Union of Pernambuco (Sindmetal) has had great difficulty to recruit affiliates and be present on the shopfloor. But according to union leaders, the very low level of unionization of workers reflects the company's anti-union strategy (Rodrigues, 2020), and they accuse Jeep management of persecuting and firing workers who approach Sindmetal.

12.1 Summing up

The Automotive Pole of Goiana has brought significant transformations into the local economic environment. The growth in the share of manufacturing industry allowed Goiana to go unscathed through the crisis that devastated the country in 2015 and 2016. Formal employment expanded even in the worst moments of the country's recession. One reason for this performance is that the implantation of the automobile company in Goiana also reverberated in the service sector. However, the earnings in the Jeep factory are only slightly higher than the average wages in the municipality as a whole and therefore the low purchasing power of the population is considered an obstacle to a wider spread of development.

13 A synthetic view of the Northeast production system

The above case studies have shown that the productive structure and the patterns of labour use varied greatly across economic sectors. The wide variety of production arrangements gives rise to heterogeneity in the levels and conditions of employment. The importance of structural heterogeneity in Latin American economies has been widely recognized and been reflected, for instance, in the work of ECLAC, and in dualistic models of development built around notions of formality and informality, or distinguishing capitalist and non-capitalist production (Chapter 1). But dualism fails to capture the complexity of the production system. Different types of production arrangements function side by side and are interconnected. The following axes of differentiation are relevant for the labour regime:

- i *The form of organization of the enterprise or production unit.* We can distinguish capitalist firms, in the sense of profit-seeking enterprises organized around the accumulation of capital and use of hired labour; household or individual production units, varying from marginal self-employment to substantial family firms; cooperatives and community enterprises of various types, built on principles of sharing and solidarity; and public sector activities (which may include some commodity production in public sector enterprises but also extends to education, health and administration). The borders between these categories may be quite soft; for instance, large family firms may operate much like capitalist enterprises.
- ii *Capital intensity and technological level.* There may be a detailed division of labour around the operation of machines, and a mechanized

production line; or production may require only simple tools and the application of specific skills; with many intermediate variants. New communications technologies also modify the labour regime, for instance when work is managed through an impersonal internet-based platform economy. These differences in the technological nature of the production process generate a wide variety of employment relationships.

iii *The integration or disaggregation of the production process.* Some enterprises are autonomous producers, connected with suppliers and clients only through the market. But many form part of a production chain or network, in which each enterprise provides only one element. This may take the form of a dominant firm outsourcing work to external suppliers, or there may be a network of producers who share resources and distribution systems.

iv *The type of product.* This also has a direct influence on the labour regime. Service activities often involve personal interaction between worker and client. Some types of production of goods connect workers directly with the outcome of their work, especially in small scale and artisanal systems; but repetitive operations within a detailed division of labour may distance them from the final product and increase alienation.

v *Consumer market profile.* Another differentiating factor of production systems refers to the markets the products and services are intended for: local, regional, national or international. In the case of consumer goods, the consumers' levels of income and consumption patterns will determine the nature of demands and quality requirements.

Without trying to be exhaustive, the following are important components of the production system in the Northeast:

a *Large, capital-intensive factories organized along Taylorist or Toyotist lines*, built around intensive and closely controlled formal employment, including some skilled work; frequently using suppliers and services which may use a similar model, though often with inferior working conditions. These are illustrated in our case studies by the FCA Jeep factory in Goiana, the shipyards in the industrial zone of Suape, and the production of havaianas at Alpargatas in Campina Grande. There are many other such enterprises in the region producing textiles, beverages, food products, medical supplies and other goods. One important characteristic is that capital mainly comes from outside the Northeast, and decision-making and research and development activities remain outside the region.

b *Capitalist firms which employ a core of formal workers but also make extensive use of informal or indirect employment.* The construction sector provides the clearest example among our case studies, where large firms may hire temporary casual workers, or use a network of informal suppliers instead of hiring wage workers, especially for particular building skills. Some manufacturing firms follow a similar model (part of the shoe production sector, for instance). Plantation agriculture (sugar and fruit production in our case studies) depends on a substantial seasonal workforce alongside a permanent core of workers. The same is true of some activities in the tourism sector, which is also seasonal.

c *Small and medium firms, often family owned, operating in production networks (sometimes outsourced from large firms) employing both formal and informal workers.* The most prominent example in our case studies is the garment pole in the Agreste region of Pernambuco, where there is a division of labour in the preparation of garments among networks of small firms, which take advantage of shared marketing arrangements and a local labour force with skills learned on the job. There are also larger firms which provide specialized services, such as the laundries that dye and process denim garments. A wide variety of employment relations and labour statuses are found in the different production operations concerned.

d *Workers and small enterprises supplying inputs to larger systems of production and distribution.* This can involve individual self-employed workers operating under subcontract as well as commission workers and agents. In our case studies the small-scale mining sector, where there are many individual *garimpeiros*, provides an example. It differs from the previous case (garment pole) in that the organization is vertical rather than horizontal, and individual workers are dependent on middlemen or larger firms.

e *Modern service operations using information technologies.* This is a diverse group which includes call centres and software production and extends to business and banking services. There are economies of scale, which tends to lead to fairly large capitalist enterprises dominating the market, with a local monopoly or oligopoly, but there can be specialized small enterprises too. Employment is polarized. Typically, within the workforce there is a small group of technical and white-collar workers, responsible for development and management, along with many low- to medium-skilled workers. Two examples in our case studies are information technology in Pernambuco and call centres in Paraíba. Another type of modern services is provided through the growing platform economy, including transport and delivery services. The labour force involved is notionally self-employed but in practice dependent on the allocation of work online through an app, managed by a central enterprise, and subject to controls on working hours and remuneration. In our case studies this type of activity is represented by a study of Uber taxi services in Rio Grande do Norte.

f *Firms providing private education and health services.* These are built around a skilled workforce (doctors, nurses, teachers, managers), who may be either wage workers or self-employed, supported by a low-skill but regular work force. Some enterprises are quite capital-intensive, and technologically advanced (e.g. in the health sector). There may be a chain of outsourced low-cost suppliers of ancillary services and other inputs.

g *Formal enterprises engaged in trade and commerce – commercial centres, shops, wholesalers, transport firms, hotels and restaurants, garages, etc.* This category includes both household enterprises and large capitalist operations. It provides employment for many low-skilled but regular workers as shop assistants, drivers, cooks, waiters, security guards and so on. We do not have examples in our case studies, but it accounts for a substantial part of the labour market. Larger firms in this category may operate like category (b) above (for example, in the case of large retail and wholesale commercial networks).

h *Public sector administration, police and public services.* Much of this consists of regular civil servants, with secure employment and above-average incomes, but there is also a substantial component of temporary and informal public sector employment (in this case mainly in the areas of health, education and public administration, in the municipal sphere). Public sector enterprises (such as public utilities) might be considered a separate category. In some the employment status is much like regular civil servants, but others may function as a somewhat more bureaucratic version of the private enterprises in the first category above. The same is true of public education and health services.

i *Informal work in trade and personal services.* This is mixed category, including domestic service, and 'marginal' street or beach work involving hawking, carrying, informal transport, personal care, scavenging and similar activities. This group of workers is vulnerable to various forms of social control and exploitation. There is also an element of criminal activities, involving drugs, prostitution and the recycling of stolen goods. At the upper end this category merges into "productive" household enterprises, and the dividing line is somewhat arbitrary (we used an income equivalent to the minimum wage as a dividing line in defining labour status in Chapter 3).

j *Small family farms.* In rural areas these often provide some subsistence production as a backup for precarious or seasonal occupations in other sectors (notably including seasonal work in large-scale agricultural enterprises and seasonal employment in civil construction). This is the case for some of the workers in our case studies of the sugarcane sector and fruit production.

k *Workers in cooperatives and in the solidarity economy.* These can be found both in the small-scale rural economy, in "marginal" activities such as waste-picking, but also in some small-scale manufacturing. The mining case study included a cooperative of *garampeiros.*

The relative importance of these components varies across the Northeast, and between regions within each state. Most of the larger, capitalist enterprises are concentrated in metropolitan regions, as is much of the formal service sector. The spatial distribution of production across the region depends on the forces driving economic development. The above case studies illustrate four modalities: (a) the State is the initial planner and financing agent, and private companies come in at the second stage when the infrastructure is in place; this is illustrated by the Petrolina/Juazeiro fruit-growing pole; (b) the State conceives and finances a project but establishes partnerships with large private companies right from the beginning, while also maintaining public enterprises, as happened in Suape; (c) the driving agent consists of one or more large private companies (generally coming from outside the region or even the country), that almost always benefit from state incentives and support, and that may or may not already have a production base in the sector, as happened with FCA in Goiania and Alpargatas in Campina Grande; (d) the production and marketing cluster results entirely or mainly from family-based activities, which support each other and are modernized over time, as happened with garment production in the Agreste of Pernambuco. Other modalities may emerge as hybrids of those four patterns.

This pattern of production leaves small municipalities of the interior of the region in dire difficulty when it comes to generating employment and income. Furthermore, deficits in basic training and professional qualifications are challenging. A study of the state of Paraíba (Carvalho and Farias, 2022) illustrates the disparities between the four mesoregions of the state. The incidence of formal employment varied, from east to west, between 57% in the coastal region of the Mata (where the state capital, João Pessoa, is located), 26% in the Agreste (where Campina Grande, the second biggest city, is located), 4% in the mesoregion of Borborema, and 12% in the semiarid Sertão in the interior. Small municipalities are in a relationship of dependence on bigger urban centres located in their mesoregions for the circulation of goods and services. Most workers are engaged in service activities, commerce and public administration. Informal microentrepreneurs and the self-employed dominate economic activities. Those municipalities are greatly dependent on public sector resources for institutional transfers through the Municipal Participation Fund (FPM), while the federal government provides resources for education and health through special funds. This concentrated and dependent pattern of development contributes to persistent spatial inequalities within the region and the states.

We do not have data that would permit us to accurately assess the contribution of each type of production unit to output and employment. But on the base of the labour status analysis of Chapter 3 and the case studies in Pernambuco and Paraíba we can say that the larger capitalist firms (categories (a) and (b)) in industry generate a significant share of output in the larger cities, but their direct share of employment is substantially less (probably less than 5% of all employment, judging by the estimates in Chapter 2). Small firms in production networks (category (c)) are of local importance, particularly because of the high levels of employment that they generate, but are relatively small contributors to regional output as a whole. Small-scale suppliers and commission workers (category (d)) are a significant category, but their contribution to overall output is also small, and much value is captured by larger enterprises. It is the service activities which are the principal contributors to both output and employment. This is a very diverse group; the public sector (category (h)) is the largest but there is a substantial presence of private enterprises, especially in modern and financial services (categories (e) and (f)). At the other extreme it also includes supply driven, low quality and low-income survival activities (category (i) and to some extent (j) and (k)) that constitute up to 20% of employment. There is a great deal of precarious self-employment and wage employment within many of these categories, as well as in the platform economy (part of category (e)).

14 Consequences for the labour regime

These different situations and arrangements form the core of the overall labour regime within the region. But this labour regime is not simply the aggregation of different labour statuses in different parts of the production system, because different sectors and activities are interrelated. Labour statuses have their own dynamics within a heterogeneous system in which formal and informal modalities of production intersect and generate a labour regime which is more than the sum of its parts.

First, enterprises and production units are directly interdependent. For instance, in the Pernambuco Garment Pole, a local production system is built on a network of enterprises of different types, with a variety of employment relationships. Large factories too depend on a local economic system which services the production process (infrastructure and transport systems for inputs and outputs and for the daily travel of workers, cleaning and catering services, security, etc.), as was noted in the case of the Alpargatas factory in Campina Grande. The enterprises concerned may hire workers under different employment relationships, often less secure or lower paid than in the central factory. A hierarchy of labour statuses is created, with corresponding differences in rights and welfare.

Second, an important aspect of interdependence derives from the incomes generated in the production process. In particular, the expenditures of workers on daily consumption and other needs may sustain a substantial local economy, involving trade, personal services and local production of consumer goods; public services including administration, policing, education and health; construction, notably through the development of infrastructure and the building of dwellings; and private finance. Regular, protected wage workers in industry are likely to purchase a variety of services in the informal economy, at a lower price than in the formal sector, and produced under labour conditions that are very different from those in the factories, with lower incomes and less social protection. Because prices in the informal economy are lower, this also reduces pressure on wages in the formal system. So, the labour regime in large formal enterprises is dependent on the parallel existence of an insecure, low-income labour regime in other parts of the economy.

We have seen that average labour earnings are lower in the Northeast than in Brazil as a whole. While this does attract investment from outside the region that aims to take advantage of wage differentials, the lower purchasing power of the local population tends to perpetuate the informal economy and be an obstacle to a wider spread of development.

The pattern of consumer demand is influenced by the overall inequality within the development regime. At low income levels, wage income will mainly be spent on local food and other daily consumption, transport, personal services and housing. Higher incomes will generate greater demands for imported consumer goods, financial services, private health and education, and domestic service. The high degree of inequality observed in the region therefore has a direct impact on the pattern of employment creation.

Third, production sectors are also interrelated through the labour market. It is true that labour markets are segmented by sex, education and other factors, which limits labour mobility, but the creation of job opportunities in one sector will nevertheless affect the supply of labour to other activities. For instance, the implantation of a large factory like the Jeep factory in Goiana draws in labour from other economic sectors, including traditional activities in agriculture and fishing, reducing the supply of labour to those activities. It also draws in migrants and commuters from outside the local area.

In fact, there is a more general interdependence through the functioning of regional labour markets. Enterprises and local production systems depend on the availability of workers with particular types of experience and qualifications. In the Pernambuco Garment Pole, for example, this is met through a constant regeneration of a pool of workers with knowledge of and appropriate skills for the sector. Another example of a regional labour market concerns seasonal workers, who may move from one sector to another within the region, such as agricultural workers who move between wage work on plantations and subsistence farms, as in sugar and fruit production, or between agricultural work and construction, so connecting agrarian systems with urban economies.

These relationships and their consequences for employment, unemployment and inequality depend not only on the different components of the production system, but also on the nature and functioning of labour institutions within the region. That includes the pattern and effectiveness of trade union activity; labour legislation and its effective application; training systems; and the social and economic institutions that govern labour market access, including mechanisms of discrimination and exclusion as well as formal employment services such as SINE. Each of the production arrangements identified above is influenced by these institutions. The routes for access to employment differ between these different production arrangements, but in all cases, they reflect a set of social institutions, which generate both inclusion and exclusion. Labour law is effective to a greater or lesser extent. Workers are organized in different ways. There are gender and race differences: women, especially black women, are less likely to be in formal wage work, and more likely to be in 'marginal' self-employment; men are more likely than women to be in productive self-employment, and black men are more likely to be in small firms or marginal self-employment. Each situation has its own institutional characteristics, which influences the quality and quantity of employment and levels of living.

Should this be characterized as a single, regional labour regime, or as a number of distinct but interrelated labour regimes in different parts of the economy? In some sense, these are just two ways of formulating the same question, for while there are distinct labour regimes in, say, the Pernambuco Garment Pole, the Jeep factory and the construction sector, they are interrelated. So, we need to conceive the labour regime at both the sectoral and regional levels.

The overall labour regime at the regional level is highly unequal. In particular, a large fraction of the working population has only a precarious, insecure insertion in the production system, and is therefore vulnerable to poverty and unemployment. It is striking how this inequality has persisted over time. Although the character of the economy has changed considerably since the 1970s, the patterns observed today still have a lot in common with the segmentations that could be seen at that time. In particular, disparities in access to employment, combined with differences in conditions of work and levels of living, seem to be endogenous to the functioning of the labour institutions. In other words, inequality is embedded in the overall labour regime, reflecting the structural heterogeneity of the production process. This unequal labour regime seems to be more stable than the overall development regime, which has gone through several incarnations. It is true that there were important advances in labour rights, in the formalization of labour relationships, in the minimum wage and in other aspects of the labour regime in the period up to 2014. But these do not seem to have changed the underlying, fundamentally unequal character of the employment system, in which different groups in the population have very different levels of access to opportunities for work and income, different levels of vulnerability and security, and different living standards.

Notes

1 These studies were published in full in Véras de Oliveira and Rodgers (2022).
2 This section is based on Eduardo Danato and Maressa Fauzia Pessoa Dantas' study "A agroindustria canaviera de Pernambuco e Paraíba" in Véras de Oliveira and Rodgers (2022).
3 In 2019/2020 Brazil produced 642 million tons of sugarcane and 35 billion of litres of ethanol; the Northeast contributed 49 million tons of sugarcane and 2.3 billion of litres of ethanol (Vidal, 2020).

4 Ramos (2016) estimated that international groups were responsible for about 25% of all sugar and alcohol production.

5 More recently, the production of sugar cane has been expanding to the Centre-West, a region where a large volume of agribusiness investment is concentrated.

6 The Brazilian government stopped regulating the price of sugarcane, crystal sugar and hydrated alcohol (Ramos, 2016).

7 The peasant movement called *Ligas Camponesas* (Peasant Leagues) gained great regional and national prominence in the 1950s and 1960s. However, it was harshly repressed after the 1964 military coup. The struggle for land was resumed in the areas occupied by sugarcane monoculture only in the 1990s. Subsequently, rural workers mobilised and actively resisted through the landless workers movement (MST – *Movimento dos Trabalhadores Rurais Sem Terra*) and two unions affiliated to FETAPE (*Federacão dos Trabalhadores Rurais Agricultores* and *Agricultoras Familiares do Estado de Pernambuco*). According to the Pastoral Land Commission (CPT –*Comissáo Pastoral da Terra*), the number of land occupations in the Northeast jumped from 3 to 135 between 1992 and 1998.

8 This section is based on Camilla de Almeida Silva and Guilherme Jose Mota da Nóbrega's study "O polo de fruticultura irrigada de Petrolina-PE e Juazeiro-BA: Dinâmicas produtivas e trabalho na agricultura de exportação" in Véras de Oliveira and Rodgers (2022).

9 The São Francisco Valley Development Company (CODEVASF) was created in 1974. The Sobradinho dam in Bahia was built in 1977.

10 Harvest contracts are fixed-term employment contracts regulated by Law No. 5,889 of June 8, 1973.

11 In the Collective Bargaining Agreements negotiated over the last 26 years, the value of the minimum wage for the fruit farming category was on average R$ 16.00 above the national minimum wage.

12 In 2020, for the first time in the 26 years of the collective agreements, the employers' union presented an extensive list of 31 demands which included the request to cancel 24 of the 84 clauses negotiated in the 2018 convention.

13 This section is based on Jose Aderivaldo Silva da Nóbrega's study "Oito décadas de mineração no Seridó Paraibano: Uma análise das configurações do setor de minerais não metálicos" in Véras de Oliveira and Rodgers (2022).

14 The housing bubble in the United States at the beginning of the 2000s stimulated Brazilian exports of non-metallic minerals.

15 For example, in 2018, a ton of raw kaolin cost R$ 11 while a ton of processed kaolin started at R$ 550 and may be more expensive depending on the size of screening and the whiteness.

16 This section is based on the study by Ana Marcia Batista Almeida Pereira, Eugenio Pereira, Bruno Mota Braga and Claudia Freire entitled "O padrão de relações de trabalho no polo de confecções do Agreste de Pernambuco" in Véras de Oliveira and Rodgers (2022).

17 90% of the Pole's production is carried out in the municipalities of Santa Cruz do Capibaribe, Toritama and Caruaru.

18 It originated among rural women who made garments at home to supplement their income and sold them in local *Sulanca* fairs located along city streets (Véras de Oliveira, 2013).

19 The highest point was 2014, with 1,708 manufacturing enterprises (1,552 operating in the garment segment and 156 operating in the textile segment).

20 This section is based on Roseli de Fatima Corteletti and Kerilin Laine Andrade Chang's study "Possibilidades e limites na produção de calçados em Campina Grande-PB" in Véras de Oliveira and Rodgers (2022).

21 In 2018, Brazil was the fourth largest footwear producer of the world. National production reached 944 million pairs of shoes, produced by 6,439 companies,

which together generated employment for around 271,000 persons (Abicalçados, 2019).

22 Nowadays half the shoes produced in Brazil are based on plastic and rubber (including the famous *havaiana* sandals), 29% are synthetic laminated shoes, and only 18% are made of leather.

23 The retail price of a pair of *havaianas* in Brazil ranged from 9.99 reais to 179.99 reais (official havaianas website in Brazil, June 2020).

24 On 1 January 2019, national minimum wage was R$ 998 per month.

25 Four micro-enterprises (with between 3 and 19 workers) and three small enterprises (between 24 and 60 workers) were surveyed in 2017. Among workers, twenty men and three women were individually interviewed.

26 This section is based on the study by Eugenio Pereira, Anderson Cardozo and Victor de Oliveira Rodrigues entitled "Caracterização do regime de trabalho no setor da indústria naval no território de Suape-Pernambuco" in Véras de Oliveira and Rodgers (2022).

27 The *Estaleiro Atlantico Sul* was created in 2005, through a partnership between the groups Camargo Corrêa and Queiroz Galvão. Its partners and technological partners were the Japanese shipyards IHI and JMU. The *Vard Promar* is part of VARD, a global designer and builder of specialized vessels, headquartered in Norway. It is part of the Italian FINCANTIERI group, one of the world's largest shipbuilding groups.

28 The shipyard workers are formally represented by the Union of the Metallurgists of Pernambuco, Sindmetal-PE, officially registered as the Union of Workers in the Metallurgical Industries, Mechanical and Electrical Materials of Pernambuco.

29 This section is based on the study by Mauricio Rombaldi, Maria Clara Lima de Menezes and Luciana Waclawovsky entitled "Regime de trabalho no setor da construção no Brasil e na região Nordeste" in Véras de Oliveira and Rodgers (2022).

30 The impact of the 2014 football World Cup alone was estimated at R$33 billion of investment in infrastructure and the creation of 710,000 jobs (330,000 permanent and 380,000 temporary jobs).

31 IBGE, *Pesquisa Anual da Indústria da Construção* (2007–2017).

32 The *Lava jato* investigation revealed that, over two decades, Odebrecht paid bribes to the presidents, former presidents or government officials of 12 countries in order to obtain preferential treatment in public tenders.

33 This section is based on Roberto Véras de Oliveira's study "Os trabalhadores de tecnologia da informação em Pernambuco" in Véras de Oliveira and Rodgers (2022).

34 The analysis is based on two data sources: (1) RAIS and (2) a survey of IT workers in the Metropolitan Region of Recife carried out in 2017. Both sources focus on activities classified within codes 620 and 631 of the national classification of economic activities (CNAE) of IBGE. For details of filters applied, see Véras de Oliveira and Rodgers (2022, p.622).

35 The increases in other regions were: North +188%; Southeast +93%; South +160%; Centre-West +71%.

36 The gender balance in telecommunications employment is similar to that in IT, but it is more equally divided in audiovisual production (48% women and 52% men), and the gender balance is reversed in call centres where women dominate employment (72% women and 28% men).

37 The value of the minimum wage in nominal terms was R$ 998 in December 2019 (then equivalent to U$250).

38 SINDPD/PE = *Sindicato dos Trabalhadores em Empresas de Informática, Processamento de Dados e Tecnologia da Informação de Pernambuco.*

39 This section is based on Ana Carmen Navarro de Moraes's study "*Call Centres* na Paraíba: Expansão, perfil dos trabalhadores e ação sindical" in Véras de Oliveira and Rodgers (2022).

40 In 2007 only Paraíba, Bahia and Ceará had call centres, while in 2019 there were call centres in all Northeast states.
41 Sintelmark: Sindicato Paulista das Empresas de Telemarketing, Marketing Direto e Conexos.
42 See Chapter 3 on the 2017 labour reform.
43 This section is based on Jose Cleyton Neves Lopes' study "A emergência dos serviços por aplicativo no Rio Grande do Norte" in Véras de Oliveira and Rodgers (2022).
44 Uber Technologies Inc. (Uber) is a global company that operates a digital platform supporting a variety of mobile applications. Founded in 2009, the company initially offered a passenger transport service and later extended its activities to cover delivery services such as food.
45 Personal interviews were carried out in the first half of 2020, during the Covid-19 pandemic, and through online video conference. They refer to the interviewee's work schedule prevalent before the confinement.
46 *Cooperativa de Motoristas de Aplicativo de Mobilidade Urbana* of Rio Grande do Norte (Compar/RN).
47 Though collective actions are rare, in June 2020 more than 1,000 food delivery drivers in Brazil participated in a strike to demand better working conditions (Rochabrun and Mello, 2020).
48 This section is based on the study by Mario Henrique Ladosky and Victor de Oliveira Rodrigues entitled "Regimes de acumulação e trabalho no território socioprodutivo de Goiana/ PE" in Véras de Oliveira and Rodgers (2022).
49 The region was one of the main bases of sugar and ethanol production in Pernambuco, and a certain level of activity still remains in this sector.

References

Abicalçados (Associação Brasileira das Indústrias de Calçados). 2019. <https://www.abicalcados.com.br/noticia/abicalcados-apresenta-relatorio-setorial-2019>, accessed 01-05-2022.

Abílio, Ludmila Costhek. 2020. "Plataformas digitais e uberização: Globalização de um sul administrado?". *Contracampo*, 39(1): 12–26.

Abreu e Lima, Maria do Socorro. 2012. *Construindo o sindicalismo rural: Lutas, partidos e projetos*. 2ª ed. Recife: Editora Universitária da UFPE.

ADEPE (Agência de desenvolvimento econômico de Pernambuco). 2019. *Câmara setorial têxtil e de confecções é oficialmente formada em Caruaru*. Recife. <https://www.addiper.pe.gov.br/index.php/camara-setorial-textil-e-de-confeccoes-e-oficialmente-formada-em-caruaru/>, accessed 01-05-2022.

Almeida, Marina Castro. 2014. "Das centrais de atendimento aos contact centers: Uso e reprodução do desenvolvimento geográfico desigual brasileiro" in Anais do VI Congreso Iberoamericano de Estudios Territoriales y Ambientales (VI CIETA): 2355–2377.

ANAMT (Associação Nacional de Medicina do Trabalho). 2020 <https://www.anamt.org.br/portal/2019/04/30/construcao-civil-esta-entre-os-setores-com-maior-risco-de-acidentes-de-trabalho/>, accessed 14-04-2022.

Andrade, Manuel Correia de Oliveira. 2001. *História das usinas de açúcar de Pernambuco* (2da ed.). Recife: Editora Universitaria da UFPE.

Araújo, Tânia Bacelar de. 2004. "Northeast, Northeasts: What Northeast". *Latin American Perspectives*, 31(2): 16–41.

Avritzer, Leonardo. 2019. "O pendulo da democracia no Brasil: Uma analise da crise (2013–2018)" in Leonardo Avritzer, Heloisa Murgel Starling, Pauliane Braga and Priscilia Zanandrez (eds.): *Pensando a democracia, a república e o estado de direito no Brasil* (pp. 17–38). Belo Horizonte: Projeto Republica.

Bono, Andrea del and Marcia Leite. 2016. "El impacto de la tercerización y la deslocalización en el trabajo de telemarketing: Una comparación entre Argentina y Brasil". *Cuadernos del CENDES*, 33(93): 15–35.

Braga, Bruno Mota. 2014. *A dinâmica formal-informal do trabalho no território comercial de Toritama: O que está mudando?* Dissertation (Mestrado em Ciencias Sociais), Programa de Pós-Graduação em Ciências Sociais, Universidade Federal de Campina Grande. Campina Grande-PB.

Braga, Bruno Mota. 2019. *O informal como tecido social: Os arranjos econômicos, sociais e laborais que constituem o Agreste das confecções.* Thesis (Doutorado em Sociologia), Universidade Federal da Paraíba, João Pessoa-PB.

Brazil, Government of. (2001). *Relatório CPI Finor.* Brasília: Câmara dos Deputados. https://www2.camara.leg.br/atividade-legislativa/comissoes/comissoes-temporarias/parlamentar-de-inquerito/51-legislatura/cpifinor/relatoriofinal.pdf, accessed 02-10-2022

Cardozo, Anderson Matias. 2020. *Trajetórias ocupacionais de trabalhadoras da construção naval no Complexo Industrial e Portuário de Suape: Identidades e reformulações a partir da divisão sexual do trabalho.* Thesis (Doutorado em Ciências Sociais), Centro de Humanidades, Universidade Federal de Campina Grande. Campina Grande-PB.

Carvalho, Rejane Gomes and Wanderleya dos Santos Farias. 2022. "As condições diferenciadas de desenvolvimento nas mesorregiões da Paraíba" in Véras de Oliveira and Rodgers (2022).

Castro, Barbara. 2013. *Afogados em contratos: O impacto da flexibilização do trabalho nas trajetórias dos profissionais de TI.* Thesis (Doutorado), Instituto de Filosofia e Ciências Humanas, Universidade Estadual de Campinas (UNICAMP). Campinas-SP.

Cavalcanti, Josefa Salete Barbosa. 1997. "Frutas para o mercado global". *Revista do Instituto de Estudos Avançados da USP*, 11(29): 79–93.

Cockell, Fernanda Flávia and Daniel Perticarrari. 2010. "Contratos de boca: A institucionalização da precariedade na construção civil". *Caderno CRH*, 23(60): 633–653.

Costa, Luciano Rodrigues. 2011. "Subcontratação e informalidade na construção civil, no Brasil e na França". *Caderno CRH*, 24(62): 413–434.

Coutinho, Grijalbo Fernandes. 2015. *Terceirização: Máquina de moer gente trabalhadora.* São Paulo: Editora LTr.

Damiani, Octavio. 2003. "Diversificação agrícola e reducção de pobreza: A introdução no Nordeste Brasileiro de produtos agrícolas não-tradicionais de alto valor e seus efeitos sobre pequenos produtores e trabalhadores rurais assalariados". *Revista Econômica do Nordeste*, 34(1): 42–84.

Danato, Eduardo and Maressa Fauzia Pessoa Dantas. 2022. "A agroindustria canaviera de Pernambuco e Paraíba" in Véras de Oliveira and Rodgers (2022).

DIEESE (Departamento Intersindical de Estatística e Estudos Socioeconômicos). 2012. "Copa do Mundo 2014: Algumas considerações sobre a realização do evento no Brasil". *Nota Técnica No.110*, maio. <https://www.dieese.org.br/notatecnica/2012/notaTec110Copa.pdf>, accessed 14-04-2022.

Ferreira, Marcos Antonio da Silva. 2018. *Corporação e Geografia: A organizaçáo territorial produtiva do grupo Alpargatas S.A. na Paraíba.* Dissertation (Mestrado

Académico), Programa de Pós-Graduação em Geografia, Universidade Estadual do Ceará. Fortaleza-CE.

FETAPE (Federação dos Trabalhadores Rurais Agricultores e Agricultoras Familiares do Estado de Pernambuco). 2018. *Zona da Mata: A história do movimento sindical dos trabalhadores e das trabalhadoras rurais começa aqui*. Pernambuco: FETAPE.

Freire, Claudia. 2019. *Da condição de trabalhador à condição de empresário: Estratégias de sobrevivência em um contexto de subdesenvolvimento*. Curitiba: Appris.

IBGE (Instituto Brasileiro de Geografia e Estadísticas). *2000 and 2010 Censuses*. Rio de Janeiro: IBGE.

———. Various years. *Pesquisa Nacional por Amostra de Domicílios* (PNAD and PNADC). Rio de Janeiro: IBGE.

———. Various years. *Pesquisa Anual da Indústria da Construction*. Rio de Janeiro: IBGE.

———. 2021. *Produção Municipal Agrícola 2020*. Rio de Janeiro: IBGE.

Leite, Ângelo Antônio Macêdo. 2013. *O desenvolvimento da viticultura irrigada na região de Juazeiro-BA e Petrolina-PE: O trabalho na contramão do discurso dominante*. Thesis (Doutorado em Ciências Sociais e da Terra), Universidade Federal de São Carlos. São Carlos-SP.

Macêdo, Caroliny Wanderley de. 2017. *Interação Universidade-Empresa-Governo: Uma análise do arranjo institucional do Porto Digital*. Dissertation (Mestrado em ciência política), Programa de Pós-Graduação em Ciência Política, Universidade Federal de Pernambuco. Recife-PE.

Medeiros, Leonilde Servolo de. 1989. *História dos movimentos sociais no campo*. Rio de Janeiro: FASE.

Moraes, Aline Fábia Guerra de. 2015. *Novo desenvolvimentismo e velhas condições de trabalho? Uma análise da dinâmica de subcontratação no complexo de Suape*. Dissertation (Mestrado em Administração), Universidade Federal da Paraíba. João Pessoa-PB.

Navarro, Vera Lúcia and Taísa Junqueira Prazeres. 2010. "Reestruturação produtiva, precarização e saude do trabalhador na indústria de calçados de Franca/SP" in Edvânia Lourenço, Vera Lúcia Navarro, Íris Fenner Bertani, José Silva and Raquel Sant'Ana (eds.): *Avesso do Trabalho II: Trabalho, precarização e saúde do trabalhador*. São Paulo: Expressão Popular.

Nóbrega, José Aderivaldo Silva da. 2019. *Estudo sobre as inter-relações entre formalidade e informalidade do trabalho no segmento de minerais não metálicos no Seridó da Paraíba*. Thesis (Doutorado em Ciencias Sociais), Centro de Humanidades, Universidade Federal de Campina Grande, Campina Grande-PB.

Oliveira Júnior, Moacir de Miranda (coord.). 2005. *Relatório da indústria de call centers no Brasil 2005*, Programa de Pós-Graduação em Administração, Pontifícia Universidade Católica de São Paulo. São Paulo: PUC-SP. <https://docplayer.com.br/8203542-Relatorio-da-industria-de-call-centers-no-brasil-2005-the-global-call-center-industry-project.html>, accessed 16-04-2022.

Oliveira, Valéria Costa Aldeci de. 2017. *De marisqueiras a operárias: Percepção das mulheres sobre desenvolvimento, trabalho e gênero nos territorios pesqueiros de Goiana/PE*. Thesis (Doutorado em Sociologia), Programa de Pós-Graduação em Sociologia do Centro de Ciências Humanas, Universidade Federal da Paraíba. João Pessoa-PB.

Pereira, Ana Márcia Batista Almeida. 2018. *Dinâmica formal-informal em lavanderias de jeans do Polo Confecções PE*. Thesis (Doutorado em Administração), Centro de Ciências Sociais e Aplicadas (CCSA), Programa de Pós-Graduação em Administração, Universidade Federal da Paraíba. João Pessoa-PB.

Pereira, Eugenio, Anderson Cardozo and Victor de Oliveira Rodrigues. 2022. "Caracterização do regime de trabalho no setor da indústria naval no território de Suape-Pernambuco" in Véras de Oliveira and Rodgers (2022).

Pereira, Eugenio Vital. 2019. *Caminhos sinuosos, trajetórias precárias: Os sentidos da qualificação profissional de trabalhadores da Indústria Naval do Complexo Suape (PE)*. Thesis (Doutorado em Sociologia), Universidade Federal da Paraíba. João Pessoa-PB.

Pereira, Monica Aparecida Tomé. 2012. *Fruticultura, emprego e migração: O caso da região de Petrolina-PE e Juazeiro-BA*. Thesis (Doutorado), Instituto de Filosofia e Ciências Humanas, Universidade Estadual de Campinas (UNICAMP). Campinas-SP.

Porcaro, Rosa Maria. 2013. "Economia da Informação: Mercado de trabalho e competencias". *Cadernos Temáticos do Observatório: Economia da Informação e Internet*. Brasilia: Softex. <https://www.softex.br/wp-content/uploads/2013/07/Cadernos-tematicos-do-observatorio-economia-da-informacao-e-internet1.pdf>, accessed 08-05-2022.

Queiroz, Allan Souza and Raf Vanderstraeten. 2018. "Unintended consequences of job formalisation: Precarious work in Brazil's sugarcane plantations". *International Sociology*, 33(1): 128–146.

Queiroz, Pedro Henrique Santos. 2014. *Trabalhadores de SUAPE: Estudo sobre a diversidade de experiências operárias*. Dissertation (Mestrado em Sociologia), Universidade Estadual de Campinas (UNICAMP). Campinas-SP.

Ramos, Pedro. 2016. "Trajetória e situação atual da agroindústria canavieira do Brasil e do mercado de alcool carburante" in Gesmar Rosa dos Santos (ed.): *Quarenta anos de etanol em larga escala no Brasil: Desafios, crises e perspectivas* (pp. 47–81). Brasilia: IPEA.

Rochabrun, Marcelo and Gabriela Mello. 2020. *In Brazil, delivery drivers for Uber, Rappi and others protest amid pandemic*. REUTERS, July 1. <https://www.reuters.com/article/us-brazil-uber-protests-idUSKBN242735>, accessed 01-04-2022.

Rodrigues, Victor de Oliveira. 2020. *Trabalho, desenvolvimento e ação sindical em Pernambuco: O Sindmetal-PE diante do polo naval e do polo automotivo*. Thesis (Doutorado em Sociologia), Universidade Federal da Paraíba. João Pessoa-PB.

Rombaldi, Maurício. 2014. "A copa de 2014 e os trabalhadores da construção: Estratégias globais, mobilizações locais". *Revista da ABET*, 13(2): 184–198.

Selwyn, Ben. 2007. "Labour process and workers' bargaining power in export grape production, North East Brazil". *Journal of Agrarian Change*, 7(4): 526–553.

———. 2009. "Labour flexibility in export horticulture: A case study of Northeast Brazilian grape production". *The Journal of Peasant Studies*, 36(4): 761–782.

———. 2010. "Gender wage work and development in North East Brazil". *Bulletin of Latin American Research*, 29(1): 51–70.

———. 2013. "The global retail revolution, fruiticulture and economic development in Northeast Brazil". *Review of International Political Economy*, 20(1): 153–179.

Sigaud, Lygia. 1980. *Greves nos engenhos*. Rio de Janeiro: Paz e Terra.

———. 1986. "A luta de classes em dois atos: Notas sobre um ciclo de greves camponesas". *Dados*, 29(3): 50–72.

Silva, Elias Gomes da. 2017. *O complexo portuário de Suape e suas implicações para o município de Ipojuca*. Trabalho de Conclusão de Curso, Universidade Federal da Integração Latino-Americana. Foz do Iguaçu-PR.

Silva, Guilherme José Mota. 2016. *Os frutos da resistência: Sindicalismo e luta dos assalariados da fruticultura irrigada no Submédio São Francisco*. Dissertation (Mestrado em Ciencias Sociais), Programa de Pós-Graduação em Ciências Sociais, Universidade Federal de Campina Grande. Campina Grande-PB.

Souto Júnior Fernano. 2013. "Se parar, a fruta aprodece: Fordismo e sindicatos no Vale do São Francisco". *REDD-Revista Espaço de Diálogo e Desconexão*, 7(1): 1–20.

Srnicek, Nick. 2016. *Platform capitalism*. Cambridge: Polity Press.

Tribuna do Norte. 2019, March 29. <http://www.tribunadonorte.com.br/noticia/-motoristas-de-uber-superam-ta-xis/443402>, accessed 20-03-2022.

Uber. 2020. "Fatos e dados sobre a Uber". *Uber Newsroom*. <https://www.uber.com/pt-BR/newsroom/fatos-e-dados-sobre-uber/>, accessed em: 28 abr. 2020.

Vasconcelos, Santiago Andrade. 2006. *O uso do território do município de Pedra Lavrada-PB pela mineração: Elementos de inserção do lugar do fazer no contexto atual da globalização*. Thesis (Doutorado em Geografia), Universidade Federal de Pernambuco. Recife-PE.

Véras de Oliveira, Roberto. 2013. "O polo de confecções do Agreste de Pernambuco: Elementos para uma visão panorámica" in Roberto Véras de Oliveira and Marco Aurelio Santana (eds.): *Trabalho em territórios produtivos reconfigurados no Brasil* (pp. 233–278). João Pessoa-PB: Editora da UFPB.

———. 2020. "Os trabalhadores de TI em Pernambuco: Perfil exploratório de um segmento diferenciado" in Marcia Leite, Magda Biavaschi, Carlos Salas and Jacob Lima (eds.): *O trabalho em Crise: Flexibilidade e precariedades* (pp. 131–149). São Carlos: EDUFSCAR.

Véras de Oliveira, Roberto and Gerry Rodgers (eds.). 2022. *Desenvolvimento e regime de trabalho: A trajetória do Nordeste do Brasil*. São Paulo: Annablume.

Vidal, Fatima. 2020. "Produção e mercado de etanol". *Caderno Setorial ETENE*, 5(121): 1–9.

Zanatta, Mariana Scussel. 2016. *Quando o fabrico se torna fábrica*. Thesis (Doutorado em Sociologia), Instituto de Filosofia e Ciencias Humanas, Programa de Pós-Graduação em Sociologia, Universidade Federal do Rio Grande do Sul. Porto Alegre-RS.

5 Towards a more equal development

1 Development and crises

The development of Brazil's Northeast mirrors the story of Brazil as a whole, one of uneven growth and high inequality. Poverty, informality and precarious work are all more widespread in the Northeast, and the gaps have persisted over time. The region has benefitted from the periods of economic growth, when there have been signs of convergence towards the national level. But it has likewise suffered from successive economic and political crises, and the gains are lost when crisis strikes. These crises have arisen from the tensions and contradictions in the development regime at both national and regional levels, involving both endogenous and exogenous forces.

This section considers four major economic and political crises that have led to a reconfiguration of political and social institutions and economic relationships: in the early 1960s, culminating in the military coup of 1964; in the 1980s, a "lost decade" in much of Latin America, which ended with the dominance of neoliberal economic policies; at the turn of the century, when the Workers' Party came to power in the wake of international financial crises and economic recession; and the period of economic and political turmoil since 2015, which continues at the time of writing.

At the heart of this process is the labour regime – the rules and institutions, both formal and informal, that govern the dynamics of the labour market and determine the pattern of employment relations. The labour regime plays a key role in the long-term economic, social and political trajectory, through its influence on production, on income and its distribution, and on social organization. Attempts to reform the labour regime have been a central issue in each historical crisis, as part of the struggle over political and economic power. How this has impinged on the Northeast has varied with the nature and outcome of each crisis.

A state-led process of industrialization was established in Brazil in the first half of the twentieth century, based on import substitution and national capital, without undermining traditional agrarian structures and institutions. This gave rise to an oligopolistic industrial production structure, centred on the Southeast of the country, where an urban proletariat was

DOI: 10.4324/9781003326670-5

formed. The Northeast remained on the margins of this process. As we saw in Chapter 2, by the end of the 1950s state action to overcome economic backwardness, notably through the creation of Sudene, had started to promote the development of the region. But there was resistance to change from traditional interests, and industrialization was slow, and dependent on the production structure and capital of the more developed regions of the country.

Economic and political crisis in the early 1960s and the military coup of 1964 brought a conservative and authoritarian regime to power at the national level, leading to "a new pattern of capital accumulation in the country – one that should not be jeopardized by redistributive pressures" (Barbosa et al., 2017, p.22). This resulted in a period of high economic growth which lasted well into the 1970s, dubbed the "Brazilian miracle", based on an alliance between the authoritarian State and private capital. Although individual labour rights were maintained for a part of the workforce, trade union leaders were persecuted, and workers were subjected to a systematic "wage squeeze", which prevented them from sharing in the high productivity gains of the period. Instead, the gains from high economic growth, apart from benefitting a capitalist class, which kept the largest share, were concentrated among a growing middle class and a protected group of skilled workers, especially in industry.

The Northeast was integrated into this process, within a model in which it increasingly became a low-cost supplier of intermediate goods to industrial production in the Southeast. By the latter part of the 1970s, the economy of the Northeast was growing faster than the rest of Brazil. Capitalist agriculture also expanded, but exploitative labour relations persisted in traditional plantations such as sugar cane. Because of the type of policies promoted by Sudene, especially those involving large-scale and capital-intensive investment, the growth of production in the Northeast was concentrated in a few metropolitan centres, which became the destination for large numbers of migrants from impoverished rural areas. The growth of formal employment was slow, and inequality widened even more sharply than in the rest of Brazil.

The seeds of the next crisis already started to germinate in the 1970s. At the end of the 1970s, impacted by the two oil shocks and the adverse international economic environment, Brazil's balance of payments deficit rose sharply, external indebtedness increased, and austerity policies drove the economy into recession in the early 1980s (Baer, 2014). This led to renewed precarity in the labour market, as unemployment rose and protected jobs were lost. A process of deindustrialization started and workers were faced with declining wages in real terms as inflation rose, culminating in hyperinflation at the end of the decade. Resistance by workers and popular movements grew everywhere and the demands for democratization intensified, undermining the military regime's project of a gradual and controlled political transition.

While the crisis of the mid-1960s led to a swift restructuring of political and economic institutions, the crisis of the 1980s was long and uncertain. This was a period of deep economic transformation, at the same time as new social institutions emerged and political structures were rebuilt over the wreckage of the discredited military regime. The trade union movement underwent an unprecedented renewal, and social and workers' rights returned to the policy agenda, in a process which led to the 1988 "Citizen Constitution" and the 1989 presidential elections. But the decade of the 1980s was marked by persistent economic instability and political tension. In the early 1980s the Northeast maintained an average growth rate higher than the rest of Brazil, reflecting the expansion of investment in the 1970s, but by the end of the decade it had converged to the national level. In the labour market, informality and unemployment, already high, rose further.

Once again, the emergence from the crisis of the 1980s sowed the seeds for the next crisis. The decade of the 1990s saw a neoliberal agenda of privatization, trade liberalization, and deregulation. But economic and administrative reforms did not lead to a viable growth process. Volatile international capital flows and increasing competitive pressure from abroad created a situation that "was unfavourable for Brazilian corporate capital, which reacted by reducing product lines, importing capital goods, and outsourcing many activities" (Barbosa et al., 2017, p.93). Attempts to flexibilize the labour market increased tensions further. While some efforts were made to introduce social and redistributive measures that could offset the disequalizing effects of neoliberal policies, and inequality started to decline from the peaks reached in the early 1990s, the model could not be sustained in the face of successive international financial crises (notably the "tequila" crisis in 1994–1995 and the Asian financial crisis in 1997–1998).

The Northeast was particularly affected by the abandonment of earlier developmental policies and a fall in public investment. Competition among states to attract private capital delivered only modest advantages for local economies. Earlier public-sector investments in the region were vulnerable to privatization, with adverse consequences for employment. Unemployment rose, as it did in the rest of Brazil, and informal employment relations not only continued to dominate the labour market but expanded further, while real incomes of workers fell and inter- and intra-regional inequalities persisted. As noted in Chapter 2, the Northeast reproduced the weak performance of the Brazilian economy as a whole.

A return to economic recession in the latter part of the 1990s paved the way for political reconfiguration in the early 2000s. The PT (Workers' Party)-led government that came to power in 2003 brought a return to state intervention in the process of accumulation, a renewal of employment and income policies, the recognition of trade unions and social movements as legitimate actors, an increasing real minimum wage, and a considerable expansion of social transfers. The result was not only higher economic growth but also a rising share of formal employment, lower poverty and falling inequality.

Nevertheless, the Brazilian economy remained heavily dependent on mining and commercial agriculture to produce commodities for global markets. And while incomes rose among poorer groups, the income share of the top 10% was hardly reduced, showing that there was some accommodation with middle class and bourgeois elites. The PT-led government remained dependent on the support of regional and landed interests, and there was relatively little advance on agrarian reform. But this was clearly a period of social progress.

The Northeast was one of the main beneficiaries of the new policies. Since poverty was higher than in other parts of Brazil, the region benefitted more from social transfers and from the rising minimum wage, while the PAC (Growth Acceleration Programme) provided support for an increase in both public and private investment in the region. Manufacturing, construction and service sectors expanded as firms headquartered in the Southeast shifted new investment towards the Northeast. Over the period from 2003 to 2015 the Northeastern economy grew faster than Brazil as a whole, and – largely because of social transfers – inequality fell in the region as well.

The next major crisis struck in 2015. Once again, the political and economic tensions had already been building up. The Global Financial Crisis of 2008 changed the macroeconomic conditions. But unlike the national crises discussed above, which were both economic and political, the impact on Brazil of the international crisis of 2008 was mainly economic in nature, causing growth to drop sharply in 2009, but not resulting in political instability or pressure on the labour regime. On the contrary, it helped to reinforce the neodevelopmentalist strategy and policies for productive inclusion of the most vulnerable. But an attempt to maintain the growth path through expansionary public policies in an unfavourable international context, though initially successful, raised the fiscal and external deficits and led to higher interest rates. Investment dropped in 2014, and in 2015 the economy went into deep recession. At the same time, there was growing political instability. The redistributive policies of the PT-led governments had generated a backlash among the emerging middle class, and corruption scandals fed a conservative movement that attacked the PT governments, provoking widespread street demonstrations and increasing polarization. This culminated in an "institutional coup" in which President Dilma Roussef was impeached in 2016 and a new government installed with the goal of implementing an orthodox programme of austerity and renewed liberalization.

Like in the 1980s, the crisis that started in 2015 was long drawn out, indeed still continues seven years later. The governments that came to power after Dilma's impeachment attempted to engineer a new growth regime around neoliberal principles, with changes in the key institutional dimensions, including a reduced economic role of the State, flexible wage labour relations, and a deregulated competition regime. But like in the 1990s, growth rates have remained low, and labour reform did not reverse the growth of unemployment and high levels of informality; on the contrary, it worsened the general situation of precarious work. As in earlier periods, the neoliberal model has met with social resistance. It is therefore not surprising that both economy and society remain in a state of crisis.

The Northeast, which benefitted substantially from the economic and social gains of the previous period, suffered disproportionately. Over the period 2015–2019, and especially after 2016, growth fell more sharply in the Northeast than in Brazil as a whole, unemployment rose more, and inequality increased. This was a direct result of the peripheral and dependent situation of the Northeast in relation to the Southeast, with capital flowing into the region in good times, but reversing course once the national economy slowed down. In fact the ratio of incomes in the Northeast to the average for Brazil remains today much the same as it was in the 1960s. Clearly the structural disadvantages have persisted regardless of the development regime; successive national regimes were built on and took advantage of the existence of a region of surplus labour with relatively low wages, which played, at the domestic level, a role similar to that of low-income countries in the capitalist world economy.

We should not imply that the whole of the Northeast follows a single pattern. Each state of the region, indeed, subregions within each state as well, connects with the regional and national development regimes in a different way. For instance, if we compare the Northeastern states of Pernambuco and Paraíba there were significant differences in growth, employment and inequality. Pernambuco benefitted more than Paraíba from inflows of public and private capital in large-scale industrial investments during the last 20 years, leading to the creation of formal, protected jobs, greater than the average for the Northeast as a whole; but by the same token it was more affected by the recession after 2015. Paraíba, in contrast, depended more heavily on service sectors, and also displayed greater informality. Each state has its own character and its own history. But there are commonalities across the region, which interact with local situations and policies.

Upon this triple layer of social, economic and political crisis a fourth layer then emerged, a health crisis, interacting with the other three. The Covid pandemic has highlighted the insecurity of many sources of income, reinforced existing social inequalities, and increased the burden on those who care for others (predominantly women). The pandemic has exposed some of the deep flaws of the current and past growth path: failure to adequately invest in public social policy, not only health but also education and social security; a short time horizon and an excessive concentration on large scale, visible, physical investment; a failure to engage a diversity of social actors in setting priorities for action; inability to deal adequately with the consequences of informality in employment and production. All of these problems are more acute in the Northeast than in the rest of the country.

2 The roots of unequal development

What factors are responsible for this alternation of development and crises? The market economy is regulated by social and economic institutions that reflect power relations and social structures. Capitalism takes many forms, and the nature of each form depends on the institutional configuration of the system of production and distribution, which varies with the character and history of each society. In Chapter 1 we outlined the approach of the "Régulation School" to this question (Boyer, 2015). Boyer and other writers in this theoretical school have highlighted five institutional forms that play a central role in the pattern of production and distribution in Europe and North America, and they all have analogues in Brazil:

- the monetary regime, notably the set of rules that governs credit and payments, and the macroeconomic policies with which it is associated;
- forms of competition, which, unlike in conventional economics depend on the relations among participants in the market and not on an invisible hand;
- the nature of integration in the international economy, and its consequences for the pattern of production and distribution;
- the wage labour nexus, or more broadly the nature of employment relationships and the relations between labour and capital;
- and the State, especially the role it plays in managing and regulating economic activity.

Among these different institutional forms, the first, the monetary regime and the macroeconomic policies with which it is associated, are essentially determined at the national level, but there are regional consequences. In particular, access to credit and the interregional flow of capital are important determinants of the performance of the Northeastern economy, and public sector financial institutions, notably the BNDES (National Bank for Economic and Social Development) and the *Banco do Nordeste*, provide capital for both public and private investment, and have facilitated the process of accumulation and growth in the Northeast. But as we have just noted, the dynamics of the Brazilian economy are such that during the boom there is expansion into the low-cost but low-productivity Northeast from the core of the economy in the Southeast, driven by the public sector and large firms, whereas capital flows dry up in the recession. Since the Northeast is subject to the same macroeconomic forces as the rest of the economy, there has a tendency for the amplitude of its economic cycles to be greater, especially since the economic liberalization of the 1990s. This can be seen, for instance, in the greater growth in the Northeast of unemployment and informal employment in the most recent crisis.

The process of capital accumulation is weaker in the Northeast, especially since it is largely driven by actors (capital) from outside the region, and this is one cause of its longer-term disadvantage. This process is closely connected with the second institutional form identified above, which relates to the dynamics of competition and the market. Within the Brazilian economy there are no barriers to flows of goods, capital and people within regions, other than those due to distance and social forces (such as discrimination against migrants). But the oligopolistic nature of larger scale industry in Brazil, along with the limited number of institutional sources of finance, has led to a production structure, especially in the Northeast, in which formal industrial production is dominated by a small number of large firms with a high degree of market power, in a variety of sectors, such as automobile manufacture, beverages, and petrochemicals, concentrated in a relatively small number of locations, especially in the major metropolitan regions of Recife, Fortaleza and Salvador, and in state-promoted industrial zones such as Suape in Pernambuco and Camaçari in Bahia, alongside a much more competitive sector of small and medium enterprises without the same ease of access to capital markets. This dualism in the production structure is in turn linked to the concentration of ownership and management in the Southeast of the country, with plants in the Northeast often concentrating on mass production, while research, development, and other higher level functions are located elsewhere in Brazil or, in the case of multinational firms, abroad. There are of course locally based firms in the Northeast as well, but much profit no doubt flows out of the region – "no doubt", because this is difficult to document, but that is the logical implication of the structure. This is not confined to manufacturing. The same pattern is found in some modern services and trade – call centres, supermarket chains and commercial centres, and business services.

Productivity is generally perceived to be lower in the Northeast, though this is probably not the case in large capital-intensive investments with global technology such as motor manufacturing and petrochemicals, where labour productivity is basically determined by the technology. But wages are also lower, and there is a large supply of relatively low-skilled labour. There are reports in some of the case studies discussed in Chapter 4 of in-migration of skilled labour from other parts of Brazil, for instance in construction, suggesting that there are skill deficits in the region. In any case the dualistic production structure maintains high wage differentials in the labour market, helping to explain the pattern discussed in Chapter 3.

"Dualism" is in reality an oversimplification. The production system is extremely heterogeneous, as the discussion in Chapter 4 shows, with a variety of enterprises and production arrangements outside the large-scale capitalist structure, especially outside the major metropolitan areas, some of them connected to large firms through outsourcing and subcontracting, others serving local or national markets. The informal network of small family businesses producing garments in the Agreste region of Pernambuco, with a high level of coordination and cooperation, is an example, discussed in the last chapter, and similar structures are observed in other parts of the region, in Rio Grande do Norte and Ceará, for instance. The production system as a whole is built on a close integration of different types of enterprises. Formal and informal are deeply intertwined and interdependent.

The third set of institutions, concerned with the integration in the international economy, is a major determinant of the development regime in the Brazilian economy as a whole, but also has specific impacts in the Northeast. There is, for instance, international capital in the tourism industry and in property in the region, and many enterprises export directly – for example, havaiana sandals produced in Campina Grande, Paraíba, or fruit production in Juazeiro/Petrolina (Bahia/Pernambuco) – indeed, some have been established explicitly to export to international markets, such as the Chinese-backed investment in iron ore mining in Pará, linked to the construction of a port in Maranhão,[1] and exporting directly to China. These enterprises are then directly subject to fluctuations in international markets. The drive for exports is one of the source of political pressures for labour market flexibility in order to reduce national production costs and gain international competitiveness. But in the international economy, the Northeast of Brazil is the periphery of a periphery, with little autonomy, and international relations are dominated by the export of commodities or are managed from São Paulo.

This brings us to the fourth set of institutions, concerned with the labour regime, which we have discussed in some detail in Chapter 3. The structure of employment relations is in large measure determined by the shape and the institutions of the production system (see Chapter 4) – so the formal segment of the wage labour market in the region is dominated by larger firms in industry and services, respecting and replicating the national institutions of labour regulation and representation. These larger firms have access to a substantial supply of labour at the minimum wage or a little higher – considerably lower wages than in most other parts of Brazil, even for unskilled labour.

Chapter 3 showed that the labour regime is very unequal, in that there are large differences in wages and incomes across different labour statuses, and this accounts for a substantial share of overall inequality. There are several factors involved. First, there is a declining but still significant number of low-income small farmers, and a considerable volume of agricultural wage labour without carteira, generally paid below the minimum wage, working in plantations or in seasonal activities. These traditional employment relations are replicated to some extent outside agriculture, in mining, for instance. Second, the formal wage labour market accounts for only about one third of employment, against almost half in the rest of Brazil. Within formal employment, there is a substantial income difference between upper white-collar and public-sector workers on the one hand, and lower white-collar and production workers on the other. Third, the Northeast labour market is characterized by widespread informality in both wage labour and self-employment. Informal is not equivalent to unproductive, and there is a part of informal self-employment that delivers decent incomes. Nor does informal mean unregulated, for there is a social organization of informal economic activity which manages opportunities and facilitates coordination. But informal work is very heterogeneous, and there is a large segment of marginal self-employment, as well as unprotected wage work in small enterprises and domestic service, which delivers incomes well below the minimum wage.

These segmentations in the labour market are both cause and consequence of the economic disadvantage of the region. They are a consequence, because shortfalls in investment and growth directly affect labour demand, and in a situation of employment deficit, some parts of the labour market are better protected than others. The bottom end of the informal economy consists of survival activities for those who are unable to gain access to decent jobs. But segmentation can also be a cause of disadvantage, if it results from employer strategies to differentiate among workers, maintaining a reserve of precarious workers alongside a segment of regular jobs, and thereby reducing labour costs overall. Labour market segmentation also facilitates discrimination by gender and race – and wage and income differentials by gender and race are a substantial component of overall inequality. And it may perpetuate the existence of groups of workers with inadequate skills and qualifications, and little scope for upgrading.

Alongside the segmentation of the labour market there is not only high unemployment but also a substantial dropout from the labour force, higher in the Northeast than elsewhere, and especially concerning young people, leading on the one hand to reduced labour commitment and on the other to social dysfunction and underground or illegal activities.

A wide variety of institutional actors are present in the labour regime. As in the rest of Brazil there is a substantial structure of representation of worker and employer interests through trade unions and syndicates. But by virtue of the smaller share of formal employment in the Northeast, these organizations are less influential than elsewhere, and have difficulty penetrating larger private enterprises in both industrial and service sectors. They may then have a formal role in wage negotiations with little effective presence in the enterprises concerned. The decentralization of production processes through outsourcing, often to the informal economy, fragments worker interests and makes their representation more difficult. Beyond the traditional trades unions, a variety of organizations and associations defend the rights of workers in agrarian settings, in informal work and in the solidarity economy. There are examples of successful interventions by unions and other groups to raise wages and improve conditions of work, through collective bargaining, direct action and other means. However, this does little to reduce the disadvantages of the region as a whole.

Apart from the institutional actors of the economy – enterprises, employers, unions and other associations – a variety of other organized groups play a role in the development process, including churches, activists and various non-governmental bodies. But it is the State that, at least in principle, is the dominant force through the regulation and management of economic activity, tax and fiscal policies, public-sector activities in investment, production and services, and its overall social policy and regulatory stance. The State may attempt to offset regional disadvantage, support employment growth and promote a fair and inclusive development path. But state action responds primarily to ideological agendas and the interests of particular groups.

In terms of economic and social policy, there are three levels to consider: federal, state (province) and municipal. Each has its own constitutionally defined mandate, but it is at the federal level that the key decisions are taken that have influenced the development regime in the Northeast. The interest of the federal government in reducing the gap between the Northeast and the rest of the country has varied over time. The "developmental State" that emerged in the 1950s treated this as a priority, notably through the creation of Sudene and public-sector investment in the region. However, this process involved tax incentives in favour of large economic groups, often with foreign capital, leading to a concentration of the benefits. The rise of neoliberalism in the 1980s and especially in the 1990s further deepened the concentrationist character of this model, while at the same time leading to a shrinking of state intervention in the economy. Then the neodevelopmental ideology of the 2003–2014 period renewed the emphasis on public investment in infrastructure and public-sector enterprises, increased expenditure on education and health, and introduced redistributive social programmes aimed at reducing hunger and homelessness (*Fome Zero*, *Minha Casa Minha Vida*, *Bolsa Família*), which disproportionately benefitted the Northeast. Some large-scale infrastructure programmes also particularly benefitted the Northeast, including the creation of industrial zones such as Suape, road-building programmes and the *Transposição do Rio São Francisco* (large-scale irrigation and drinking water projects drawing on the water of the São Francisco River). But the reversion to a neoliberal model since 2016 once again shifted the agenda away from state action and back towards the private sector. And as we have seen, the market economy does not equalize; on the contrary, it concentrates and polarizes. So the gains of the Northeast in "developmentalist" periods have been lost once the neoliberal agenda prevails.

This is not just a question of public-sector investment and social policies, but also one of economic regulation. In principle, economic regulation could reinforce regional action, but that is not usually the goal. Labour market regulation is a case in point. The 2017 labour reforms, aiming to flexibilize the labour market and reduce labour costs, which we discussed in Chapter 3, impact a labour market in the Northeast which is already highly flexible because of the large informal economy, and which already has a labour cost advantage over other parts of the country, but neither aspect has led to any sustained catching up by the region. Compared to the Brazilian economy as a whole, the labour reform seems as likely to disadvantage the region, in terms of the impact on economic growth and employment, as to benefit it.

There can be and has been an important regional dimension to other national policies to influence labour market outcomes, notably with respect to racial and gender discrimination, skill development, small enterprise development, and in other fields. But overcoming the gap between the Northeast and the rest of the country would require resources of a magnitude that successive governments have been unwilling or unable to allocate. And beyond the question of resources, it would require establishing the political conditions for structural changes that are essential for a more equitable pattern of economic development, such as the reform of land ownership, the decentralization and democratization of the banking and credit system, and a more progressive tax system, among others.

The scope for intervention at the level of the state (province) or municipality to promote local development is more limited, but tax and investment incentives can play an important role in attracting private investment. Examples include the facilities offered to Fiat to build its Jeep factory in Pernambuco, and on a more modest scale, incentives in Paraíba and other states to attract call centres, as well as the more systematic effort by the state of Ceará to attract industrial investment in the 1990s. However, as noted above, this can have the perverse effect of encouraging tax competition among states for a limited number of investment projects, and raising the capital-labour ratio because the incentives apply mainly to capital and physical assets. Individual municipalities or metropolitan areas also try to attract private sector investment through the development of markets, as in the Agreste garment pole in Pernambuco, the creation of industrial zones and local production clusters such as the Bodocongó footwear pole in Paraíba, investment in urban infrastructure, labour market support, and partnerships with training organizations. These can be important, as the example of Goiana discussed in Chapter 4 shows. But their importance is local; on their own they cannot provide an effective means to reduce regional disparities.

Of course, the State is the reflection of the structure of economic and political power. Popular movements, when they have come to power, have promoted working class interests. Business and financial lobbies have played a considerable role in pressing for liberalization. Governments have been largely built on shifting alliances between three forces, a popular movement, a middle-class political force and the traditional oligarchy (Singer, 2018). In the Northeast, the role of the traditional oligarchy has been particularly important, built on clientelism and the manipulation of local institutions. Each crisis has led to a reconfiguration of these interests and alliances. The vulnerability of the State to corruption is another limiting factor. The political centrality of the issue of corruption in Brazil in recent years has clearly weakened the credibility of the State and its ability to promote a development agenda.

No single factor explains the relative economic backwardness of the Northeast. Rather there is a set of often contradictory current and historical forces which tend towards this result. In the absence of deliberate countervailing efforts, State and business tend to advantage the more developed regions of the country. When redistributive policies shift resources towards low-income groups and regions, resistance develops among those who were previously favoured, and a political crisis emerges; powerful actors defend their interests. Stereotypical attitudes towards the Northeast and Northeasterners in other parts of Brazil may also play a role, influencing attitudes to workers and perceptions of their work. Many of the social institutions concerned have deep historical roots – there is a history of discrimination and resistance, and of the emergence of social networks which can play an important economic or political role. Informality is pervasive. It may be a response to lack of opportunity, or an escape from state regulation. But it is above all embedded within the production system and the labour regime. Much production activity spans formal and informal, sometimes because informal activities contribute to formal production through outsourcing, sometimes because informal production is distributed through formal markets, sometimes because there is no sharp dividing line between formal and informal. Households may have income from both formal and informal sources. This is true of Brazil as a whole, but it is particularly important in the Northeast.

Perhaps it can be said that in Brazil the social and political forces that support periods of economic stability are relatively less inclusive, leaving out the most vulnerable working populations, who live on the edge of survival, and the less favoured regions. This weakens the domestic economy and increases dependence on external demand (and its fluctuations). The dynamic balance between the accumulation regime and the mode of regulation takes place, in the case of Brazil, on a permanently unstable ground.

3 Issues and scenarios

The economic crisis that started in 2015 was not yet over when the Covid-19 pandemic struck in 2020. The Northeast was particularly vulnerable because of high levels of poverty and unequal access to health systems. The pandemic severely affected labour markets, not only directly, due to the fall in production and morbidity among workers, but also indirectly, due to policies to limit the spread of the disease (confinement, social distancing, etc.). Between May and November 2020, unemployment increased by 70% in the Northeast, while the national average increased by less than 40%. It is striking that informal workers were more affected than formal workers. In the second quarter of 2020, the country experienced a 15.6% drop in employment in the informal sector and 5.5% in the formal sector (Corseuil et al., 2021). Up to the third quarter of 2020 the PNADC showed a reduction of approximately 11 million informal jobs in Brazil as a whole, compared with 3 million formal jobs lost (Al Masri et al., 2021).

> while labor income fell across the entire income distribution, poor households were the most affected. Households in the bottom income decile lost about 1 percentage point of their percentile share in total income as their monthly labor income decreased by 30 percent. Our analysis shows that poverty and the Gini index would have increased sharply as a consequence, to about 13.9 percent and 0.58 respectively, compared to about 4.7 and 0.53 pre-COVID for May (ibid., p.21).

Neri (2021) shows the Gini coefficient of labour income per capita rising from 0.628 in the fourth quarter of 2019 to 0.667 in the third quarter of 2020, before falling to 0.646 in the second quarter of 2021.[2]

Government policy to contain the pandemic was widely seen as inadequate or negligent, but some policies to limit its impact on incomes were put in place. They involved two types of measures, aimed, respectively, at formal wage workers and at informal workers. Measures aimed at formal workers, intended to limit the rise in unemployment, were broadly in line with business interests, pursuing the flexibilizing and deregulating policies of the 2017 labour reform, with suspensions of contracts and of workers' rights and expansion of the discretionary power of employers. More significantly, an Emergency Aid Program (PAE) was launched in 2020 aimed at informal workers and microentrepreneurs. According to PNAD Covid data, 39% of households received some government aid related to the pandemic in May 2020 and 42% in October of the same year. This programme effectively offset the negative short-term impact of the pandemic on poverty and income, at a cost in 2020 of around 4% of GDP (Roubicek, 2021). Al Masri et al. (2021, p.27) calculate that it reduced extreme poverty from the 13.9% cited above to 4.4%, and the Gini coefficient of household income inequality from 0.58 to 0.51, both lower than their pre-Covid levels. However the scheme was phased out in 2021.

It is not yet possible to assess the long-term impact of the pandemic on work and income. But with many families suffering deaths or other consequences of the disease, small businesses losing workers and customers, investments cancelled or delayed, young people's entry into work impeded, widespread loss of labour protection and a weakening of collective action, it is clear that many problems will persist, even if economic recovery is rapid. There is already evidence that the high prevailing levels of inequality influenced the impact of the pandemic, in that infection and mortality were higher in low-income areas (e.g. Demenech et al., 2020), presumably reflecting the lesser ability of low-income households to protect themselves, because of crowded housing conditions or labour market vulnerability, and less access to health facilities (Leal, 2020; Meireles, 2020). There are reasons to fear that there will also be longer-term consequences for inequality, particularly where there has been loss of livelihoods or an impact of illness or death on household incomes.

This book is not about the pandemic, which is not yet over at the time of writing, and its longer-term consequences will take time to emerge. But we see in this crisis some of the mechanisms observed earlier – and, in particular, that crises disproportionately affect lower income groups and poorer regions. The adverse short-term income shock was largely compensated by state policy, but the shape of the longer-term recovery will depend on the underlying institutional forces. Whether or not these forces will give rise to a fairer and more inclusive development regime in the Northeast depends on whether a new, reasonably stable constellation of institutional relationships emerges which can overcome some of the past disadvantages of the region.

We have no crystal ball, but some of the issues that will have to be faced can readily be identified.

3.1 Dependency of the production system

First, we have seen that the dependency of the Northeastern production system vis-à-vis the economic centre in Brazil, especially the Southeast, is a source of both advantage when the economy is doing well, but disadvantage when the economic context is more difficult. This is not only a source of unemployment and deprivation, but is also one of the reasons why the region has been unable to close the economic gap. The nature of competition in the Brazilian economy, and the process of capital accumulation, tends to perpetuate backwardness in the Northeast. So a change in the pattern of investment will be needed, perhaps relying more on local sources of capital. This problem has long been recognized, and public investment in the past has tried to crowd in private capital. In this respect, success has been greatest for larger enterprises, in a process has led to the dualisms that we discussed above. But there are other possible sources of economic dynamism on which a policy to promote endogenous growth in the region could rely, including a variety of local initiatives and production networks, innovative small enterprises in IT or the green economy, and solidarity-based enterprises, among others. They could enhance the autonomy of the regional economy and form the basis for a more balanced pattern of growth, and one with a greater potential for employment creation. Institutions that channel capital to these types of activities could make a large contribution to regional development.

3.2 Informality in production

Second, the issue of informality in production will need to be addressed, though not necessarily with the automatic policy reflex that the solution is to formalize. We have highlighted the close connections between formal and informal production in the Northeastern economy. The high level of informality in the Northeast can be a source of weakness, undermining social protection, preventing upgrading of skills and production capabilities, and facilitating exploitation. But it can also be a source of strength, if informal productive relationships are embedded in social reciprocity and complementarity, in cooperatives or producer networks. Pathways to stability and security are needed, and formal systems and regulations need to be adapted to the reality of the economic environment. We have seen, in discussing labour status, that a substantial fraction of the workforce in the Northeast is engaged in productive self-employment, both registered and unregistered, that has the potential to deliver high incomes. Moreover, small enterprises have much higher employment-output ratios than large ones, and account for the majority of private sector employment. Local arrangements for productive development (APLs) have the potential to make a substantial contribution. Sebrae, the public service to support small and medium enterprises, also clearly has an important role to play, especially if it can connect its business-oriented approach with the social and regional goals to which small scale producers contribute.

3.3 Informality in employment

Third, and related to the second, the issue of informality in wage employment also needs to be dealt with. This issue overlaps with, but is distinct from, the question of informality in production. Informality in wage employment is in part the consequence of a lack of employment opportunities, and so reflects the poor performance of the economy as a whole; but it also results from lack of effective representation and poor coverage of social protection. It also reflects and facilitates discrimination and differentiation in the labour market. To deal with the problem, labour institutions need to be reinforced, not weakened, contrary to the labour reform introduced in 2017. But like for informal self-employment, this needs to be done in a way that is sensitive to the needs of both workers and employers, otherwise it will not succeed. An inclusive labour regime would need stronger representation of all categories of workers, and more effective dialogue between workers, employers and the State. A striking feature of the 2003–2014 period was a growth of formal wage employment, both in the Northeast and in Brazil as a whole, during a period when labour force protections were strengthened and the minimum wage increased. The neoliberal approach, in contrast, gives priority to efforts to reduce labour costs and protections with the ostensible aim of increasing enterprise competitivity. But the evidence suggests strongly that improved labour conditions provide an alternative source of competitiveness through higher productivity, if implemented in the right social and political environment. The high share of informal and unprotected wage work in the Northeast is a weakness, and a source of poverty and deprivation, and overcoming it can be part of a strategy to raise productivity and promote decent employment.

In fact, much of the institutional policy agenda lies in the labour regime, which, as we have seen, at present delivers highly unequal employment opportunities and much low quality work. Among the many institutional issues, universalizing access to skills and abilities would be the foundation of an equitable development process. The substantial training system in Brazil, the "S" system, plays an important role in raising workforce technical skills, mainly for the formal sector, and often in partnership with enterprises and local administrations. But in reality, most skills are acquired or consolidated on the job, and an emphasis on formal qualifications may be a source of segmentation and inequality, unless the S system can achieve universal coverage. Moreover large investments are needed further upstream, in the educational system, where the roots of much labour market differentiation lie. Another concern is the representation and organization of workers, which is partial and fragmented – and elements of the old corporatist trade union system survive and limit the effectiveness of union action. An important issue is outmigration from the Northeast – a continued flow of migrants to the Southeast of the country can limit labour availability and lead to a deficiency of specific skills. Institutions are needed for the reintegration of migrants who return to the region, or to attract skilled migrants from other parts of the country, in order to encourage a two-way flow.

3.4 Embedded inequality

Fourth, high inequality is one of the causes of Brazil's unstable and crisis-prone development trajectory, distorting the pattern of demand and favouring speculative capital flows to the detriment of long-term productive investment. The forces driving differentiation in the production system remain strong, there are pressures to reduce redistributive social transfers, and progress towards reducing discrimination lost momentum during the current recession and the pandemic, as did the trend towards reducing regional inequality. Inequality is deeply embedded in social and economic structures and relationships, both regional inequality to the detriment of the Northeast, and inequality between social and economic groups and classes within the region. At the root of inequality lies the concentration of wealth. Almost half of all wealth is owned by the top 1% in Brazil (Chancel et al., 2022), and the share has been rising even during the period when the PT was in power. There are few options to address this in Brazil, but among its adverse consequences it is a source of high regional inequality because of the concentration of wealth in the Southeast of the country. Income inequality is also very high, and this is due not only to inequality in income from capital but also to large differentials within the labour market. On the other hand, there was a reduction in income inequality over the two decades up to 2014. An important feature of this period was a focus on policies which improved the situation of low-income groups, which not only reduced poverty overall, but also reduced regional inequality because of the higher incidence of low incomes in the Northeast. This was true not only of national redistributive policies such as *Bolsa Família*, but also the rising minimum wage, which, since it is uniform across the country, disproportionately benefits (formal) wage workers in the Northeast. But the political conditions which permitted these developments were no longer in place after the fall of the PT government in 2016. A new and more equalizing development regime may emerge in the wake of the on-going crisis, but that is unlikely to happen without political and institutional transformations.

3.5 The State

Fifth, a key lesson of the 2003–2014 period was the importance of state action, combining developmentalist interventions through public investment with state social policy. The swings of economic ideology, cycling between state-led and neoliberal, have highlighted the potential for state intervention to reduce regional disparities, but for the market to increase them. Public investment in regional infrastructure is clearly essential, notably social infrastructure such as education and health, and this will be most effective if local economic actors help to identify priority needs.

There also appears to be space for state (provincial) governments to play a more important role. A development strategy for the Northeast as a whole would call for coordination among the states of the Federation, rather than competition among them for public resources and private investment. It is equally necessary to provide more effective coordination of public actions at the municipal, state and federal levels. This is a role that a body such as Sudene could play, even if it is no longer an important actor in regional development strategy.

Of course, from the point of view of the federal government, the Northeast is only one region among others, and there are many competing demands, not least from the other low-income region of the country, the North. Coordination between regions, and not only between states, is also needed.

The government is also a large-scale employer in its own right, and the public sector as a whole accounts for 15% of employment in the Northeast, against 12% in the rest of Brazil. Incomes in public-sector employment are relatively high, but there is also a tendency for insecure public-sector employment to grow, mirroring the private sector. The public sector can provide an example for the private sector to follow, rather than the reverse.

3.6 Research and academic institutions

Sixth, regional disparity in output and income is also replicated in regional disparity in research and knowledge systems. We have seen that this is true of private sector production, where research and development tends to be concentrated in the Southeast of the country. It is also true of the academic and intellectual world. The major universities, research institutes and think tanks, both public and private, are concentrated in São Paulo, Rio de Janeiro, Brasilia and other locations in the South and Southeast. There are of course a number of important universities and research institutions in the Northeast, but they do not have the resources to compete. And while research on the Northeast is also undertaken in other parts of the country, strengthening the institutional knowledge base within the region would provide strong support for the development of regional strategy in many domains, while stronger educational institutions would retain more students in the region.

3.7 Building on regional strengths

Seventh, there are strengths in the region that can play a more central role in developing a strategy for regional development, for social inclusion within the region and a levelling up of incomes. Some are obvious – a strong cultural tradition in literature and music, natural resources, potential for tourism, a regional identity. The question is how these can be effectively embedded into a development regime that creates employment and incomes. Tourism, for instance, has a considerable potential as a source of employment, but creates many insecure and temporary jobs. New capabilities can also be created – in the digital economy, in cooperative enterprises, in climate-friendly investment, or in other domains, such as the recent and growing investments in wind and solar energy in the states of the region. An economic strategy can also be built around the strengthening of existing local and regional networks of small businesses, many of them showing economic dynamism but subject to institutional constraints or limited market access. They could be reinforced with public support for local productive arrangements, including subsidized credit, investments in infrastructure such as communication and transport systems, expansion of education and health programmes, development of irrigation systems, preferences in government procurement, expansion of professional training, and other targeted policies.

* * *

There are many possible lessons from the recurrent crises that Brazil has experienced. But one notable observation is that recovery from each crisis has involved both political and economic change. Overcoming crisis also involves a restructuring of the positions of competing interests, the contradictions between labour and capital, between elites and people, between middle classes and the working poor, between the different regions of Brazil. New institutions, or an evolution of existing ones, are needed to create zones of dialogue and common interest, sufficient to form the basis of an equitable future regime for labour and development in the Northeast and in Brazil as a whole.

Notes

1 The state of Pará is outside the Northeast region, but export of iron ore is through a port in the Northeast.
2 The Gini coefficients reported by Neri and by Al Masri et al. are not comparable. Neri uses labour income per capita, while Al Masri et al. use income per household.

References

Al Masri, Diala, Valentina Flamini and Frederik Toscani. 2021. *The short-term impact of COVID-19 on labor markets, poverty and inequality in Brazil.* Working Paper WP/21/66. Washington, DC: IMF.

Baer, Werner. 2014. *The Brazilian economy*, 7th edition. Boulder, CO: Lynne Rienner.

Barbosa, Alexandre de Freitas, Maria Cristina Cacciamali and Gerry Rodgers. 2017. *Growth and inequality: The contrasting trajectories of India and Brazil.* New Delhi: Cambridge University Press.

Boyer, Robert. 2015. *Economie politique des capitalismes: Théorie de la régulation et des crises.* Paris: La Découverte.

Chancel, Lucas, Thomas Piketty, Emmanuel Saez and Gabriel Zucman. 2022. *World Inequality Report 2022.* World Inequality Lab. <https://wir2022.wid.world>.

Corseuil, Carlos Henrique, Maíra Franca, Gabriela Padilha, Lauro Ramos and Felipe Russo. 2021. *Comportamento do mercado de trabalho brasileiro em duas recessões: análise do período 2015–2016 e da pandemia de covid-19.* Nota Técnica 92. Brasília: Diretoria de Estudos e Políticas Sociais, IPEA.

Demenech, Lauro Miranda, Samuel de Carvalho Dumith, Maria Eduarda Centena Duarte Vieira and Lucas Neiva-Silva. 2020. "Desigualdade econômica e risco de infecção e morte por COVID-19 no Brasil". *Revista Brasileira de Epidemiologia*, 23.

Leal, Jefferson. 2020. *Na crise, homens negros e mulheres negras são os mais vulneráveis. Mas surgem "novos vulneráveis", homens brancos e mulheres brancas em serviços não essenciais.* Nota Técnica 3, Boletim 3, 24 de abril. São Paulo: Redepesquisasolidaria. <https://redepesquisasolidaria.org/boletins/>

Meireles, Thiago de Oliveira. 2020. *A vulnerabilidade dos trabalhadores brasileiros na pandemia da Covid-19.* Nota Técnica 2, Boletim 2, 17 de abril. São Paulo: Redepesquisasolidaria. <https://redepesquisasolidaria.org/boletins/>

Neri, Marcelo (coordinator). 2021. *Desigualdade de impactos trabalhistas na pandemia.* Rio de Janeiro: Fundação Getulio Vargas, FGV Social. <https://cps.fgv.br/DesigualdadePandemia>, accessed 07-02-2022.

Roubicek, Marcelo. 2021. "Qual o impacto do novo auxílio para a população e a economia?". *Nexo Jornal*, 16 mar. São Paulo. <https://www.nexojornal.com.br/expresso/2021/03/16/Qual-o-impacto-do-novo-aux%C3%ADlio-para-a-popula%C3%A7%C3%A3o-e-a-economia>, accessed 04-05-2021.

Singer, André. 2018. *O Lulismo em crise: Um quebra-cabeça do período Dilma (2011–2016).* São Paulo: Companhia das Letras.

Postscript

The manuscript of this book was completed in June 2022. This postscript considers possible developments in the light of Lula da Silva's election as President on 30 October.

Lula's narrow victory brought to an end Bolsonaro's extreme right-wing government, whose inadequate performance was widely acknowledged, including ideologically driven economic policies, a deficient response to the Covid-19 pandemic, reductions in state support for the poor (except in the run-up to the elections), the deforestation of the Amazon, opposition to gender, racial and other identity movements and acts and attitudes which threatened democracy. These no doubt played an important role in Lula's victory. Nevertheless, his political position is fragile. He was elected by building an alliance with the centre and centre-right, but he has to govern a country in which the left-wing parties are in a minority, and the right and extreme right have been strengthened in both houses of Congress. Lula's election relied heavily on the Northeast, where he won two thirds of the vote; but with a few exceptions – some states of the North, Minas Gerais and the city of São Paulo – most of the rest of the country, especially the richer areas, voted for Bolsonaro. More than half of the states within the federal system are now governed by the opposition.

The country is thus deeply divided. There was fear of widespread violence in the wake of the election or a refusal by Bolsonaro to respect the results, or even military intervention, and there were indeed demonstrations and roadblocks, but Brazil's democratic political institutions proved to be up to the task, helped by the broad alliances created by Lula and the rapid recognition of his victory at both national and international levels. Nevertheless tensions remain high, and risks of violence and of social instability persist. For a large part of the population, the conservative values of the right – family, religion, nation – trumped questions of labour and social justice. The redistributive policies of earlier Lula and Dilma governments were also rejected by a substantial proportion of the middle class. And the revival of old accusations of corruption also contributed to the opposition to Lula. This polarization makes the task of the incoming government much harder.

DOI: 10.4324/9781003326670-6

Under these circumstances, it will be difficult to implement a development agenda comparable to that of the PT-led governments from 2003 to 2016, which included significant redistribution and extensive social policies. Lula has positioned himself in the political centre, and has called for dialogue among all sections of society to construct the future government programme. But many powerful political actors are unwilling to follow his lead.

As far as the Northeast of Brazil is concerned, in Chapter 5 we highlighted seven issues that need attention, if the disadvantage of the region is to be reduced. On some of these issues progress is likely, but certainly not on all.

The first, the dependency of the Northeast production system on the economic core in the Southeast of the country, cannot be overcome without large scale investment in the Northeast. This is part of Lula's programme, but implementation will require substantial resources. Public-private partnerships may help, and state financial institutions such as BNDES can play a larger role, as they did before 2016.

The second issue, informality in production, is a problem in the country but especially in the Northeast. Nevertheless there is space for policies to support local development and networks of small enterprises, and to facilitate their access to capital, skills, technology and markets, which will probably receive wide political backing.

The third, informality in employment, also much greater in the Northeast, is an area where substantial progress was made under the earlier PT governments; but this was largely reversed by the impact of economic recession and the 2017 labour reforms, which attempted to deregulate the labour market. There is a need to rescind some of those reforms – which generally disadvantaged workers but did not lead to employment growth – and to increase worker protections. But it is not clear that Lula will have the political support needed.

The fourth, the structural inequalities in wealth and income in the Brazilian economy, are unlikely to be addressed, if only because Lula's victory was built on alliances with political forces that reflect key vested interests. Indeed, little progress was made even during the earlier PT-led periods. But even if structural inequalities remain, some important redistributional policies which particularly benefit the Northeast, including a rising minimum wage, a new version of *Bolsa Família*, and the popular housing programme *Minha Casa Minha Vida* are back on the agenda.

The fifth issue, a renewed leading role for the State in the development process, is likely to be contested. Constitutional rules to limit public spending were introduced by the Temer government, and efforts to increase budgetary flexibility will have to overcome political opposition.

The sixth, concerned with research and education, suffered major budget cuts during the Temer and Bolsonaro periods, along with discriminatory and defamatory campaigns. There are now expectations for a renewed emphasis on federal universities, research institutions, the reinforcement of data systems and programmes to promote and encourage culture, all areas where the shortfalls are greater in the Northeast.

The seventh issue is about building on regional strengths. Most states in the Northeast are governed by Lula supporters or allies, which suggests that there is considerable scope for joint efforts between federal and state governments to create employment and overcome poverty. But to retain political support the government will have to respond to special interests all over the country.

Actions in these fields will depend not only on the government but also on others, including trade unions and other organizations. Trade unions gained space and importance during the earlier Lula and Dilma governments, but were penalized under Temer and Bolsonaro. They may now recover influence, including through new forms of organization, but this will depend not only on progress towards reregulating the labour market, but also on a growth in employment which would strengthen their bargaining power, and on a revitalization of collective bargaining institutions.

The first Lula government came to power in 2003 in the wake of a deep economic crisis, and subsequently took advantage of the expanding global economy up to 2008, including a commodity boom, to finance progressive policies and to promote growth. Could history repeat itself? At the time of writing, in late 2022, high inflation and rising interest rates make slow global economic growth likely for the immediate future and IMF forecasts suggest that Brazil will do worse than the world average in 2023. Some commodity prices have been rising, which is potentially to Brazil's advantage, but the global slowdown is likely to depress international demand. So conditions are much less promising than in 2003.

Looking further into the future, for the favourable conditions of the first Lula government to be reproduced the global economy will have to recover, but this is uncertain and will in any case take time. But whatever the international context, environmental issues are now crucial, and Brazil has the resources and the potential to build a development path that is both socially and environmentally sustainable. If this road is taken, the prospects for successful progressive policies are reasonably good in the medium term. But structural and institutional change, and significant reductions in inequality, are likely to be more difficult to achieve.

Index

Note: **Bold** page numbers refer to tables; *Italic* page numbers refer to figures and page numbers followed by "n" denote endnotes.